Political Islam, Iran, and the Enlightenment
Philosophies of Hope and Despair

Ali Mirsepassi's book presents a powerful challenge to the dominant media and scholarly construction of radical Islamist politics, and their anti-Western ideology, as a purely Islamic phenomenon derived from insular, traditional, and monolithic religious "foundations." It argues that the discourse of political Islam has strong connections to important and disturbing currents in Western philosophy and modern Western intellectual trends. This book demonstrates this by establishing links between important contemporary Iranian intellectuals and the central influence of Martin Heidegger's philosophy. The readers are also introduced to new democratic narratives of modernity linked to diverse intellectual trends in the West and in non-Western societies, notably in India, where the ideas of John Dewey have influenced important democratic social movements. As the first book to make such connections, it promises to be an important contribution to our understanding of Political Islam and will do much to overturn some long-held and pervasive assumptions about the dichotomy between East and West.

Ali Mirsepassi is professor of Middle Eastern studies and sociology at the Gallatin School, New York University. His publications include *Democracy in Modern Iran* (2010) and *Intellectual Discourses and Politics of Modernization: Negotiating Modernity in Iran* (2000).

Political Islam, Iran, and the Enlightenment

Philosophies of Hope and Despair

ALI MIRSEPASSI

Gallatin School, New York University

CAMBRIDGE
UNIVERSITY PRESS

CAMBRIDGE UNIVERSITY PRESS
Cambridge, New York, Melbourne, Madrid, Cape Town, Singapore,
São Paulo, Delhi, Dubai, Tokyo, Mexico City

Cambridge University Press
32 Avenue of the Americas, New York, NY 10013-2473, USA

www.cambridge.org
Information on this title: www.cambridge.org/9780521745901

First published 2011

Printed in the United States of America

A catalog record for this publication is available from the British Library.

Library of Congress Cataloging in Publication data

Mirsepassi, Ali.
Political Islam, Iran, and the enlightenment : philosophies of hope
and despair / Ali Mirsepassi.
   p.   cm.
Includes index.
ISBN 978-0-521-76882-5 (hardback)
1. Iran – Politics and government.   2. Iran – Intellectual life.   3. Intellectuals – Political
activity – Iran.   4. Islam and politics – Iran.   5. Politics and culture – Iran.   6. Islam and
secularism – Iran.   7. Islamic modernism – Iran.   8. Heidegger, Martin, 1889–1976 –
Influence.   9. Dewey, John, 1859–1952 – Influence.   I. Title.
DS318.825.M576   2010
320.5'570955–dc22   2010022939

ISBN 978-0-521-76882-5 Hardback
ISBN 978-0-521-74590-1 Paperback

Contents

Acknowledgments

I researched and wrote most of this book while I was a Carnegie Scholar Fellow. The generous support of the Carnegie Corporation of New York gave me the opportunity to travel and conduct research in India and Iran. I would like to express my gratitude to the Carnegie Corporation of New York and its visionary president Vartan Gregorian for helping and supporting this book project.

I have received the help of a community of colleagues, friends, and students in writing this book. I could not have written the book without the substantial editorial and intellectual help of my longtime research assistant and editor, Tadd Fernée. Tadd helped me in the writing and editing of this book, and I would like to express my deep appreciation for his considerable work. As a faculty member at Gallatin School, New York University, I feel very fortunate to be a member of such a supportive and intellectually inspiring institution. I would like to acknowledge the support of the Gallatin School's dean, Susanne Wofford, and my colleagues Laura M. Slatkin and E. Frances White, who read the introduction and gave me very helpful comments for revisions.

I would also like to express my gratitude to Marigold Acland, Senior Editor at Cambridge University Press, for her enthusiastic interest in this book and for her support in its publication. I would like to thank the anonymous reviewers whose comments and suggestions for revisions helped improve the quality of the book.

Introduction

Political Islam's Romance with the "West"

When the French philosopher and scholar Henry Corbin visited Iran in 1945,[1] Allamah Tabataba'i, the most eminent Shi'i scholar and philosopher of the time, traveled from Qom to Tehran just to meet with him. Corbin conducted several intense dialogues with Tabataba'i and a number of other religious scholars, some of whom later became the leaders of the Islamic Republic (Motahari, Beheshti).[2] Corbin was also a mentor to Darush Shayegan and Housen Nasr, two of the most prominent secular scholars in Iran.[3] Perhaps most significantly, he was highly influential for Ali Shari'ati, one of the better known Islamist intellectuals of the 1970s, who had studied with Corbin at the Sorbonne.[4]

Corbin was a scholar of spiritual Islam and Iranian-Islamic philosophy, but his importance for Iranian religious intellectuals had an additional mysterious dimension. He was known as the French Heideggerian scholar of Islam, and he wielded a particularly important influence for this reason.

Corbin had visited Heidegger in Freiburg in April 1934 and July 1936 to discuss the French translation of *What Is Metaphysics?* He also translated Heidegger's text on Hölderlin and the *Essence of Poetry*. What is interesting in the Corbin-Iran connection is the renewal of strong interest in Heidegger within Islamic intellectual circles: Heidegger, the radical critic of Western Enlightenment who ambiguously collaborated with the Nazi regime, the philosopher of existence, transcendentalism, and the jargon of authenticity. It is within the context of the Corbin-Iran link that we may fully appreciate the meaning and contribution of the three most significant Iranian intellectuals of the 1960s and '70s, Ahmad Fardid, Jalal Al-e Ahmad, and Ali Shari'ati, and their role in intellectually shaping the Islamic Revolution of 1979.

This book accordingly focuses on the contribution of certain ideas and intellectual trends, generated in the West, that have shaped the principal ideological formation of the Islamist critique of modernity and the West. I suggest that an excessive emphasis has been placed on the purely religious quality of political Islam, and that this has led to a scholarly blindness concerning "non-Islamic ideas" in the overall development of the Islamist ideology as a mobilizing and motivating force.

The tendency of most scholars to overlook the Western influence on political Islam has contributed to the perpetuation of widespread and simplifying myths that occlude the actual complex nature of this signifi-cant and often troubling political phenomenon of the late twentieth and twenty-first centuries. I propose that there is a profound influence of cer-tain intellectual trends, originating in the West, that has contributed sig-nificantly to the formation and continuing development of political Islam as an anti-Western and counter-Enlightenment ideology. In this book, I argue that Muslim intellectuals in general – and Iranian intellectuals in particular – have come to know the West, modernity, and democracy largely through the radical anti-Enlightenment ideas of German philoso-phy, as well as of certain French intellectuals. These ideas were generated in the counter-Enlightenment discourses that ultimately played so major a role in the fermentation of reactionary modernist politics in Western nations in the mid-twentieth century. These discourses, based on the appeal of nostalgia and the restoration of a "lost" shared sense of com-munity and social meaning, and feeding off of the social discontent and cultural disorientation endemic to rapidly modernizing societies, found their way into influential political discourses offering "salvation" to the newly urbanized publics of twentieth-century Iran and other Middle East-ern and Islamic societies. In this phenomenon, we see the invention of a new language and mode of describing the problems and discontents of modern social realities by way of familiar symbols that conceal a radi-cally transformed meaning and propose a solution based on the familiar modern concept of "total revolution." It is therefore very unproductive to talk about Islamic thought as such, or to discuss political Islam as if it were disconnected from crucial political discourses and issues of the modern West.

Changes in the Middle East reflect, not an autonomous or linear his-torical process, but, like all late modern history (and to a lesser extent early modern), a distribution of often fractured lines of becoming in tradi-tion, modernity, and cosmopolitanism, expressing geographical and eco-nomic realities cutting across and incorporating multiple distinct conflicts (class, colonial, political, religious, ethnic, gender, regional, ideological, etc.). These conflicts are patterned in the twentieth century by the World Wars, the Ottoman disintegration, decolonization, the Cold War, nationalism, refugee influx and state formation (particularly Israel), development and labor migration patterns, the postwar capitalist boom, and corresponding population and resource connections. We have, in sum, a complex historical-geographical configuration or multiple interconnected singularities from the Russo-Japanese War to the Marshall Plan and the Soviet politics in Azerbaijan. In this accumulation of connections and productions without an organizing center – except the minimal structural logic of capitalism in dependent populations, universal exchange value, surplus, wage labor, state-law complex, and so forth – we may identify several formative discursive moments in, first, modern Enlightenment as the French Revolutionary model of national assimilation and emancipated human nature as "intellectual virtue" (narrowly essentialized as modern/tradition, science/culture, fact/value), and, second, radical Enlightenment seeking to conceive "rights" within a more inclusive framework than autonomy as property ownership or education (Marx, Sen) and seeing in practical "moral virtue" a potential for everyday forms of democracy beyond the legislative moment of the state (Dewey or Thoreau as thinkers, Mahatma Gandhi or Martin Luther King as practical demonstrations). Third, we have the influential discursive moment of counter-Enlightenment that in rejecting the coercive universal pretences of Enlightened modernity also categorically rejects the institutional forms of secularism and liberal democracy in the name of a totalized "local" and "ontological" claim to either religious or cultural truth – the highest intellectual expression of which is probably contained in the works of Martin Heidegger. This was the discursive moment that gained ideological influence in late-twentieth-century Iran within the context of the crisis of the secular modern developing state and a history of foreign intervention and had enormously dangerous consequences for the project of building Iranian democracy.

Because of this strong identification with anti-Enlightenment discourses by many important Muslim intellectuals during the late twentieth century, the Muslim understanding of the West and modernity is often highly limited. The exaggerated association among these intellectuals of "modernity as such" with the particular paradigm grounded in French Enlightenment and revolutionary experience has resulted in many Muslims seeing modernity as secular in the sense of inherently hostile and even at war against non-Western/traditional cultural ideas and beliefs. This

French Revolutionary paradigm was the vision of modernity and secularism adopted by Kemal Ataturk and the Shah of Iran in the Middle East. In fact, a more "middle way" secular politics exists and is available as evidenced by different experiences of the secular from Britain (expressed in the eighteenth-century moral philosophers such as Shaftesbury, and the tradition of progressive and piecemeal social and administrative reform) to the independent Indian Republic (expressed in the ideas and practices of Gandhi and Nehru).

Although "secularization" may be a specific socioeconomic process, theorized by Habermas as the "public sphere" and necessary to all free societies, it is an institutional rather than cultural or moral construct. The "secular," by contrast, is an epistemic or imaginative construct shaped heavily by cultural and moral elements, but has often been taken to mean Europeanization projected as a fixed "scientific" universal (i.e., for Ataturk, with his now-dated nineteenth-century scientific determinist imaginary) – when in fact even within the West itself the "secular" can mean different things within various historical conjunctures of modernity and their unique historical-geographical variables from population to existing religious structures (from Britain to America, from France to Italy, etc.). Where the "secular" is concerned, different cultures can develop all sorts of specific cultural and moral ideas and discourses in order to imagine, discuss, and negotiate such crucial issues as freedom, agency, justice, and rationality. Within this context, the possibility of a positive contribution by religious ideas and values to the creation of a new democratic society is by no means ruled out – as with late seventeenth-century post-Puritan England, where a prophetic and scriptural structure was used to undermine clerical claims to authority in a championing of secular principles.[5] For the same reason, secularism should not be confused with a "natural" or "inevitable" process, nor should it be supposed that it is inherently linked to democratic or politically free society. The twentieth century offers numerous examples of violently authoritarian secular regimes, from the Shah of Iran to the Ba'athist regime in Iraq.

Overlooking the many rich historical examples of secularism as a "middle way," and focused on the secular regime in its authoritarian variation, many Islamic thinkers have become attracted to a narrowly Nietzschean and particularly Heideggerian critique of the West as the single source of modern inhumanity and a general loss of cultural and existential meaning in a Manichean universe. A clear case study is the rise of political Islam in Iran and the strong Heideggerian influence on a number of leading Iranian intellectuals who helped enormously to articulate the Islamist ideology that paved the way to the 1979 revolution (Fardid, Al-e Ahmad, Shari'ati, Shayegan, Davari, etc.). Therefore, this project maps out a philosophical genealogy (namely, the reception/mobilization of counter-Enlightenment thought in political Islam); at the same time, it also sets forth counterexamples of nonviolent and pluralistic political practice – within, for example, the twentieth-century Indian experience of achieving national independence – that are highly relevant and useful for modeling alternative futures for Islamic democracy in the contemporary world.

1. Discourse of Political Islam

The goal of this study is to situate the rise of political Islam in contemporary social and cultural contexts from a fresh and alternative perspective. Political Islam promises to restore a pure and unbroken order to modern society based on a claim to an ontologically legitimized higher truth and a uniform set of values grounded in this truth. Critics and analysts of political Islam, as a rule, do not look beyond the superficiality of these claims and uncritically accept them on their own terms, thereby perpetuating a vicious cycle of misunderstanding. My argument is that far too dogmatic a grip has been maintained on the contention of religious content as being intrinsic or essential to political Islam, whereas a comparative blind spot has prevailed regarding those "global" qualities that have been highly important in giving the movement its integral substance and definition. The overemphasis on the religious content has produced a deficit in public understanding and debate where this important issue is concerned, as well as creating an unwarranted sense of "mystification."

This book therefore focuses on the contributions of ideational complexes and intellectual trends that, although generated in the West itself, have ironically had a powerful influence in shaping the principal ideological formation of the Islamist critique of modernity and the West. From this perspective, I hope to raise awareness among scholars by defining the "non-Islamic" ideas that have been essential to the overall development of the Islamist ideology, disturbing at once the Islamist claim to local "authenticity" as well as the too-common assumption in the West that these radical politics somehow represent a "natural" or "logical" extension of Islamic religious or cultural history as such. For, although it is true that Islam in its historical evolution has provided conceptual, institutional, and moral resources for contemporary Islamic political movements, there have also been fundamentally important levels of the

Islamist social *imaginaire* that are interacting and interrelating deeply with core intellectual discourses of what has been called the Western counter-Enlightenment.

I argue in this connection that Muslim intellectuals in general – and Iranian intellectuals in particular – have come to know the West, modernity, and democracy largely through the radical counter-Enlightenment ideas of German philosophy, as well as of certain French intellectuals, in a genealogy that goes back to the counter-Enlightenment movement: from its various twists and turns through such early ideologues as Joseph de Maistre – who defended the French *ancien régime* – to such latter-day and more boldly aggressive defenders of the aristocratic "order of rank" as Friedrich Nietzsche, and finally Martin Heidegger, on the eve of fascist total war against the values of the Enlightenment in World War II. On the other hand, we may just as easily indicate evidence of the Enlightenment democratic tradition at work within modern Iranian political history – for example, in the Constitutional Revolution of 1905–11, or the democratic experimental interim of 1941–53. In other neighboring Asian nations, we may point to the successful political establishment of these democratic Enlightenment traditions over the long term, most particularly in India.

These expressions of Enlightenment and counter-Enlightenment heritage are always unique and specific to the evolving society in question. In this context, I argue that political Islam in Iran is in considerable part a nativist reaction to modernity that is in many ways very similar to early twentieth-century populist reactions to modern democracy in Europe. Similarly for Iran, as for Europe, there is the ever-present possibility of the establishment of democratic hegemony within the Iranian context.

2. The Philosophical Foundations of Islamism

Many Islamic thinkers have become fascinated by the Nietzschean and particularly Heideggerian critique of the West as the source of modern dehumanization and a general loss of cultural and existential meaning, or so-called roots. Through the popularity of these discourses, in turn, the West, modernity, and democracy have often been construed through a narrowly constricted lens that unjustly links the positive democratic heritage directly to such dark experiences as colonization and imperialism. It is necessary to show that the assumption of such an "essential" link is a harmful error and is based on a falsely monolithic imagining of the West popularized in counter-Enlightenment discourses.

This project presents a clear case study of the rise of political Islam
in Iran, and the strong Heideggerian influence on a number of leading
Iranian intellectuals who helped enormously to articulate the Islamist ideology that paved the way to the 1979 revolution (Fardid, Al-e Ahmad,
Shari'ati, Shayegan, Davari, etc.). These individuals reckoned with experiences of social and cultural dislocation spurred by rapid modernization,
urbanization, foreign intervention, concomitant economic marginalization, and crises in political legitimacy – all of which induced them to seek
and, indeed, invent an appropriate ideology of radical social transformation. In light of such complex evidence and genealogies, it becomes meaningless to talk about Islamic thought as such as any explanation for these
political movements and discourses, or to discuss political Islam as if it
were disconnected from crucial political discourses and issues contemporary to the modern West itself. We see, rather, how it is more productive
to discuss radical Islamist movements in terms of the troubling alternative vision of modernity that was ushered in by the counter-Enlightenment
tradition with a reactionary emphasis on rigid social cohesion, hierarchy,
and preservation of order grounded in shared public meaning and culturally rooted values and traditions. The counter-Enlightenment undertook
a fearful effort to bring final closure to the disconcerting unity of disunity
that is modern life.

The reappraisal of political Islam in this light should lead to a new
approach in public discussion and better illuminate the general predicament of Islamic societies by going beyond the current focus on two issues:

(a) The idea that political Islam is representative of Islam or the Muslim
world against the values and institutions of the democratic West or
Judeo-Christian civilization. Framing this conflict as a fundamental
clash of two essential worldviews, or competing forms of socioeth-
ical understanding, will only assist Islamists who claim that their
own political aspirations represent the historical grievances of the
Muslim world as a whole. The framing of the issue in this way,
moreover, is consistent with the Islamists' goal of presenting their
agenda in terms of opposing identity politics, and can only close
any meaningful public dialogue concerning the relationship of our
contemporary societies and the possible nature of their complex
interactions.
(b) The treatment of current tensions in terms of an idea of East-
West communication. This is something to be avoided, because we
know that this kind of discussion is prone to imagining the West

as a closed and essential entity that is situated in the context of the historical experience of Christian moral values and is hostile to the "Eastern" worldview. This project should alert us to the fact that the West is not a bounded geographical entity and has a great deal more presence in the Muslim world than has so far been adequately recognized and reflected on. Of even more significance, the Islamists themselves are far more influenced by important ideological waves in "Western" thought than they are ready to admit and than others indeed have so far recognized.

These two mainstream tendencies are embodied in the writings of, for example, Esposito and Hadad, in arguments that "Islam" represents a tradition that does not separate religion from politics. There is also the "critical theory" social science approach that interprets Islamist movements as part of larger emerging discursive movement identified, in Michel Foucault's terms, as the rise of "subjugated knowledges." From this perspective, Islam is viewed as a tradition presenting an alternative to liberal modernity and challenging the totalizing nature of rational Enlightenment. Influential writers including Talal Asad, and in a less rigid way Saba Mahmood, have declared the Islamic tradition incompatible with secular liberalism on this theoretical basis. These views ultimately entail a concept of Islam anchored in a notion of romantic authenticity.

Going beyond these two dominant interpretations (the "conventional" and the "critical") will first contribute to a demystification of Islamism, and will second indicate the extent to which we live in a critical and defining moment in the future development of Islam itself, in which an important struggle is taking place over how Islam is to be defined in the modern situation. Within this context, we see that, although political Islamism offers an important voice within contemporary Islam, there are at least two other voices with very different interpretations of Islam and an altogether different understanding of the place of this religious tradition in the modern world.

(a) The traditionalist Islamic establishment and its Ulama.

   Since its inception in the 1950s in Iran, Islamism has been and remains a major challenge to traditionalist Islamic leadership and institutions. The traditionalist establishment does not agree with the overpoliticization of Islam and religious institutions, and it is therefore an important force in quietly undermining certain Islamic radical movements. This is true in Turkey, Egypt, Iran, and many of the Gulf States.

The unfortunate tendency to treat Islamism as representative of Islam as such in today's world has made it difficult for the traditionalist forces to effectively challenge political Islam in the more serious way of which they might otherwise be capable. Making the distinction between opposing elements and tendencies within an "Islamic" world space already rich in diverse languages and ethnocultural variety will both help the existing democratic forces and, at the same time, undermine the ability of Islamism to claim for itself the role of complete embodiment of the religion.

(b) The reformist movements, intellectuals, and institutions.

In almost all Muslim countries, including Iran, Algeria, Egypt, and Turkey, the main challenge to conventional Islam comes from reformist religious intellectuals, and the many institutions with which they have been involved. Religious intellectuals such as Abdolkarim Soroush in Iran, Mohammed Arkoun in Algeria-France, Nasr Hamid Abu Zayd in Egypt, and so on, are important forces with powerful and practical ideas that have attracted and captured the imagination of both educated youth and the middle class. Those who see these religious intellectuals as representing simply more moderate versions of Islamism make a considerable error. Intellectuals of this variety have achieved a fundamentally different view of Islam and its place in society and have, moreover, set themselves and their ideas up as potential democratic forces aligned with the more progressive elements in the society.

Although it is no doubt true that these Islamic tendencies have certain shared ideas and outlooks, in looking at the social and intellectual contexts and the complex developments that have attended the ascent of political Islam over the decades we should be able to clarify the distinction between the basic aims and precepts of political Islam in comparison to those of the religious intellectuals. The larger argument of this study is that Islamist movements are a part of the larger issue of reconciling Islamic societies with modernity, a project that has opened up a variety of roads. Whereas much current literature on political Islam focuses largely on the origin or nature of Islamist movements or their failures in resolving the crisis of Islamic societies, I argue that unless a properly democratic narrative of modernity that is compatible with contemporary Islamic societies can be offered, the Islamist ideology will likely continue to dominate even in the clear absence of an ability to offer any meaningful political or socioeconomic progress.

3. Alternative Narratives of Modernity and Enlightenment within the West, in Non-Western Countries, and within Islam

One central aim of this project is to offer a democratic narrative of modernity by highlighting diverse intellectual trends in the West and in non-Western societies such as India. There were different experiences at the origins of modernity in England and the United States, with their own particular approaches to religion and secularism, and these differ from the French model that is so often taken to represent the experience of modernity as such. Yet, these often more open experiences, allowing for a far wider latitude of possible belief and a greater openness to religion, are regularly overlooked or minimized in comparison to those historically constructed and more dogmatic discourses that are repeated routinely in studies of the meaning and nature of modernity. The vision of an expanded democratic narrative of modernity is also given articulation in the philosopher John Dewey's ideas of democratic public life and his philosophy of conceptual pluralism, which critique the often unknowingly recycled metaphysical presuppositions that insist on the unique possibility of a single road to democratic modernity. Dewey goes further to argue that secularism – as merely a formal and legal system – cannot by itself maintain democratic and egalitarian principles in a society, and some additional "common" or unifying ideals and moral traditions are required to help develop our communities toward the realization of freedom.

Dewey's ideas are given an interesting practical counterpart in the social movements in both India and the United States, in which intellectual leaders – namely Gandhi, Nehru, and King – envisioned democratic social change in terms of the incorporation of values of the Enlightenment, in addition to a critique of Western oppression, with their particular moral and cultural understanding of the world.

Through an in-depth look into the ideas of visionary democratic leaders of the twentieth century, such as Gandhi, Nehru, and King, we find models for practical experiences of democratic social change that incorporate moral and cultural sensibilities while creating democratic spaces and extending the heritage of Enlightenment along new paths. Both Gandhi and King articulated nonviolent and inclusive democratic discourses suited to the growing complexities of evolving global multicultural societies in which the traditional past need be neither enshrined in dangerous dogma nor rejected out of hand as being "other" to modernity. Rather, for these thinkers and activists, the traditional past is to be engaged as a vehicle for the construction of a democratic form of social organization suited to the society in question. At the same time, Nehru articulated a vision of Indian history that in many ways expands the historical paradigm beyond the regularly reproduced limits of a "West-centric" and linear framework to include voices and experiences that have fallen under the shadow of the "unthought" in dominant historical narratives, all the while being highly important to the complex development of global modernity and its democratic possibilities.

In this context, it is crucial to examine the ideas of those important contemporary religious reformist intellectuals who offer a radically alternative, open-ended, and democratic path for Islam in opposition to the intellectually and politically totalitarian project of Islamism. We may point here to certain key Muslim intellectuals, particularly Mohammed Arkoun, in order to show a widespread and growing tendency among Islamic thinkers toward conceiving and imagining a more enlightened understanding of historical and contemporary relations between Islam and the West, as well as venturing profound criticism and reinterpretation of historical and contemporary Islamic thought and culture with a view to developing more democratic forms in existing Islamic societies. By way of these reconstructions of Islamic thought and reconsiderations of historically engrained dogmas, these thinkers explore paths along the frontier of the "unthought" in contemporary culture and politics and point to alternative democratic possibilities while also showing an often-overlooked dimension of contemporary Islamic culture and religious discourse. This project, in sum, presents a critical representation of an important, but unfortunately overlooked, dimension of contemporary Islam that is ever-growing and open to the ideas and experiences of democratic modernity along a variety of new paths.

Chapter Summary

Chapter 1. Intellectuals and the Politics of Despair

The central theme of this study is introduced in the dangers of ambitious intellectual projects for social transformation that fail to take into account, or are openly hostile to, everyday life. It is argued that existing everyday life, and not any metaphysical or epistemological plane, is the necessary intellectual starting point in projects for democratic social change.

Taking this problem into account, an epistemic historical analysis is called for to increase an awareness of the broader and unexamined frame of our received modern intellectual heritage in both Western and non-Western social contexts, and particularly in Iran. In this context we may distinguish "narratives of hope" from "narratives of despair." If the first presents a more sociological vision of change grounded in the everyday and centered around a flexible pragmatic ethics, the second disparages both the everyday and liberal institutions in the name of a supposedly higher order of social being grounded in an inflated and remote, generally totalizing, and metaphysical projection.

In light of this issue, the significance of John Dewey and Martin Heidegger are discussed, particularly the relevance of Heidegger to the rise of a powerful Islamic ideology in the Iranian context.

An analysis of the current Iranian intellectual situation, explained in terms of the "Fardid phenomenon," shows a radical separation between prevailing intellectual discourses and everyday life in contemporary Iran. Discourses tend to be either immersed in German metaphysical abstraction with dubious political aspects, or engaged in so-called radical epistemological critiques that call for the absolute overhaul of existing and traditional patterns of Iranian thought and culture in the name of a "new beginning." These equally pessimistic and totalizing forms of discourse have little to contribute in a society where an ongoing struggle for democratization continues to be the concern of most people.

In an analysis of "Fardidism" we see how Fardid, whose discourse introduced a break with Constitutional-era discourses around Enlightenment, science, progress, and so forth, established a new dominant intellectual model centered on a Heideggerian historicism and a metaphysical imaginary of "East" and "West" as hostile adversaries. Above all, Fardid introduced within this context the notion of a "master thinker" as the single key to opening up tomorrow's "new realities." This conception of the "master thinker" has shown amazing persistence in Iran, even among those intellectuals who are critical of Fardid, until it has become an almost *de rigeur* stance of contemporary Iranian intellectuals. It is this almost unconscious archetype that remains largely at the root of hostility to everyday life and democratic aspirations among too many Iranian intellectuals.

In this context, other important and influential Iranian intellectuals are examined, including Al-e Ahmad and Shayegan, who like Fardid anchor an imaginary cosmos of "East" versus "West" in a metaphilosophical framework of Heideggerian historicism and thus create a discourse of so-called Islamic authenticity that projects its absolutes beyond the mundane concerns and realities of the everyday, and beyond the democratic aspirations of most Iranian people.

On the other hand, we also find a second wave of "master thinkers," including Dustdar and Tabatabai, who argue that only by a radical destruction of existing and historical Iranian traditional religious thought – or an "epistemological revolution" – can the scene be properly set for establishing a modern democratic society. These equally pessimistic and metaphysical, not to say arrogant, ideas also project themselves on a totalizing level far above and beyond the realities of everyday life. Moreover, even as critics of Fardid, these thinkers share in the harmful archetype of the "master thinker." There is simply a shift from the premises of European counter-Enlightenment and culturalist (especially German) thought to the "certainties" of eighteenth-century rationalist and Orientalist ideas about the inadequacies of "Islam" for democratic modernity.

The chapter argues that these tendencies do have serious political implications in terms of fostering an elitist and undemocratic approach to social change, based on totalizing concepts that in no way take into account the sociological particulars and genuine issues of contemporary Iranian society.

Chapter 2. The Crisis of the Nativist Imagination

It is argued here that at stake in the type of discourses initiated by Fardid and others is a larger crisis of security rooted in the decentering experiences of modernity and a consequent will to project a future based on some vivid imagining of a stable and authentic past. This landscape of the imagination is far from unique to Iran and can be found in many writers from both the West and the world over. An analysis of Rimbaud's influential *A Season in Hell* shows a similar obsessive anxiety over loss of roots and obliterated memory, a critique of modern reason interwoven with Orientalist imagery and a search for a spiritual "home." Indeed, we can find a similar "landscape of the imagination" in the thought of such illustrious figures as Gandhi and Hegel. This chapter seeks in some measure to map out the main features of this powerful subterranean geography of the unconscious imagination.

The chapter offers a detailed analysis of Sudanese writer Tayeb Salih's *Season of Migration to the North*, arguing that this novel depicts the inherently violent dangers and antidemocratic character of anti-Western discourses centering roots and authenticity. The narrative reconstructs the Orientalist 'landscape of the imagination' as it is deployed from both "Eastern" and "Western" angles and simultaneously deflates its claims to any true reality beyond mere fantasy and violence of thought. We are urged to fully face up to the radical and disturbing nature of changes that have taken place throughout the history of the modern world without recourse to either fantasies of "return" to an unchanged precolonial past or dreams of revenge in the form of violent discourses of nativism.

We may read this book as a warning against political definitions of nation or religion centered on authenticity and thus based inevitably on the exclusion and denial of other ideas and experiences. Conversely, it is argued that open and democratic societies avoid the imposition of a narrative of authenticity as a principle or basis for inclusion and exclusion within modern society.

Chapter 3. Modernity beyond Nativism and Universalism

Contemporary Iranian discourses of authenticity that express a crisis of inner security and a bid for "wholeness" depend on the use of certain notions whose meaning is taken as self-evident: the West, universalism, tradition, nativism. As a result the level of debate is contained on a simple level of binaries (inside/outside, East/West) and does not extend to the more serious level of debate at which these very concepts in themselves contested and were redefined. Moreover, this tendency overlooks the reality of a particular Iranian experience and understanding of modernity and sees a falsely imagined option between a dichotomous inside and out-side. These ideas, in turn, are anchored in certain metaphysically inspired "philosophies of history."

The chapter presents these Iranian discourses in the broader global context of discourses of Enlightenment and counter-Enlightenment. We can make much sense of seminal Iranian political discourses of the late twentieth century in terms of their affinity with counter-Enlightenment thought and ideology as a somewhat unselfconscious global movement that is given expression in a great variety of modernizing national settings. It is argued that such discourses are inherently hostile to democracy.

The initial focus of the chapter is a presentation of the main debates that have animated intellectual life in postrevolutionary Iran, over "historicism" and "positivism," mainly between Soroush and Davari. These views, in turn, are discussed in the context of larger issues of modern political thought touching on the views of Hegel, Heidegger, and Dewey. In particular the discussion focuses on the relevance of movements in modern hermeneutics to such debates, as well as the dialectics of the nation-state. Here, we may take cautionary example from projects that combine hermeneutical interpretation with dogmatic and totalizing truth claims of an ontological nature, as we find in Heidegger and the many Iranian intellectuals who are influenced by him. On the other hand, we may point to different and more pluralistic uses of hermeneutics in the works of Arkoun, Soroush, and others.

By opening up these horizons for discussion, it is possible to investigate the potential grounds for a reflective and democratic enlightenment project in the contemporary Iranian context in terms of nontotalizing critique of national tradition centered on the strengthening of existing democratic possibilities. Such a project seeks a way to democracy through openness and pragmatism and presents an alternative to discourses of authenticity that center around forced and violent conceptions of closure.

Chapter 4. Heidegger and Iran: The Dark Side of Being and Belonging

Considering Heidegger's work, particularly *Being and Time*, from a political point of view, the chapter locates the philosopher's discourse in the historical context of the counter-Enlightenment tradition including Maistre, Rivarol, Nietzsche, Kierkegaard, and Junger, leading up to European fascist ideologies and World War 2. The chapter analyzes the importance of this tradition, and Heidegger's key place in it, for the Iranian Islamist discourses that took shape leading up to and provided the ideological base for the Iranian Revolution of 1979.

It is argued that Heidegger contributed to creating an alternative vision of modernity, one opposed to the values of Enlightenment and 1789 and indeed secular democracy as such. In contrast to the conservatism of the counter-Enlightenment tradition, Heidegger (like Nietzsche and also Junger before him) made a call for total and radical change combined paradoxically with a call for absolute authority in tradition. His alternative vision of modernity is thus totalizing in its call for what amounts to a "spiritual purity" and restored "rooted" community. These political ideas of "home," or being and belonging, had very strong resonance in Iran during the rapid modernization program imposed dictatorially by the Shah, and greatly helped to shape the "nativist" philosophy of the revolution in terms of both a "spiritual" sensibility and a defense of "local" culture against universalism grounded in a dangerously conceived "return" to a "pure source" of being or "authentic" identity.

The chapter analyzes Heidegger's ambiguous relation to the heritage of the "West" and his hermeneutical reconceptualization of the "West's" history as a decline or "fall from being." In an effort to reckon with the vertigo of modernity, Heidegger redefines the proper and "rooted" relation to the past in the name of a "new beginning" to be ushered in through language and action.

Heidegger is ultimately arguing for the institutionalization of "authentic being" in opposition to the "rootless" cosmopolitanism that is constructed on a "superficial" primacy of knowledge (from the Cartesian ego to the Hegelian dialectic). The institution of an "authentic" being grounded in "lived depth" necessitates a relation to the past as a "productive force." Such "authenticity," in the first place, amounts to an "ontological" privileging of cultural particularism as the "primordial phenomenon of truth" (in opposition to the "superficial" modern intellectual truth of representation). Such an idea of "truth" is further wedded to a set of "heroic" values of "active nihilism" in which "resoluteness" anchored in a strong tradition leads to the "primordial truth of existence." Heidegger accordingly identified two levels to Western tradition, the dominant inauthentic level, and the authentic level ("aletheia") buried under layers of corrupted interpretation awaiting resurrection.

It is argued that this series of philosophical positions in Heidegger is based on a totalizing truth claim as a hidden "authentic" ground accessible only by way of "revelation" and not reasoned argument, an experience of authenticity rather than any system of knowledge, and a matter of courage rather than understanding. A higher and deeper goal is realized in a "moment of vision" to revitalize and extend the "absolute tradition" grounded in "authentic being." Heidegger thereby establishes a paradigmatic conception of a clandestinely grounded essence of history as invisibly competing truth claims with apocalyptic moments of overall transformation.

Heidegger's is ultimately a religious discourse, calling for a social structure to impose an act of witness and remembrance of the unknowable "mystery" of being. In this way it is a political discourse that is antisecular, and in its call for a single overarching meaning, it is antipluralistic. His philosophy amounts to a philosophy of the will in the grip of a higher power as the basis for a radical and "authentic" social reconstruction. Finally, it is elitist in its privileging of moments of inspiration sent from being for the few as the basis for authentic action in an aesthetically conceived framework of truth. The idea complex in *Being and Time* points to the need for a totalitarian state power to carry out its vision and the disappearance of formal liberal freedoms under the promise of a rooted experience of being.

Chapter 5. Democracy and Religion in the Thought of John Dewey
The chapter considers the contribution of John Dewey's philosophy of Pragmatism to debates on the historically received paradigm of

modernity, particularly with regard to the question of democracy and religion in modern societies.

In his critique of dualisms, Dewey contended that Western historical epistemology, tacitly influenced by religious tendencies, had conceived a great wall between an imaginary higher and perfected order of being and the continuous change of an always unfinished lived experience, to the inherent denigration of the later. In defense of the rich pluralism of everyday life, Dewey sought to emancipate thinking from a metaphysics that he viewed as fostering a closed and antidemocratic paradigm of a "pure" and "completed" beyond. In this sense Dewey was a philosopher of openness and immanence in contrast to, for example, both the universalist dialectic of Hegel and the ontologically sanctioned hermeneutic of Heidegger – that is, the pitfalls of both liberal development schemes and cultural or religious essentialisms. Dewey sought answers in the complexity of moral experience as lived – a premise that begins from the existing world of lived cultures and traditions in their specific dynamism within the broader framework of the modern social universe. Dewey evolved a concept of "conceptual pluralism" grounded in a politics of "deliberative democracy," envisioning a decentered rather than statist political framework where sites of deliberation occur at multiple points beyond the narrow voting-based institutions controlled by elites.

"Conceptual Pluralism" opposes a conception of truth as a "fixed object of knowledge," beyond lived experience, proposing instead a specific and relational view of truth. Seeing Dewey's affinity with some poststructuralist thought, the chapter presents a comparison between Heidegger and Dewey in terms of their similar preoccupations over the basic problems of modernity as a universalizing end. Unlike Heidegger's insistence on protecting "being," or the insular stasis of traditional social forms, Dewey sought a balance between the "being" of tradition and the "becoming" of global scientific modernity. For Dewey, the conventional modern metaphysic of excluding or "transcending" traditional social forms was in clear error, and yet rather than protecting these traditional forms, Dewey saw in modernity an opportunity for their radical regeneration and growth toward the realization of a democratic politics. As an ethical premise, Dewey argued for the unity of ends and means, opposing the "grand plans" from above of totalizing modern ideologies that commit atrocities to attain their "ideal" ends, and he therefore introduced an alternative to the excesses of both liberal and "counter-Enlightenment" modes of political thought. These insights will prove to have great importance regarding the potentially positive relation between democracy and tradition, and the cautioning against the dire consequences of epistemic violence in roads to national liberation.

"Conceptual pluralism" may be understood principally in terms of its refusal of a transcendent "Reason" as the search for "immutable truths" and rather its emphasis on the application of intelligence and imagination to specific problems. Dewey's refusal of an "antecedent" or "pure" truth has implications for "deliberative democracy." In line with the shift into a pluralism and immanence of lived experience that is story structured rather than "beyond," we also see how democracy cannot be governed by any fixed or final principles of either the ontological or epistemic sort, but is at once a goal and a means requiring a broad participation inclusive of the diversity of existing social forms to be effective. In this way Dewey creates a nonfoundationalist framework or conceptual openness to modernity, potentially open to trajectories of reason traditionally linked to non-Western contexts. Dewey, being aware of this, urged philosophical thought to move outside the narrowly conceived and closed historical framework of "Western Civilization" from ancient Greece to the modern West, anticipating the pluralistic historical meditations of Nehru explored later in this study.

Dewey's thought has considerable relevance to current debates over modernity in the "Third World" with respect to any secular democratic project. It is "rooted" and "meaningful" while avoiding any totalitarian pitfall, reducible neither to a "scientific secularism" nor to "ontology" of "roots" and "authenticity." In his radical democratic vision, he emphasizes the social nature of knowledge and imagination as well as the importance of community and tradition. In this context, Dewey is open to the potentially positive role of religion in democratic modernity as he opposes received "foundationalism" to a "conceptual pluralism."

Key to "conceptual pluralism" are the ideas of "imagination" and "intelligence," and in this chapter we focus on Dewey's *A Common Faith* with its distinction between "religion" (closed institutional doctrine) and the "religious" (the evolving historical imagination) and critique of historic epistemology. For Dewey, the supernatural, or "transcendent object," is the defining limitation of traditional Western faith and intellectual thought. Rejecting the dogma of any specific kind of experience that is religious experience – the exclusive claim of each particular religion – and arguing that *all* experience can be potentially religious, Dewey argued for an understanding of God as the "unity of all ideal ends arousing us to desire and action." Hence the "religious" needs to be liberated from the narrowly dogmatic claims of "religions" so that the virtues, moral traditions, and contemplative sensibilities of traditional religions may survive and flourish in an increasingly secular modern culture and contribute positively to its growth.

Here Dewey opposes a dogmatic substantive metaphysical reason to a principle of growth in everyday life and proposes a corresponding cognitive structure of considerably wider range beyond "known objects." In this Pragmatist framework, there is no inflatedly conceived "utopia" beyond, for which existing cultures must be violently transcended; rather, existing cultures in their living immanence are to be developed with full realization of their flexible and dynamic potential through reflexive thought and action. Dewey therefore at once calls for a reflexive modernity and a radical reconstitution of our intellectual and practical relation to our inherited traditional past: a combination without the "completion" of absolutely new beginnings or final ends, but rather evolving options between sometimes incompatible conventions grounded in the open terrain of everyday experience guided by democratic principle. Dewey's work makes an important case for cultures, including religions, as being not monoliths defined by fixed essences but rather sites of multiple evolutions in a perpetual becoming and regeneration where non-violent democratic potentialities may always represent possible roads to the future.

Chapter 6. Enlightenment and Moral Politics
This chapter explores the idea that Enlightenment may be viewed on a far broader spatiotemporal basis than is regularly supposed in conventional narratives that center the eighteenth-century French Enlightenment and Revolution. The experience of the British Enlightenment centers a notion of "moral sense" that is more inclusive than the more restricted and elitist French Enlightenment discourse of Reason. This alternative emphasis has ethical implications, pointing to a politics of broadly based dialogue and localized democratic transformation, while permitting the valuable contribution of religious and other traditional values/ideas in the process of modern democratic nation making. The ideas of the British Enlightenment have certain continuity in the radical Enlightenment ideas that drove the Indian National Movement, itself a rich blend of Indian political and philosophical ideas as well as Western and other intellectual elements. The core ethical and practical precepts of the Indian National Movement under Gandhi and Nehru, following their success in achieving a democratic Indian independence, were adopted by Martin Luther King

in his leadership of the American Civil Rights Movement. In this history of ideas and practices we see a broadly inclusive, creative, and flexible tradition of Enlightenment that is derived from global ideational sources and far more adaptively open and nonviolent than the conventionally recognized French Enlightenment paradigm.

I

Intellectuals and the Politics of Despair

Intellectual work and ideas exist in a complex relation with the material and practical world, being neither the pure products of the individual mind (or "genius") nor simply the passive reflections of material and economic reality in a given time and place. Although intellectual works and ideas are shaped by the institutions and material conditions in which they are born, they also have a measure of autonomy in their ongoing dialogue with historical intellectuals across the seas of time, and among specific contemporary intellectuals from near or far. In the dialectic between structure and agency, moreover, the modality of culture is a dualistic combination of constraints and enabling functions involving an ongoing negotiation of norms. These overall destabilizing and patterned "long" moments, involving the living and the dead, may be called intellectual communities. They form the material and imaginative source and space for the development of intellectual ideas on the conscious surface level of what is said, and the more buried unconscious level of a historical field of possible questions, outlooks, alternatives, and lines of formation. On this basis, it becomes important to explore and understand how intellectuals relate to and are influenced by other intellectuals, the way in which they imagine their own role and identity within the larger intellectual community and its history, and the often unconscious regularities that guide their thought.

In this chapter we sketch the grounding for such an analysis within the modern twentieth-century Iranian context, in what we could call a history of the present. To look at the conditions for emergence and changes in Iranian intellectual culture during the twentieth century is above all to analyze the network of possibilities and constraints around ethical concepts and the construction of "absolute values" that took place. To analyze the intellectual conditions that produced the affirmation of such "absolute values" is to come to understand the emerging historical ethics in Iran in their direct relation to political power. This form of author-itarian political order, which obtained power through the revolution in the name of such "absolute values," is above all notable for its hostility to those powers animating everyday life or civil society that drove earlier moments in Iranian history such as the Constitutional Revolution or the National Front Coalition.

The danger presented by the wedding of "absolute values" to intellec-tual enthusiasms is hardly unique to Iran and has constituted a general political danger to liberty throughout the modern period. Intellectuals and their labor, by virtue of a social location less grounded in any particular class and at greater liberty to unleash the impulses of inner subjectiv-ity, are relatively removed from the constraints and realities of everyday life. For this reason, intellectuals are best situated to offer imaginative ideas on their respective societies. On the best and rarest of occasions, they may even help in some measure to bring about change in local or even global realities. However, the force of the intellectual imagination can only assist with realizing a spirit of hope or a fantastic creativity, or unveiling real new social possibilities, when the intellectual imagination leaves a particular space for the world of everyday life in existing actu-ality as a key reference point for all socially oriented intellectual work. It is most often only the pragmatic ethics, or concern with social good, that can help prevent intellectual reflection from being seduced by nar-cissistic expressions of subjectivity, the tyranny of ideas, and the violence of thought. Intellectuals are often in conflict over how to negotiate their relationship with the societies in which they live. If they give up hope of the possibility of a meaningful life as it actually exists, they are prone to creating their visions of reality based on fantasies of nostalgia, and their vision thereby becomes utopian, impractical, and unconcerned with the practical or ethical implications of the ideas produced. As a result, the intellectual attitude develops into one that is brutally hostile toward all social realities as they currently exist, or simply all that *is* in some wildly conceived and apocalyptic ontological critique. Deeming the world to be without hope in its present state, such intellectuals look to some imag-ined society in the past for inspiration, or even some dreamed-up science fiction-now vision of the future. We may remember that almost all tragic social projects of recent times, particularly in the last century, have had strong intellectual influences that were generally calls for some absolute overhaul of all existing social or historical realities. The memories of the previous century should teach us to mistrust such absolute beginnings.

When grounded in everyday reality, intellectuals can offer and often have offered a social narrative about the future that may be one of hope or healing, social solidarity, or cultural tolerance. Their work may explicitly connect the contemporary situation to the past, or it may contribute to assembling stories about traditions of struggle for justice and freedom and celebrate the sufferings for social good and human hope. In so doing, such intellectual work may strive to bring out the best aspects of any tradition. In the case of Iran, the history of Iranian political culture and popular movements prior to the 1960s–1970s period tells of precisely such a story. The national democratic struggle was firmly anchored in the experience of the post–World War II democratic interval (1941–53), where the public prevalence of secular Left and nationalist politics had culminated in Mohammed Mossadeq's 1951–53 Popular Front Government – a mass movement dedicated to a secular-democratic and independent national politics. Mossadeq promoted a democratic political line in part by appealing to the values of Iranian religious tradition, while also asserting the novel ideal of secular reason as supreme over other forms of traditional law. His ideas and the political practices he initiated were powerful attempts to integrate Enlightenment ideals with existing Iranian traditions. Mossadeq's efforts were grounded in the already existing Iranian political culture traceable to the 1905–11 Constitutional Revolution, which was itself a mass movement dedicated to a parliamentary constitutional and independent form of government.

Genealogies of intellectual roles in the public space, however, all too often tell a far darker story as well. The history of intellectuals in general is one filled with extremes of contradictory and often painful tendencies and impulses. Among Iranian intellectuals, Sadeq Hedayat (1903–51) stands out in this regard: setting out as a very bright foreign student of privileged origins living in Paris, he befriended Jean Paul Sartre and passionately explored European literature and ideas. A prolific writer, he attempted to introduce modern European literary conventions to Iran (Kafka, Sartre, and Poe) but steadily found himself morally and politically estranged from his home country. After his failed attempt to return home and live productively in Iran, he became an exile in France who voiced bitter criticism of the Iranian monarchy and society. While sinking deeper into spiritual despair, he wrote his famous *The Blind Owl*, a labyrinthine tale of the soul's journey through a bleak landscape of petrified traditional forms (mixing Buddhism, Hinduism, and Islam) and warped modern structures embodying paranoia, tyranny, and oppression. The degree of his inner despair led to his suicide in a Paris hotel room in his late forties. Thus, one of the more widely acknowledged literary talents of twentieth-century Iran ultimately left behind an intellectual legacy of nihilism and despair tinged strongly with the irrationalist and angst-laden themes of Surrealism and Existentialism. His works, though banned in today's Iran, are still illicitly available in popular bookstalls and are widely admired – despite the underlying hopelessness and circularity of his later and most well known works – as visions of resistance to dehumanizing political authority. Certainly his social class at once permitted him to travel and alienated him from the popular traditions of his country, contributing to his cosmopolitan sense of loneliness. His very social class was the abrupt product of the national modernization drive from above that persecuted him politically and artistically, and which he hated violently in the form of the reigning state. Perhaps this explains the abundance of police spies populating *The Blind Owl*, the graphic violence, and the frightful mood of schizophrenia running through the mysterious split narrative. Hedayat's traveling and study permitted him to learn foreign languages and meet influential intellectuals in other societies. For all of these structural or socioeconomic elements constituting his life path, he generated a deeply personal and original (if highly metaphoric) vision of Iran's fate in modernity that spoke to literate Iranians on an emotive level across a wide spectrum in ways the author surely never consciously intended.

The mood of despair mixing existential and political themes that gripped Hedayat also found its way into the thought of more theoretically minded Iranian intellectuals, particularly of the post-1953 coup period. With the 1960s–1970s period in Iran, notably, the more cosmopolitan and secularly oriented critical political and intellectual tradition shifted insidiously in favor of an alternative vision as cosmopolitan intellectuals started losing ground to intellectuals promoting nativist or Islamist discourses claiming "absolute values." This Iranian example, among many others in a variety of countries, has forced contemporary intellectuals to look this reality in the face: where national democratic institutions are young, the irresponsible embrace of violent and fanatical ideologies by influential young intellectuals of secular learning seeking "roots" can have painfully tragic results.

This lesson concerns a political shadow and intellectual hazard that is particularly modern, rather than a survival from the traditional past. Throughout modern history, the psychological boundaries between hope and despair, the temporal ones between past and future, the ethical and existential ones between self and others, and the very border between real and imagined are not always as clearly defined and recognizable as some would like to think. This fact, as a reflection of a growing awareness of the complexity of human and natural reality (our growing realization of what the universe is), is not necessarily a problem in itself. If, however, one is or becomes blind to the consequences of the ideas or theories that one embraces within the "immature sciences" of sociology and politics, then this basic fact of life ambiguity can take on disastrous and dangerous dimensions.

We need to critically take into account an epistemic history underlying received ideas. It is important to have a clear and full awareness of the intellectual heritage, the broader and often unexamined frame, being taking in hand as one reckons with the puzzling and often volatile issues of contemporary modern societies and social ideas in their evolving and radically overlapping global trajectories. This warning was buried implicitly in Foucault's *The Order of Things*, but because of his insistence on "determining systemization" over "meaning and intention" in human affairs, he could not take the message of his own work fully to heart. For today's Iranians who experienced the 1979 revolution and reflect critically on these events, this lesson is unforgettable. In a discussion with Alireza Alavi Tabar in 2005, a Ph.D. in political science and a prominent figure in the 1990s for his journalistic writings and essays on the politics of the Iranian reform movement, he points out that the Iranian Revolution began with the combined intellectual influences of Shari'ati and Motahari on social and epistemological thought. The central role assigned to the State, he recalls, was mostly based on Shari'ati's stance on leadership which envisions the responsibility of the government as being to elevate the population on cultural and moral grounds – a notion Shari'ati drew largely from his understanding of German nihilist thought (including Heidegger and Junger) reconstituted for the Iranian setting by important Iranian writers (Fardid, Al-e Ahmad) influenced by this movement for a higher purpose to modern politics than mere democracy or public welfare.

To illustrate these dilemmas, this study addresses two elements in comparing what I call, first, narratives of hope – a more sociological approach or vision of social change with particular emphasis on the here and now, the category of the everyday, the framework of pragmatic ethics, and a guiding commitment to the democratic possibility of modernity to, second, narratives of despair featuring broad philosophical and ontologically

grounded critiques of modernity, disregard for the everyday, and hostility toward the supposed mediocrity of liberal institutions and democratic
forms of social organization in the name of an allegedly higher and elitist
order of social being that is often imagined to have been lost somewhere
and somehow.

John Dewey, with his theory of conceptual pluralism, is among those
best representing the first category in narratives of hope. Dewey's critique
of metaphysics was a basically political stance in which he insisted on the
ethical and epistemic primacy of the everyday world in its richness and
diversity of possibility as a basis for democratic transformation. This conviction, in turn, was grounded in a critique of ontological and epistemological dogmatisms that sought to explain human experience reductively
in terms of any fixed essence or principle, thereby denying all others as
inauthentic, irrational, or any other excluding binary structurally integral
to such dogma in any form. Dewey's work is at once a deep critique of the
more totalizing and intolerant tendencies in historical Western modernity
while being nevertheless also an endeavor to champion and preserve the
enormously valuable aspect of this heritage in the democratic project. For
Dewey, everyday experience is the necessary starting point for intellectual
inquiry, and so there can be no fixed metaphysical conception of a timeless democracy floating in a pure transcultural modernity to exclude those
complex contributions of local cultures that must inevitably project themselves onto the struggle for democratic modernity in any concrete social
setting. Dewey's ethical critique concerned the insight that the means
must be one with the ends in projects of democratic social reconstruction on both moral and practical grounds. He was therefore opposed to
gigantically conceived utopian social projects that aimed for the realization of some new dawn in the form of a violence inflicted on the past
and hence on human life itself. For Dewey, as a result, although the critical sociological tools of enlightenment in the everyday context were an
indispensable opportunity for a selective social and cultural growth of
all existing traditions, even a purging of their more deplorable elements,
the destructive idea of progress as total transformation – as championed
by the model of the French Revolution – could lead only to tragedy and
further cycles of violence that obliterate democratic aspirations. Dewey's
articulation of this complex crossroads serves as a balanced and sensitive
theoretical alternative to the extremes between ideologies of hegemonic
Western modernity and nativist authenticity that have too often dominated discourse in the loudest and harshest of terms, dividing it artifi-
cially into two camps. We find examples of this outlook in the story of

twentieth-century Iranian politics and nation making, notably in the thought and practice of Prime Minister Mossadeq, who argued that democratic legal reform is possible within the context of Iranian Islamic society through a framework integrating examples from Turkey, Tunisia, and Japan, as well as a "synthesis between Iranian and European ideas, values and techniques."[1]

The most representative as well as impressive example of the second category in narratives of despair is Heidegger, to say nothing of the great many who have been, and continue to be, influenced by a Heideggerian critique of modernity as an expression of their own longing for cultural roots. Heidegger ventured a critique of modernity that, though at first sight nondogmatic and immanent in its rejection of Western metaphysics, in fact instituted a discourse of authenticity as a substitute category of value and enshrined a notion of heritage as an overarching social meaning to be imposed by force of violence if necessary in the quest for a pure identity in being. The admirable focus on everydayness in the early part of *Being and Time* is lost in the later part and later works as everydayness is reviled as an expression of inauthentic historical being in comparison to the new beginning. This is a discourse with an obvious hostility to any conception of democratic social organization and is therefore inherently prone, on simple pragmatic grounds, to the violent excesses and intolerance of a totalitarian state structure. It is in terms of this issue that we may explain the relationship between Heidegger's philosophical views and his friendly attitude toward German fascism. This relationship can very likely be traced to Heidegger's philosophical disregard for the everyday and the corresponding privileging of certain grand ideas at the expense of living human predicaments.

It is telling that although debates on Heidegger's philosophy as a political legacy have been passionate and plentiful, and debates on Islamist political movements and particularly Iran have been equally if not more intense, there has been no space whatsoever devoted to the profound entanglement of these two deeply timely and problematic issues. This reflects at once the continuing and stubborn insistence, no doubt largely unconscious, on an Orientalist divide at an essential level between Western and Eastern thought, an entrenched tendency of noncommunication and an easy way out as harmful as it is misleading. In fact, Western ideas are at the very heart of the so-called Islamist ideology in its many forms and partake at this level in an identical and equally erroneous notion of the essential East/West divide. This serves to obscure what is in fact a broadly shared cultural and intellectual ancestry, and not only in the modern period, to say nothing of a highly dangerous shared contemporary political conjuncture made only more volatile by the ignorance and fear perpetuated by Orientalist and Islamist essentialist discourses alike. This study is intended as a step toward clearing the path of such distortions toward the goal of productive communication with the shared aim of constructing forms of democratic social organization.

The Fardid Phenomenon

In Iran, where Heidegger's influence on intellectual life has been profound, intellectuals are of special importance to contemporary Iranian society. In the absence of such well-established and strong institutions in the public sphere as long-lasting political parties, independent media, and institutions of higher learning, as well as unions and professional organizations and societies, intellectuals are seen as public leaders in defining cultural visions and possibilities for the future, conditions of the present, as well as articulating narratives of past traditions. It is somewhat ironic that in the supposedly religious postrevolutionary Iran it is the role of intellectuals, in their debates and ideas, that has become the critical and defining core of the world of Iranian political and cultural discussion. Those who are unhappy with the rise and establishment of the Islamic state and religious domination of the public space condemn the status quo based on the left-leaning and anti-Western intellectual discourses that were so dominant in the 1960s and '70s. Others, who identify with the current power structure, dismiss any critical intellectuals as alien and irrelevant to the authentic cultural and historical experiences of Iran and Iranians.

One unfortunate consequence of the exaggerated position of Iranian intellectuals in social and political affairs, coupled with their endless obsession with fighting one another, is that in recent years they have increasingly isolated both themselves and their ideas from the issues and struggles of everyday Iranians and the society at large.

Intellectuals are far away from what is ostensibly the subject of their intellectual inquiries, namely, the current political conditions and cultural crisis of Iranian society. Many leading intellectuals have sought refuge in, most notably, German philosophical traditions and, in the most imaginative fashion, have succeeded in creating an intellectual environment where the ideas of Heidegger and his philosophical tradition became the dominant discourse among university students, Islamic intellectuals, and some secular intellectuals. One leading intellectual recently announced that it is almost impossible to understand the current Iranian situation unless one is fully trained in Hegelian philosophy.

The intellectual arrogance of many leading Iranian intellectuals in what is the so-called contemporary epistemological revolutionary stream has led to their insistence that all of the social and cultural ills of the society are a result of the way Iranians think or, more precisely, the inability of Iranians to think, as linked to the decline of rational or critical thinking in Iranian history. This is a kind of absolute epistemological critique that, in its stark pessimism regarding existing culture and society, obviously partakes of the tradition of narratives of despair. What is most interesting and ironic about this is that these intellectuals attack each other opinions and also the history of modern ideas in Iran as an expression of *Enhetat Tafakor,* or the decline of thinking. Some even go so far as to condemn the entire history of Iran as the history of a dogmatic and unthinking cultural experience. Others identify the decline of rational thinking in Iran with the post-Islamic period. The grandiose and vague philosophical general-izations about Iranian history and its current predicament make it almost impossible to identify what it is that many Iranian intellectuals of this stripe are considering as the real sources and origins of the Iranian crisis and precisely what problem the philosophical rethinking they propose will supposedly address.

From the point of view of an outsider, there appears to be a strug-gle for democratization going on in contemporary Iran. A large part of the Iranian population, including women, youth, and the middle class, would like to see a more open and democratic as well as prosperous soci-ety. These groups are therefore at odds with those in power who have imposed a closed and restricted Islamic state dominated by conservative *Ulama* who do not recognize women's rights and see human rights in themselves as representing an alien social discourse, and who are gen-erally very suspicious of secular and modern ideas and lifestyles. One may conclude from this that the secular intellectual concerned with the current situation in Iran would try to articulate ideas suited to bringing democratic change to the society. Yet the intellectual scene in Iran unfor-tunately tells a different and very depressing story. Some of the leading Iranian intellectuals, taking part in the narrative of despair, have decided to reject and fundamentally question any possibility of hope in Iran. It would seem that, according to them, unless Iranians give up their reli-gious beliefs and affiliations and willingly submit to some kind of great epistemological transformation, they are condemned to live a life of self-inflicted brutality, destruction, and despair.

Ironically, the core ideas, worldviews, and social/cultural projects advocated by many Iranian philosophers are almost exclusively drawn from a particular tradition in German philosophy, a tradition that has also very often grounded its principal claims and ideas in a despairing vision of reality as it now exists or modernity as such. Hegel, of whom this is of course true to a lesser extent, Nietzsche, and particularly Heidegger are embraced, introduced and reintroduced by intellectuals in Iran as if the German project had been responsible for producing only the most democratic societies of our time. These Iranian intellectuals have fantastic imaginations that permit them to totally disregard the reality of contemporary Iran as well as the real historical experiences marking the German involvement with a harsh reality produced by radical antiliberal discourses in the tradition of Nietzsche and Heidegger. They would have us believe that in contemporary Iran, it is Nietzsche's critique concerning the innocence of becoming or even postmodernist hostility to formal democracy that can offer solutions to the already strange Islamic discourse growing amid the antiliberal and antidemocratic political realities of today's Iran. What is it that makes these seemingly very clever intellectuals believe that ordinary Iranians, in their desire for a democratic society, are unable to think rationally and critically? Moreover, how is it possible that these philosophers might have, even after the tragedies of German fascism and so many other dreadful political experiences of radical antimodernism, a way of thinking that will help Iranian society to live peacefully and democratically? Those who unreflectively succumb to the seductions and gigantic promises of a narrative of despair may or may not realize that this discourse is antidemocratic even at the elementary level of its founding precepts and can therefore pave a road only to an enormous degree of human suffering in its quest for either a pure (and therefore violently exclusive) home in modernity or a clear epistemological break with the corrupting past.

The thinker whose work contributed most to setting the ground for a Heideggerian political discourse in the Iranian context was Ahmad Fardid (1890–1994). He was the leading authority on German philosophy and Heidegger in particular from the 1950s on. Ultimately, he contributed enormously to the evolution of the intellectual discourses that culminated in the Iranian Revolution of 1979. His work involved redressing the Orient-Occident binary in a language of philosophical conceptions borrowed from Heidegger. In a historicist vein, he argued that the dominant "truth" of the era had been, since the eighteenth century, that of a Western civilization that robbed all "Islamic countries" and "oriental nations" of their "cultural memoirs" and their own "historic trust."[2] This position is constituted first of an anti-Enlightenment claim that the growth of empty and external Western civilization is a direct threat to the vitality of local non-Western cultures, and second of the claim that this threat must be met by way of a reclaiming of what is an erased cultural memory and seizing hold of a stolen past. In the dualistic framework of Orient-Occident, Fardid insists that *Gharb* (the West) has to be abandoned as both an ontology and a way of life. The West, then, is conceived as an ontological unity immersed in the "moon" of reality while the "sun" of truth in an ontologically opposed Iranian Islam has gone into eclipse.[3] This outlook may perhaps be compared to Zizek's idea of reality as a kind of desert accessible by science, whereas experience is invariably bounded by the colorful and illusionary world of imagination. Yet here one variant of imagination is given ontological and religious sanction. The highly imaginative hermeneutical work of reconstructing this Iranian Islamic "sun" of truth as an ontological figure therefore becomes the work of intellectuals and the aim of "authentic" political practice.

One can argue that Fardid, by having established himself as a prophetic philosopher and claiming to be an all-knowing master thinker, helped to create a broad intellectual habit among Iranian thinkers that is still alive and well represented even among those who disagree with his political views, his harsh and intolerant attitudes toward all who disagreed, and his many self-promoting claims and personal flaws. In an ironic turn, it now seems that attacking Fardid's political beliefs, his flawed character, and his confusing and obscure ideas has become part of the accepted intellectual self-definition in Iran, and that it is only the Islamicism ideologues who continue to praise him as their master philosopher. Yet by focusing on Fardid's personal and character shortcomings and rejecting his Islamic politics, many intellectuals in Iran have found an easy way to merely scratch the surface of what the Fardid phenomenon actually represents and, despite themselves, continue his legacy. I would venture to argue that many of the leading Iranian intellectuals are still working and thinking very much within the unconscious framework of the Fardid discourse. It seems that the battle in fact concerns who is to be the new Fardid, or who is to boast the title of the master thinker, rather than being about the more important purpose of transcending the very idea of a prophetic philosopher in the name of something more pragmatically grounded in everyday life and experience.

Fardid helped to create an intellectual model in Iran that is unique and constituted a sort of break from the intellectual model that, coming out of the constitutionalist movement, embraced an enlightenment discourse of progress, liberalism, and modern science. Fardid created an alternative framework with phantasmagorical ontological precepts that deeply captured the imaginations of other prominent intellectuals of the time such as Jalal Al-e Ahmad, Dariush Shayegan, Ehsan Naraghi, and Reza Davari.

The philosophical universe conceived by Fardid, very much within the tradition of narratives of despair, represents a kind of proto-Nietzschean aristocratic, high-culture, anti-Enlightenment intellectual worldview, which imagines society as existing somehow in an organic mode of total cooperation and sees the function of the intellectual/philosopher as filling a prophetic role. It seems that the nostalgic call for the grounding of society in a higher and more sublime order is necessarily linked to the promotion of an aristocratic model of social organization, and certainly such a tendency was very present in the writings of Nietzsche. The high-handed calling of the intellectual in Fardid's thought is to mold the people according to higher design or inspiration. The consequences of imagining intellectuals as master thinkers with prophetic callings, already dangerous in principle, have been extremely destructive in reality and have devastated the Iranian intellectual environment. Here I identify three main aspects of this problem:

1. *Fardidism* values only ideas that are at once grand and highly abstract, unfamiliar and mysterious. Fardid himself and later his disciples invented an intellectual language that is hardly comprehensible, a meta-philosophical discourse that exploits all of the most obscure aspects of modern philosophy while combining Islamic theology, Sufism, and ideas of a literary nature. Such an intellectual project finds itself inevitably very much at home inside the particular trend of German philosophy embraced by these Iranian thinkers. In this case, however, it was above all Heidegger who offered the supreme model of the master thinker. Fardid accordingly became known as the Iranian Heidegger. The language, in its obscurity, is meant to give the impression of reaching beyond the frail limits of mere human reason to some profound ontological truth hidden beyond and only accessible to the master and those who follow the path illuminated by his thought.

An important and violently suicidal quality of the Fardid phenomenon – which is to say, prophetic intellectuals in Iran in general – is the almost total intolerance for the everyday common man, for social realities as they presently exist, and the call for the radical destruction of all

ideas, structures, habits, and ways of thinking. If intellectuals are master thinkers with prophetic callings, then all other ways of thinking (and
other intellectuals) need to be converted to the master way of thinking
or, failing to do so, must be humiliated, rejected, and violently critiqued.

Fardid's own critique of the West and Iranian modernity was certainly
radical and totalizing in itself, but of more importance for our discussion is
what one of Fardid's more gifted students, Jalal Al-e Ahmad, managed to
construct based on the model and its presuppositions. Al-e Ahmad's two
most important books are the best representations of radical epistemic
violence that prophetic intellectuals have inflicted in the Iranian intellectual and social context. *Westoxication* is a totalistic condemnation of
modernization in the Iranian context, a radical and intolerant attack on
every facet of modern life in contemporary Iran. In its scathing account
of an Iranian society gripped by inauthenticity and spiritual decline as if
by a disease, it raises the genre of narrative of despair to new imaginative
heights. His other book, *On the Service and Treason of the Intellectuals*,
is an even harsher and more violent critique of modernist intellectuals in
Iran. If one looks at the ideas, concepts, and theories that Fardid and his
students have used to criticize other intellectual trends, current cultural
situations, or the history of ideas in Iran, they use notions such as Westoxication and treason. These intellectuals call on the common people to
reject an unworldly universe and convert to their preaching of a future
utopia of Iranian and Islamic authenticity.

In the 1960s and '70s, intellectuals such as Fardid, Al-e Ahmad,
Shari'ati, and many others imagined themselves in the role of prophetic
intellectuals and rejected the entire Iranian experience of modernity, its
socioeconomic development, and all Western influence as evil and cancerous.

Influenced by Fardid, Al-e Ahmad's critique of the West (*Gharbzadegi*)[4] did the most to popularize the concept of a hermeneutically
resurrected Islam as the authentic counterpart to the "Western sickness." Al-e Ahmad's use of these ideas is a complex and contradictory
concept that cannot be simply reduced to an anti-Western polemic or
variation on religious dogma. His "return" seems to have been kindled
by the decade he spent doing "ethnographic works," traveling through
the Iranian countryside and seeking to acquaint himself with the "true"
masses, their culture, and his own "true" roots. By finding a supposed
"purity" in these villages, he implied the corruption, or Westoxication,
which plagued the new and rapidly growing urban centers. By celebrating
the "wisdom" of the peasantry, he disparaged the emptiness of modern
scientific thought. His later rejection of a job offer at Tehran University

supervising the publication of ethnographic works, on the grounds that his aim was not "objective science" but the self-realization of the Iranian people, testifies to this emerging conviction that neither history nor social studies should be a process of collecting facts but rather a radical process of self-realization: "my aim in (this) endeavour was a renewal of self awareness and a new assessment of the local environment by our own criteria."[5] For a man with a strong background in the social sciences and modern political thought, this remark reveals a significant turnaround. This rejection of "universal" learning in favor of deeper currents of mood and local know-how is decidedly Heideggerian, and the notion that truth should serve vitalistic self-empowerment rather than "objective" knowledge is a strongly Nietzschean idea. We thus see how through the works of Fardid and others the German "narrative of despair" was set in place as an episteme, that is, an unconscious system of thought that served as an automatic resource in the writings of future thinkers and political activists.

There were also establishment intellectuals of the time who created still more variations on the same basic discourse. An important example is Dariush Shayegan, who studied in Switzerland, England, and finally France under the famous Orientalist scholar Henri Corbin (whose own extensive field research on Iran claimed to be phenomenological in its approach). Studying Hinduism and Sufism under Corbin, Shayegan became immersed in the works of Heidegger, and from this experience he evolved his influential vision of the relations between "East" and "West." His work was highly influential in the 1970s, while he was teaching Sanskrit language and literature and Indian religion and thought. His interests also included other Asian countries such as China and Japan. Yet his studies of various Asian cultures generally pointed back to the influence and issue of the West. He hosted an international symposium in Tehran in 1977 entitled, "Does the Impact of Western Thought Render Possible a Dialogue between Civilizations?"[6]

Shayegan, like others of the time thinking through a Heideggerian lens, distinguished Orient and Occident based on separate ontological essences. "Western" thought, at the outset, is fatally hostile to "Eastern" thought:

My research of many years on the nature of Western thought, which in terms of dynamism, variety, richness, and mesmerising power is a unique and exceptional phenomenon in our earthly world, made me conscious of the fact that the process of Western thought has been moving in the direction of gradual negation of all articles of faith that make up the spiritual heritage of Asian civilizations.[7]

Again, we see a notion of heritage or memory as under attack by a "Western thought" conceived idealistically as an almost autonomous force of destruction. This observation is based on a reading of the ontological differences between Oriental societies (the world of Islam, Buddhism, and Hinduism) and that of the West. Whereas the first is grounded in revelation and faith, the second is grounded in rationalist thinking: "If occidental philosophy is a question of existence and being and if philosophy answers 'why' questions, in Islamic mysticism the questioner is God, and humankind only answers."[8] The answers, in the East, were provided long before the questions were formulated. He argues that on the "Western path," in which "existence (is) reduced to a mere subjectivity or a process such as in the philosophy of Hegel," the replacement of revelation by reason leads ultimately to the negation of all metaphysical values.[9] From such a Manichean point of view, it is hardly possible to acknowledge what is in fact the reality of a radical overlap and co-development of intellectual thought between modern nations beyond simplified and fanciful East-West binarism on the common horizon of globalized modernity. Looking beyond such primarily imaginary binarisms to what are underlying shared systems of thought is another hermeneutical possibility, as Arkoun has attempted to do in the case of medieval Islamic thought and logocentrism, or as is being done here between Islamic radicalism especially in the Iranian context and the tradition of German anti-Enlightenment philosophy that laid the intellectual foundations for the politics of fascism.

Shayegan's argument links metaphysical thought with the lived spiritual traditions of non-Western societies as if they existed together in an unbroken flow. It amounts in a political sense to an elaborate attack on institutionalized secularism, which for Shayegan leads to "cultural decadence, the twilight of the gods, the demise of myths, and the collapse of spirituality."[10] Here we hear the "narrative of despair" expressed in full force: an apocalyptic scenario is evoked in which modern society, having gone radically spiritually astray, is in need of a higher authentic guidance to find the way home through the darkness. It is very far from an exact sociological analysis of even the most wildly imaginative sort. The onset of historical decline is identified in the sixteenth century as the point in Western history when civil society replaced religious order. Shayegan implies that any separation of the social and religious world is both blasphemous and inconceivable in the Orient where existence, by contrast, "never became mundane, and nature never got separated from the spirit governing it, and the manifestations of divine blessing never left the realm of our universe."[11] Thus a sublimated and hazy spiritual notion serves to establish a supposed antithesis between what are allegedly opposed civilizations in the "East" and "West." The social nihilism that is the "inevitable end of Western thought" is clearly conceived along Heideggerian lines.[12] Shayegan extends this Heideggerian line of thinking still further to tackle the issue of technology. He insists that far from being merely tools, technology and science embody metaphysics of being which imprisons humanity by extending its own power limitlessly outward. The logical outcome of modern technology, itself a manifestation of Western metaphysics, is a nihilism that leads to the "gradual negation of all oriental articles of faith."[13] Such an ontological point of view represents a considerable departure from an older generation of Islamic reformers, al-Afghani for example, who sought a reconciliation of Islamic thought with modern science.

Accordingly, Western thought is conceived as if it were a driven by a single ontological determinism. Shayegan conceived four descending movements of the spirit in the evolution of Western thought: technicalization of thought, materialization of the world, naturalization of man, and demythologization.[14] For Asian civilizations to avoid falling prey to "a way of thought that is the most dominant and aggressive worldview on earth," they must break free from what he calls a "double illusion."[15] Asian intellectuals of the late nineteenth and early twentieth century, he contends, saw themselves as being at once ahead of their own civilization and behind the West. They had mistakenly sought to acquire modern technology while maintaining their own cultural identity: "One cannot say that we borrow technology (from the West) but would abstain from its annihilating consequences because technology is a product of a transformation of thinking and the outcome of a process lasting a millennium."[16]

Conceiving technology as being ontologically one with Western culture and the inseparable whole as harmful in itself, Shayegan's position on accommodating modernity was both less radical and less clear than Al-e Ahmad's. Al-e Ahmad's originality was in his creating a dialectical synthesis of traditional Iranian Shi'ism and modern radical secular ideology. Yet on this point they were agreed: "Today the class that is more or less the protector of the ancient trust and despite its weak health keeps alive the treasure house of traditional thought is to be found in the Islamic theological centers of Qom and Mashad."[17] We see at this point where the elaborately dreamed metaphysical fantasy suddenly makes a crude and unreflecting connection to the reality of contemporary politics in a manner at once dangerous and sensational.

Shayegan wrote: "Against a (western) culture that is threatening our existence we have no right to remain silent." This alarmist and paranoiac language invites Iranians to combat this threat and preserve cultural identity through initially engaging in a dialogue with "ethnic memories" and subsequently entering a dialogue with the West, because ethnic memories could "expedite the flourishing of Asia's ancient, glorious heritage."[18] It is clear that there is something here of Heidegger's historicist idea of calling a "great past" to the foreground of present time in a bid for the world of tomorrow, or "repetition." Heidegger himself never really talked about memory in any direct way, loathing individual subjectivity as he did, but everything he wrote so obsessively about the crucial importance of heritage points to a conviction concerning the need to control memory, individually and collectively, to cast it into alignment with the "authentic" traditions of the past, to control the past so as to control the future.

In the context of "ethnic memories" Iranian Shi'ism supposedly had a unique historical destiny: "Iran has the same mission in the Islamic world as Germany has had in the West. If, according to Hegel, the Germans were the ones who kept alive the torch of Greek thinking, Iranians have been the guardians of the light of the Asian legacy in Islam."[19] Interestingly, here "Asian" is inflated to the level of an all-purpose ontological category, naturally in opposition to the "Occident," with Iran set at the helm in this utopian odyssey to a liberated authenticity. In Shayegan's writing, there is an imaginative combination of colorfully nationalistic German metaphysical thought and a highly unconventional vision of Shi'a Islam as a kind of primordial identity. He mistook this phantasm for the reality of the social world that surrounded him and believed that "If Shi'ism was Iran's primary spiritual asset, and then the *Ulama*, by necessity, would be its most conscientious custodians."[20] Following the revolution of 1979, he had cause to publicly regret many of his earlier positions.

Yet there is a lesson to be drawn from the discourse shared and given renewed life by Al-e Ahmad, Fardid, and Shayegan. This discourse of authenticity, with its anti-Western and utopian frame of reference, could not help but be disconnected from the realities of Iranian life in its Heideggerian preoccupation with the pure realm of metaphysical philosophy that supposedly underlies and overdetermines events in human history. In spite of Heidegger's insistence on the "concreteness" and "everydayness" of his own philosophy in *Being and Time*, we see how severely he slipped and lost his footing when he attempted to take political action on behalf of his own philosophical ideas through the National Socialist Revolution

of 1933. In spite of Heidegger's claim to "deconstruct" Western metaphysics, his central preoccupation with "ontology" as a total claim both
philosophically and socially guarantees a totalitarian political frame and
a blindness to the *situated* character of real political and ethical problems.

Above all, we need to be aware of the dangerously seductive element
in these philosophies, very much shared between "East" and "West,"
which is in the vivid and compelling if imaginary and phantasmagorical
"narrative of despair" that at once condemns the world in its entirety and
promises its total salvation on dubious religious grounds widespread in
the modern literary imagination (we find similar attitudes, for example, in
the very popular fictional writings of Burroughs or Rimbaud, we may well
think of the case of Celine, and a similar apocalyptic mood is powerfully
evoked in Hedayat's *Blind Owl*).

In terms of the paradigm of the master thinker and the new beginning,
the Fardid legacy continues among even contemporary Iranian intellectuals who call for an absolute epistemological break with Iranian religious
and cultural traditions.

Aramesh Dustdar, an Iranian intellectual who was educated in Germany and now lives in Berlin, argues that the historical dilemma of Iran
has been its genealogy in religious worldviews that he defines as being
a refusal to think or even the fear of thinking. For Dustdar, the main
characteristic of what has come to be known as philosophical or social
thinking in Iran is *Din-Khoo-i* (religiousness or religiously oriented, or
habitual religiosity), which he defines as the art of nonthinking. Its roots
in Iranian culture, he argues, are deeper than they first appear to be.
Dustdar believes that Iranians, from ancient times to the modern era,
have suffered an erosion of thinking as a result of their *Din-Khoo-i*, and
that their habitual cultural behavior is marred by the art of nonthinking. We have been condemned, in the totality of our existence, to remain
habitually religious.[21] His definition of religiously oriented ideas and reasoning is that "religion always prohibits all those inherent developments
that question or subvert its foundational principles and values, and upon
encountering such developments it smashes them."[22] Dustdar operates
on an abstract and philosophically technical terrain. He never bothers to
examine other forms of beliefs and value systems, what anthropologists
and ethnologists call the thick body of culture, including popular culture
and folklore, where one can find all kinds of deviations from mainstream
religiosity.

The other Iranian philosopher who studies Hegel in Europe and is
influenced by the philosophy of history discourse, Javad Tabatabai, sees

the art of unthinking as being the core political problem of Iranian history. He has attempted to give a new interpretation of modernity in Iran through a vigorous critique of the philosophical foundations of Islam in Iran. His rejections, like most such philosophical endeavors, can be understood as the binary opposition of two concepts: Islamic tradition and modern Reason. And for him the prevalence of Islamic tradition is the root cause of many of the major problems in contemporary Iran:

> To find a way out of this double impasse would be possible solely through modernity that is the establishment of modern philosophical thought. On the one hand, we need to acquire a modern historical consciousness, which should not be based on repeating the sociological ideology But, on the other hand, regard for tradition must be a reminder based on modern thought and not based on inherited anecdotes, so that this reminder itself becomes a firm foundation on which we can extrapolate the degree of our proximity to, or break with, the past, to aim at strengthening our modernity, not demolishing it.[23]

Both Dustdar and Tabatabai are superficially opposed to the Islamic ideology of Fardid in their insistence on the need for a total critique of the Iranian religious tradition in the name of a championing of modern thought Yet in their posturing as master thinkers with a prophetic calling, they unwittingly inherit the basic framework that is Fardid's lasting discursive legacy to Iranian political and cultural thought. Moreover, in applying the conception of opposed and absolute categories in Islamic religion and modern thought, they draw from the same metaphysical resource articulated regularly in Orientalist discourse. We find it expressed again in an especially imaginative manner, if dangerously, in the German tradition of philosophy both for purposes of affirming the West (in Hegel) and for critiquing its soul-deadening power (in Heidegger).[24]

2. *Philosophical arrogance and the everyday*: The fascination of Iranian intellectuals with abstract philosophical ideas has led to the tragic assumption that all specific social and political concerns are, in one way or another, linked to a philosophical category. Al-e Ahmad used a Heideggerian notion of Westoxification to explain the spread of consumer culture, political autocracy, poverty, and the decline of religious practices among the middle class. None of these important sociological claims came from any serious field work or even theoretical analysis of Iranian society. The master thinker already possessed the key to knowledge, which was, in this case, Westoxification and a few personal observations linked

to scant evidence from here and there, and this was supposedly enough to establish a causal relationship explaining all that was wrong in Iran and concerning Iranian encounters with the West. The fact that the idea of the West or enlightenment as being the cause of the decline and death of authenticity is itself a Western construct (from Nietzsche, Kierkegaard, Heidegger) and that Fardid himself had openly claimed to be influenced by this philosophical tradition could not make the slightest difference to the advance of these robust metaphysical claims on behalf of Iranian authenticity. More importantly, none of these master thinkers pay any serious attention to the fact that for the common man in Iran, the politics of authenticity or nostalgic return to the old ways of a preconstitutionalist era will very likely bring nothing but a considerable increase in misery, poverty, and oppression. Moreover, it escapes them that the ideas of cultural isolation and rejection of technological progress are more in tune with the desires of aristocratic intellectuals than with the average Iranian, who is far more concerned with the standard of living, political rights, and general peace in the society.

Shari'ati, too, engaged in similarly metaphysical intellectual endeavors as a means to explain real situations in Iran. He very conveniently put forward a few quite abstract ideas such as Western nihilism and *Shi'a alavi*. In his writings and lectures on the history of Islam, Shi'ism, and Iran, Shari'ati rejects a more traditional narrative as inauthentic and constructs a new ideological narrative of the authentic Islam. In a similar manner to Al-e Ahmad, he did not bother to engage with Muslim Iranians and their issues, nor did he conduct research or field work of any kind. Instead, he simply asserted a clearly defined metaphysical explanation of the problem and articulated a single powerful solution in a "return" to authentic Islamic identity. Interestingly, Shari'ati, too, was deeply influenced by Western ideas and particularly by the anti-Enlightenment philosophical tradition of Heidegger, Corbin, and so forth. He indeed praised Heidegger for his project of searching for God in the world along new paths while rejecting the nihilism of Western reason. He similarly integrated elements from French existentialism and Massignon. In some respects it can be said that none of these intellectuals, including Fardid and Shayegan, ever in fact engaged with Iranian history, ideas, or even the reality of contemporary Iranian society. In an ironic way, they were not really master thinkers so much as soldiers left out on a remote island fighting a war that had ended a decade earlier.

In contrast to the prerevolutionary period, Iranian intellectuals now are different in several respects:

(a) If figures such as Al-e Ahmad and Shari'ati condemned Western influence as a sign of social and cultural ills and overall decadence, now Tabatabai and Dustdar consider hostility to the West and its philosophical tradition as being the cause of the current crisis and decadence. Whereas the earlier Iranian intellectuals were more influenced by radical counter-Enlightenment, contemporary intellectuals, although still influenced by Hegel, Nietzsche, and Heidegger, are more likely to identify themselves with the eighteenth-century rationalist tradition and particularly with European Orientalism. In a way the main theory advanced in the 1980s by Aramesh Dustdar, *Din-Fhoi* (religious thinking), and later in a different context by Javad Tabatabai (unthinking), came from the European Orientalist literature on Islam. Following the Orientalist tradition, these thinkers assert that Islam in itself, and religion in general, somehow constitutes an inherent obstacle to thinking. There is presumed to be a dualism dividing the free realm of rational thought and its opposite in an unreflecting and blind religious obedience that excludes all questioning. This notion is more essentialist and metaphysical than historical or sociological, and is hardly sustainable as a thesis against the rich diversity of philosophical debate that has characterized and shaped important periods in Islamic history. As Arkoun has argued, Islam and all religions present a discourse, and like all discourses are subject to the limits of the thought and unthought that is itself undergoing transformation on a continuous historical basis. The idea that Islam or any religion should have some fixed essence is certainly fanciful.

Therefore, in just the same way that Al-e Ahmad and Shari'ati never realize that their discursive construction of the politics of Islamic authenticity does not in fact originate in the Iranian context – or that such a political project had indeed been tried before with tragic consequences for millions of lives – the current project of today's prophetic intellectuals is presented without any real awareness of its proper historical origin and context at the discursive level.

(b) On a more positive note, Iranian intellectuals today are more serious and their writings more professional relative to earlier times. However, intellectuals in the current Iranian situation are less relevant and the public is more critical of their claims and fundamental theories. With the exception of Soroush, leading Iranian intellectuals enjoy very limited public attention. On the other hand, this fact of being isolated from the public actually contributes to the positioning of some of these intellectuals and their ideas at very far remove from the practical realities of contemporary society.

(c) One interesting consequence of the obsessive attention paid to philosophy by intellectuals as the key to explaining Iranian reality has been the Orientalist approach that individuals such as Dustdar, in particular, and Tabatabai, to a lesser extent, have adopted.

(d) At the same time, one can see an anti-academic tendency among master-thinkers. They do not perceive their work as being part of the larger scholarly literature on Iran, and they hardly ever engage with other scholars, Iranian or non-Iranian, in the same field in any dialogue or exchange of ideas. Dustdar, after a few years of living in Iran in the 1970s, has been studying and living in Germany for almost three decades. Yet amazingly he writes only in Farsi and there is no indication that he is engaged in any way with the intellectual or academic community in Germany or in Europe.

> 3. *Elitist thought.* One very important but unproductive quality of the new master thinkers is their narcissistic intolerance, harsh and brutal language, and absolute refusal of dialogue, exchange of ideas, or openness to criticism. One might in fact argue that intellectuals in general are prone to being self-absorbed and intolerant of other ideas – and yet the extent of self-glorification and harsh language used by individuals such as Dustdar and Tabatabai far exceeds any usual degree of intellectual arrogance. This particular quality can in fact be linked to Fardidism. Fardid was most brutal and exceedingly hostile to those who would dare to disagree with him and would engage in regular attacks of a personal and unethical nature. Al-e Ahmad was also very harsh and intolerant toward others.

My goal in this book is to offer a radical intellectual turning away from grand theories, master thinkers, philosophical/prophetic, utopian/suicidal projects, discourses, and images, toward a more limited and imperfect, yet pragmatic and hopeful, and above all democratic intellectual project. I see the phenomenon of Fardidism as an intellectual paradigm that has considerably transcended the figure of Fardid himself and exists embodied in the prophetic model that is used habitually and apparently with so much appeal among contemporary intellectuals. It is crucial to emphasize the point that mere critiques of Fardid on the level of his personality and philosophy, which limit themselves to the thinker while ignoring the deep and powerful legacy of Fardidism as an unconscious paradigm appealing to the worst of narcissistic intellectual tendencies, may risk legitimizing an intellectual tradition that, though not perhaps as crude as the original, is nevertheless part of the same dangerous legacy.

2

The Crisis of the Nativist Imagination

In considering three types of modern narrative that have commonly dominated post–World War political action and state building in the twentieth
century – varied ideological combinations of philosophy, religion, and
nationalism with their intellectual roots stretching back to the eighteenth
and even seventeenth centuries – we may ask what they offer us today
in terms of a home, a familiar and intelligible place for our collective
imagination, and security and protection from others as either a physical
threat or a disturbance on the level of grounding ideas and beliefs. The
interweaving threads of these three forces – each asserting at times its
own claim to absolute truth in the secular annihilation of "false belief"
(philosophy), religious fundamentalism (a totalizing millennial promise),
or ethnic nationalism (a claim to immediate certainty in violence and
authenticity) – constitute the powerfully shaping discursive material of
salvational modernity from the Naxalite Maoist uprising in contemporary India to the ongoing Taliban resistance in Afghanistan. Those many
people worldwide who yearn for existential certainty and rootedness as
promised in different ways by these threads, who seek shelter from political and economic violence on the wrong end of uneven global development, and who generally hope to escape the inherent change inflicted by
modernity via these various modern ideologies of closure, demonstrate
the profoundly ambiguous and contradictory relation of modernity to
utopia as an irreconcilable tension and temptation – one can never pay
too high a price in violence for attaining the promised land of permanent
peace.

Yet the irony is that modern reality and imagination can offer us a
home only if we can dare to leave behind what is familiar and make a

home in whatever new and troubling situations we are tossed into. Change is inescapable, but change can help us to re-create lives of our own only if we participate and become agents of change – beyond the tacitly Jacobin utopian notion of absolute agency linked to violence and transcendence of the everyday. Such an open and pluralistic notion of agency is appropriate to the institutional functioning of democracy at the level of civil society and political process, itself the prerequisite for nonviolently confronting problems of social justice. Of all countries that crossed the furious river of the twentieth century, from grass roots political movements involving the wretched of the earth to high-tech military-backed states dealing in colossal global capital, Iran learned this lesson of the ideological pit of violent absolute agency from all points of view. What the Iranian population – and those non-Iranians either directly or indirectly involved in their local-global struggle – experience today is a crossroad. On the one hand there is a society trying to define itself as a place with a unique identity, pure and different from all others, and a world of native Muslims living a morally good life in Qom. On the other hand, there is the sometimes harsh reality of the existing world in its complex and changing global structural dimensions, or the globalizing trends and high technologies of the market. It is almost impossible, shaken between these two states of existence, to tell what is of us and what is foreign to us. One set of ideas and practices may be familiar to one group of Iranians while also being alien to certain others, and common ground can be consequently lost from sight. The old paradigm of official modernization as an austere and singular state control over national economics, politics, and cultural production increasingly slips into the past amid the unruly energies of globalization.

This national existential dilemma is what we describe as the crisis of Iranian society. The crisis involves many facets from economic to cultural, but at bottom represents the inability of many to come to terms with the reality that in the postcolonial world, there is no option of returning home. The challenge to Iranians is therefore to participate cooperatively in building a new home, resolving contradictions in economic and political power nonviolently in the process, via a modern-democratic society anchored within the specific historical context of Iran. Modernization as a world historical process can be a liberating experience, but it is necessary to rectify those flawed ideological priorities of the nation-state paradigm to steer into a more pluralistic and creative unleashing of the nation's potential. Iranians are themselves part of the modern world and very much influenced by it, as well as attracted by its possibilities and

potentials, while also being afraid of its unsettling and unfamiliar qualities. In some respects, the contemporary predicament of Iran is the history
of Iranian anxieties linked to the decentering experiences of modernity,
and the crossroad faced diverges between open negotiation through creative thought/action and self-destruction through ideological denial.

The intellectual debates and discussions fashionable in Iran today,
weighing the merits of constructing nativist modernity, or a modern
democratic Islamic state, or a secular Iran, in all of their importance,
constitute a certain sort of obstacle. They obstruct the process of coming
to terms with the reality of world historical events that have occurred
over the last two centuries: the rise of modern Europe and colonialism,
the experience of colonization and modernization, and the interdependence of our cultural, economic, and political realities at the global level.
These conditions irreversibly set up new realities and render, despite any
deep desires to ignore them, any construction of Iranian society based
on a nativist discourse an inherently self-defeating project. If we agree
that Islamist movements are the latest manifestation of a nativist desire
to construct contemporary societies in the image of the imagined Islamic
past, the extremely high cost of such a self-defeating project very quickly
becomes visible.

There is a universe of the imagination at work in the writings of Fardid and those inspired by the paradigm shift he had so seminal a role
in initiating. We see a combination of entrenched Orientalist imagery
interwoven with a certain narrative around the fear of a loss of roots or
spiritual home. As an evocative imaginative framework it is hardly new
to Iran, though Iranian intellectuals of the 1960s and '70s certainly put
an original twist on it in their local variation. We can see very much the
same cosmogony put into motion in the Symbolist poetry of Rimbaud.
A Season in Hell presents a culturally archetypal vision of the metaphysical wanderer who is plagued at once by an obliterated memory and a
lack of any roots to a collective heritage capable of providing a sustained
meaning for life. Throughout this poem, which can be read almost as a
kind of philosophical sketch of modernity, the hero undergoes a series
of transformed, contradictory, and religiously obsessed identities – even
at one point assuming the very voice of God – while consistently railing
against the soul-erasing effects of the age of reason or modernity. Moreover, in expressing his need to escape from the deadness of the West, he
projects the Orient as an ideal alternative in which primitivism, wisdom,
paganism, dark skin, and so forth are presented as life-affirming and

positive attributes and counterparts to the amnesia and spiritual death of progress, science, democratic qualities, and so on.

The very title of this poem implies a religious crisis in the temporalizing of hell, which is supposed to exist as an eternal realm in the traditional Christian thought against which Rimbaud mounted his spiritual revolt. The opening lines express a doubt in memory, "If I remember rightly," which is followed by the claim of suffering from having swallowed an excess of the poison of forgetting.[1] There is a bemoaning of a lack of roots in one's own country: "If only I had antecedents at any point whatsoever in the history of France! But no, nothing." It is the paradigmatic crisis of modern experience: "I do not find myself again in any time other than the present." This crisis of rootlessness is set in the world of families "owing all to the declaration of the Rights of Man," or democratic modernity, and a world of doubt where through science "everything is revised."[2] The narrative resonates with related anxieties about purity. Innocence, the search for a lost eternity, and the loss of memory are frequently repeated themes and often linked to politics, as with the image of "republics without memories."[3] In his preoccupation with the last shred of innocence, the narrator has "returned to the East and to the first and eternal wisdom." He speaks of "the delight of escaping from modern sufferings" that are "far enough away from the thought, from the wisdom of the East, the primeval birthplace." He asks: "Why a modern world, if such poisons are invented!" He taunts: "But you wish to speak of Eden. Nothing for you in the history of the Oriental peoples. – It's true; it's of Eden that I was thinking! What does it have to do with my dream, that purity of the ancient races!"[4] Eden is here associated with the Orient, as it was described as being so in Genesis. These evocations of the Orient as a site of purity and alternative to the bindings of Western modernity are no doubt largely tongue-in-cheek in Rimbaud. More importantly, the evocations attest to the power and availability of such resources in a collective imagination. Rimbaud's projections of the Orient are obviously pure, if purposeful and meaningful, fantasy. Yet we could say very much the same of how Fardid and other Iranian thinkers have used the ontological categories of "West" and "East" to evoke a certain ideological vision of social reality irrespective of what it actually might be. The creative power of language is enormous in its impact on thought and action, and the mere demonstration that it does not hold up to scientific scrutiny is rarely adequate to cause the enthusiasm it invokes in the human heart and mind to subside.

Finally, addressing the frail and rootless world of modern intellectuals, Rimbaud concludes: "Philosophers: The world has no age. Humanity simply moves about." This is obviously an attack on any idea of a linear framework of historical progress. He continues: "You are in the West, but free to reside in your East, as ancient as you require, – and to live well there. Do not be a loser. Philosophers, you belong to your West."[5] The self-conscious juggling between the categories of East and West as geographical areas and pure states of mind is obvious here, as is the association of the "West" with a notion of repressive modern reason and the "East" with some unchanging (yet: "as you require") and ancient condition. Rimbaud provides a vivid landscape of the modern imagination beyond the more limited conscious aim of destroying the wall of morality and bourgeois tradition in his own society of nineteenth-century France. His reconstruction of the world through scattered symbols and revitalization of imagination through the unreal state of reality, or the delirium of modernity, holds a considerable resemblance to Tayeb Salih's *Season of Migration to the North*. It does so not in terms of ideological content, which is considerably different, but rather in terms of a common symbolic landscape of the imagination used also by Fardid and other diverse thinkers discussed in this study, including Gandhi and Hegel. Tayeb Salih uses these realms of the imagination to point to a very different road of modernity beyond the traps that these essentialisms lay out for those thinkers who stumble into them unawares.

This shared landscape of the imagination visited by diverse writers across centuries, from nineteenth-century France to twentieth-century Sudan, is visible as well in the political mindscape of twentieth-century Iran, where all traditional institutions, values, and ideals came under accelerated siege.

Season of Migration to the North

Within the overarching vision of *Season of Migration to the North*, Sudanese novelist Salih's first and acclaimed work on Sudanese living in the space of exile between newly independent Sudan and England, we are given a vivid insight into the imaginary and often violent nature of discourses that privilege rootedness and authenticity along anti-Western lines. This novel shows how such a political discourse can work only on the level of sheer imagination, whereas in practical reality its consequences are necessarily violent, contradictory, and destructive to all concerned. It questions the obsession with "place" and transfigures received notions of its meaning. At the same time, this is a novel about modernity as a social and ethical possibility beyond the shelter of dogmatic thought that provides brutal fantasies of large transitions.

Season of Migration to the North does not so much represent *the* modern condition as piece together multiple conflicting sites of movement, or migration, none of which can be reduced to either one another or any single underlying reality, and thereby undoes a received representation of modernity as a world flattened into simplified essences along either the geographic axis of East/West or North/South, or the cultural-historical axis of tradition/modernity or Islam/the Occident. Salih substitutes these for axes of absence and presence as intermingled existential conditions of modernity, with panic over hybridity and the aspiration to purity as responses of deep uncertainty to the haunting effects of globalized conditions. *Season of Migration* is therefore a work about the crisis of cultural authenticity. Its narrative can be read as an attempted migration from displacement to authenticity that ultimately points to a middle way that attaches itself to no single claim to existence as an ontological or epistemological dogma.

This remarkable and acclaimed novel was written in the 1960s and was hence one of the earliest novels to deal with the postcolonial contradiction that came to be a defining issue of so many academic and literary projects in the ensuing decades, and which has framed the general context for the enormous amount of public debate and critical reflection that remains very much alive and productive to our own day. The novel is pioneering in its tackling of these issues in terms of a problematic that continues to be highly relevant in our time. The complex issue of "us" and the "others" illustrates the great range of available forms in nationalist discourse and is made clear in its ethical import by the stark difference between "violence" and "nonviolence" as the chosen path toward realizing the communal and national ideal. These issues in turn define the relation between "community" and "individual" on the road to national modernity and determine the political character of the national order. In this novel we also glimpse a rich psychological tableau in what was an early literary figuring of Deleuze's later articulation of the schizophrenic interior space of capitalist modernity, as the central characters in the novel are often suggested to be different sides of a single person.

The story in *Season of Migration to the North* covers a brief span of time in a late twentieth-century Sudanese village. The village is engulfed in the at once ominously remote and disturbingly intrusive political and economic process of national modernization under the newly independent

Sudanese state. Most of the members of the village have remained in the village throughout their lives, struggling on an everyday level to make the best of a situation in which they are more the objects than the agents of the modernization process, whereas others in higher positions have spent a part of their lives in Khartoum as functionaries in the frustrating pursuit of endeavoring to shape this process. Only the two central characters in the novel, the narrator and Mustafa Sa'eed, have traveled and lived abroad.

As the story opens, the narrator returns to the village after several years of having completed a doctorate in English literature at a London university. He is disturbed to notice an unknown stranger among the villagers whom he has known intimately since childhood. On questioning the identity of the stranger, he is told by his family that the man is Mustafa Sa'eed, a farmer who simply appeared one day and settled in the village. It is gradually revealed through a series of chance moments and investigations, however, that the man has concealed his genuine past, which included a considerable period of time abroad. It turns out that in his secret life he had achieved a considerable status and notoriety in the postwar British intellectual scene as a professor of economics in London, preaching radical theories based on an "economics of love," but that at the apex of this career he was tried and imprisoned for the murder his English wife as well as having been at the probable root of the suicides of several other young English women. On his release from prison, he underwent a passage of wandering and eventually made his way back to the Sudan, where he attempted to live a purified and anonymous existence in the world of the Sudanese village. Only he and the narrator share knowledge of this secret past.

The narrator's encounter with this stranger and the discovery of the secret ultimately has grave effects on the village. After disclosing his secret to the narrator, Mustafa Sa'eed insists that in the event of his death the narrator be entrusted with responsibility for all of his belongings, the care of his wife, and the upbringing of his sons. He gives the narrator the key to a mysterious room that no one has ever entered. When Mustafa Sa'eed later mysteriously disappears in what may or may not have been death by a flash flood, the young village woman who is his widow thwarts village custom by trying to refuse marriage to an old man who is determined to marry her. Bound by village custom, she is unable to refuse, and begs the narrator to marry her in order to spare her from this unwanted fate. His response is indecisive, and when the young widow vows to him that she will kill both the old man and herself in the event of being forced to marry, the narrator nevertheless permits events to unfold without intervention. All the while, he is haunted by a rising awareness that he is deeply in love with the young woman.

It is while away working in Khartoum that the narrator hears that a diabolical disaster has transpired in the village. It is with great difficulty on his hasty return that he learns from the reluctantly silent villagers that the young widow has carried out her promise some weeks after the wedding. The narrator, driven to near madness, enters into violent altercation with old friends as the village drifts into a general atmosphere of tension and previously unknown conflict. Late one night, the narrator at last enters the secret room to find that Mustafa Sa'eed has documented his entire life with an enormous collection of notebooks and diaries, books, ornaments, photos, and paintings. The narrator burns down the house with the entire collection in it. He subsequently wades out into the river, and only when he is near the point of drowning does he call for help, for the first time seemingly conceding his interdependence and involvement with the community.

The unnamed narrator returns to his native village and his people at the twilight of colonial Sudan from living abroad and studying in England for a period of seven years: "for seven years I had longed for them, had dreamed of them, and it was an extraordinary moment when I at last found myself standing amongst them."[6] The preoccupation with his people suggests an awakening sense of nationalism at some raw emotive or pre-ideological level. The text invites us to reflect on the many possible forms that nationalism may take. Since the national revolutions of the eighteenth and nineteenth centuries, the association of nationalism with modernity has been deeply embedded in Western thought. It is well known that in this development, "European culture gained in strength and identity by setting itself off against the Orient as a sort of surrogate and even underground self."[7] The legacy of these experiences sets the context for Salih's work in a narcissistic economy of images at once permeating and sustained by a corrupted order of power relations both at the national and international levels, and above all within the interstices between.

The narrative is structured around mirrors and doubling. To mimic Western modernity means to roam around within the boundaries set up by the Western Orientalist discourse itself. The two main characters both endure double lives, and the narrative is itself a double. It is like a diamond shape divided into two parts, and each half has a double aspect: (1) the narrator's return from London/his subsequent life in Sudan; and

(2) Mustafa Sa'eed's life in Sudan/his recollections of his life in London that contaminate, fuse with, and ultimately transform the narrator. Not only is the narrator finally compelled to obsessively reassemble the scattered pieces of Mustafa Sa'eed's old life, but in some moments he experiences his own identity collapsed with that of his counterpart. In a dramatic instant, he recognizes: "This is not Mustafa Sa'eed: it is a picture of me frowning at my face from a mirror."[8] Both main characters, in their different ways, reckon with a world of masks that are at once the aftermath and the continuing reality of a centuries-old willed imaginative and geographic division between "East" and "West." This involves a peculiar violence that leaves invisible traces, marks and hauntings, within the absence created by colonial representation.

Accordingly, the two principal characters in *Season of Migration* inhabit a world of hauntings: broadly defined, ghosts "bring absence into presence, maintaining at once the 'is' and the 'is not' of metaphorical truth."[9] The rhythmic haunting of the novel is generated through the process of doubling that begins with the encounter of Mustafa Sa'eed and the narrator at the outset of the story. This doubling in turn sets up the central theme of absence and presence as a counterpoint to the cultural and geographic dualisms of dominant discourses of modernity. The phantoms in this novel, in effect, are social imaginaries, or a "created consistency" or "regular constellation of ideas . . . about the Orient" that cannot be understood without their "configurations of power."[10] Their effect, without the necessity of corresponding to anything real, is of course dramatic. This atmosphere of haunting permits the structuring of the narrative around doublings and mirrors as ghosts "are always double (here and not) and often duplicitous (where?). They mirror, compliment, recover, supplant, cancel, complete."[11] Mustafa Sa'eed is regularly described as "the mocking phantom," as "inducing a "nightmarish feeling of the world being not a reality but merely some illusion," as "a nightmare," "a lie," or "a dream."[12] In the second half of the work, following his death, he haunts the narrator on three occasions: on a train, in the presence of a university lecturer and the English Minister of Finance, and at a government conference in Khartoum. As a ghost, Mustafa Sa'eed represents a critique of institutions of Western modernity in postcolonial Sudan that unsettles any conception of national identity as a part of a natural order.

The metaphoric structure of the text seems to ask: is the claim of national identity as a coherent and total system, grounded in the imaginary and geographic counterposing of East and West, not lodged in the very fragility of identity and memory – which stands out today as an ever more singular obsession? How, in this context, is a postcolonial society to come to terms with a modernity in which "the unmixed or 'intrinsic' is as impossible as it is undesirable"?[13] These problems point to the very contemporary reality of an ongoing struggle over the meanings of national identity, Islam, and other categories within postcolonial societies. *Season of Migration* is about this struggle over meaning and the basically multiple roads it may take in the form of discourses that are not a matter of indifference in their consequences or in their claims on the future. These are issues that have been directly relevant to Iran, a land that has historically been of great ethnic, religious, and linguistic variety, social complexity, and regional diversity. Nineteenth-century Iran included varieties of Christian communities from Armenians to Nestorian and Catholic Assyrians, Jews, and Zoroastrians, as well as varying branches of Shi'i and Sunni Muslims including Babism. The democratic movement of 1910, citing the "constitutional movement" as uniting "the many communities," argued that "Iran must treat all its citizens – Muslims and Jews, Christians and Zoroastrians, Persians and Turkic speakers – as equal, free, and full Iranians."[14] Yet with the rise of Reza Shah in 1921, and his obsession with restoring the purity of a "Pre-Islamic Iran," we hear of the need for the state to eliminate "local dialects, local clothes, local customs and local sentiments," and for the masses to be freed from religious superstition.[15] The alternative conceptions of modernity and the nation evoked metaphorically by Salih have produced dramatically differing political experiences of nation making, between experiments in democratic pluralism and authoritarian bids for racial purity.

Salih's narrative presents a detailed phenomenological picture of the sometimes schizophrenic circumstances under which these differing worldviews are formed. The combined experience of prolonged study abroad and nostalgic dreaming places the narrator in the interstice between his people and the outside. In this way, *Season of Migration* posits the experience of learning and the value of knowledge in relation to dreaming at the core of concern. This is somehow paradoxical: knowledge and dreams should be opposed. Yet in the interstice, everything is made from dreams: "because of having thought so much about them during my absence, something rather like a fog rose up between them and me the first instant I saw them. But the fog cleared and I awoke...."[16] The fog is the fantasy conceived in long-term absence. This awakening, we very quickly learn, is only the prelude to a second sleep. Recurrences of bad faith or slippage back into old metaphysical abstractions establish the context for a struggle for wakefulness against the seductions of the underground self in Said's sense, or "collective imaginaries constructed and maintained on both sides through unthinkables and unthoughts cultivated by education systems, the discourse of political establishments, and the media."[17] These questions of identity concern, significantly, the "disposition of power and powerlessness in each society."[18] Ultimately, moreover, the novel concludes that in political globalization, we all live to varying degrees in the interstices and hence in a modernity of such dreams where "human identity is not only not natural and stable, but constructed, and occasionally even invented outright."[19]

In the narrator's case, sleep is a "nostalgia desirous of putting things back in their place (which) has to do with the adventure of a being of flesh and bones who, like Ulysses, is in his place as much in the places visited as upon his return to Ithaca." Yet the feeling of uneasiness – *Unheimlichkeit* – joined to the feeling of not being in one place, of not feeling at home, haunts us, and this would be the realm of emptiness.[20] This unease manifests itself in a desperate seeking after the meaning of life. The experience of time and place inside this mental framework is not fluid, but organized according to a hierarchy of value. The lowest order of value is that of being lost or a stranger to oneself and alone, and the higher and inevitably collective order the narrator describes thus: "I feel a sense of stability, I feel that I am important, that I am continuous and integral." This experience entails a union with a larger order of existence than the self and a productive contribution to the future: "no, I am not a stone thrown in the water, but seed thrown in a field." It also depends on a vital relationship to the past: "I go to my grandfather and he talks to me of life forty years ago, fifty years ago, even eighty, and my feeling of security is strengthened."[21]

Within the localized village setting of the novel, the outside represents the menace to this inner security longed for by the narrator as he endeavors to fill the absence. The early part of the story is the narrator's resistance to acknowledgment of his fear of and contamination by this outside that is at once his personal crisis and that of the Sudan in the aftermath of British colonialism. As much as he wants to pretend that nothing has really changed and life is as before, he is destined to experience a set of irreversible migrations. His most important migration is the inner migration that begins on his return to the Sudan from abroad, and it is initiated by his encounter with his mysterious double, Mustafa Sa'eed. Mustafa Sa'eed, in a sense, functions as the outside even as he obsessively shares the narrator's dream of an authentic being and belonging in Sudanese society and almost in the manner of a bitter rival. As two outsiders, they feud quietly over which is the more authentically belonging. The narrator is particularly obsessed with his exclusion from the village: "Just like everyone else, I said, I want to know what happened. Why should I be the only one who mustn't be allowed to know?"[22] Again, knowledge here is very much on the level of a sense of cultural inclusion.

Mustafa Sa'eed is like mirrors within mirrors – when a mirror is reflected by another mirror, there appear numerous mirrors, without recognition of the original one until we have an infinite play of empty mirrors. Although his life appears more the expression of a multitude of symbols than the story of a man, unlike the narrator, he has the strength to choose one side. Yet like the narrator, he is trapped in a double life. In the first and secret life, his single-mindedly cold intellectual pursuit of knowledge is initially triggered in childhood by his attraction to a colonial officer's cap, and hence by an image of power. After studying in both the Sudan and Egypt, he goes to London where, ultimately, his learning blossoms into the exacting of vengeance on British colonizers through cultural stereotyping as a weapon of seduction[23] against a number of English women. He in effect becomes many images in taking on the mirror image role of the colonizer as "a place of romance, exotic beings, haunting memories and landscapes, remarkable experiences."[24] The sadism of his many relationships is simultaneous with his rise to fame as an esteemed economist preaching a global economics of love. He endeavors to transcend his fake life by acting as a mightier imperialist from the South than the one who had abused his soul. The successive suicides of the women under the duress of psychological torment culminate at last in Mustafa Sa'eed's murder of his wife with a dagger during lovemaking and his subsequent trial. Having followed a path of violent revenge against the West, and having killed the symbol of the West in his humiliatingly yet excitingly dominant English wife, he comprehends that his life is necessarily over as a symbol that can only exist in relation to that other symbol now lost: "My life had reached completion and there was no reason to stay on."[25] He wants to beg them to "kill the lie."[26] But, despite his wishes, the court refuses to execute him and instead condemns him to imprisonment. These events of this first life precede his encounter with the narrator, and their meeting occurs during his second life as a self-regenerated simple farmer with an unknown past who materializes one day and purchases – implying the encroachments of a universal abstract value – a place in the narrator's native village. Again, in his second life, he finds himself once more reliving what has already been experienced in imagination, and hence as a consumer of information within a historically

fixed boundary. Geesey has argued that Mustafa Sa'eed is "locked into a
negative pattern of cultural mythologizing."[27]

Mustafa Sa'eed's pose as a simple farmer hides and denies the complex web of invisible power that still follows his every step, from his
experiences abroad, his education and knowledge of the workings of
legal and economic power, of the language and world of the colonial
master, and the sheer possibilities as a man invested in him by such
knowledge and being. Haunted by his history of misusing such powers,
he seeks to become something – a simple Sudanese villager – that he can
neither ever be nor understand. The entire history of violence, masks, and
subterfuge that Mustafa Sa'eed represents is a metaphoric reflection of
the workings of power in certain modernizing Middle Eastern societies
including Iran: we see a similar warped political imaginary at work in
Reza Shah's dream of spreading the Persian language among non-Persian
peoples by force, and driving Arab and Turkic tribes from the border
provinces into the interior regions as if to create the model Iranian citizen
of his assimilationist dreams. The ideological refusal of existing ethnic
and religious diversity reflects a project of modernity focused excessively
on the state, and overlooks the hope of reckoning with such differences
through a democratic political process via a project of modernity focused
on society itself and its civil organs.

In the narrator himself, we see other general aspects of twentieth-
century Middle Eastern and African development antinomies presented
through a metaphorical biographical unfolding. The narrator's inner
migration is set up in the very opening scene in three successive moments.
The first is the fog of isolating dreams produced by the distance, passage, and nostalgia accrued during a contradictory quest in a foreign
land for knowledge of uncertain value. The educational value of absorb-
ing a foreign culture and language in obtaining an English literature
degree in order to earn money and hence power is initially conceived
as a straightforward affair. The narrator states: "True I studied poetry,
but that means nothing. I could equally well have studied engineering,
agriculture, or medicine; they are all means to earning a living."[28] The
meeting with Mustafa Sa'eed gradually unsettles the narrator's confidence
in the immediate certainty of knowledge and wealth as neutral and simple
matters rather than permeated with the historical and political legacy of
empire. In the dualism of Nature and History (i.e., capitalist totality), he
would like to remember things in his own way: as if the historical aspect
had never happened. Caught in this dream, the narrator increasingly suf-
fers from an "inability to act in any decisive fashion" and is "paralyzed

by self doubt" through which he "sinks into deeper and deeper obsession with Mustafa Sa'eed's life."²⁹ In his obsession he is inwardly concerned with his own purity and whether he, like Mustafa Sa'eed, is a victim of cultural contagion. The narrator therefore asks, "He had said he was a lie, so was I also a lie?"³⁰

The second moment is therefore the counterpoint to the first in dreams of innocence regained. The narrator's mood is of "a child who sees its face in the mirror for the first time."³¹ His initial passing moment in the fog is followed by a remarkable impression of a world fundamentally unchanged by time and circumstance. A sudden and powerful recollection from childhood inspires the reflection that "I felt not like a storm-swept feather but like that palm tree, a being with a background, with roots, with a purpose."³² These contrasting images express at once the narrator's fear of purposelessness, of rootlessness, of being contaminated by a difference that renders him an outsider to both his community and any other and his vivid idealization of a rooted and purposeful existence within a community of shared meaning as the natural condition. Yet the very fanciful nature of this idealization is betrayed immediately after, when he continues his self-reassurances by affirming that, "Yes, life is good and the world as unchanged as ever."³³ This idealization of the past is personified in the narrator's grandfather, who, venerated by both the narrator and Mustafa Sa'eed, is "as though ... something immutable in a dynamic world" and "a part of history."³⁴ Mustafa Sa'eed later insists to the narrator that "your grandfather knows the secret," hinting at a privileged order of ontological knowledge possessed by those in harmony with the presumed simplicity of the traditional past. To this, the narrator wonders to himself in shock, "what secret does my grandfather know? My grandfather has no secrets."³⁵ We thereby see that Mustafa Sa'eed is searching for a hidden secret to explain the meaning of life, while the narrator seeks that same meaning in a faith that nothing further exists behind the sheer simplicity and naivety he attributes to the village life around him. Both testify to an order of knowledge involving forgetting as a mode of constructing an artificial innocence of consciousness. We have a real example of this in how Reza Shah hoped to politically engineer a nationwide forgetting of the entire Islamic heritage and past in Iran in the name of dreams of a lost Aryan greatness linked to what he took to be "modern knowledge," and the violent and abject failure of the project as proof of its unfeasibility.

The third moment, which is the narrator's encounter with Mustafa Sa'eed, initiates the undoing of this created memory of a pure reality in nature and tradition. As the familiar faces of the village are showering the narrator with questions concerning the imagined differences of the West, he all of a sudden spots the face of a stranger amid the crowd who "said nothing but only listened in silence, sometimes smiling in a way that was mysterious, like someone talking to himself."[36] This introduction of Mustafa Sa'eed, who functions on a symbolic level as the narrator's double and reflection, begins the descent of both men along in-part temporally dislocated but psychologically interrelated paths into an ever-deepening displacement leading to a reckoning for the whole village with an inescapably fragmented and potentially very dangerous contemporary global culture. Their paths of violent discourse and romantic nativism impute too monolithic a character to different parts of a world that is inextricably interconnected by the experiences of modernity. These experiences point finally to the interconnection of all experiences beyond the dualism of separate essences in a reckoning with the physical fact of discontinuity, the myriad possibilities for reconstructing the broken pieces of the past, and the clear perception that the illusion of partial and plural identity is itself reality through interpretation of event and context.

From this opening scene, the historical composition of postcolonial Sudanese society is shown through the two principal characters' battles, through memory and the living present, with received restricted imaginings. This shows the power of cumulative and corporate identity of imaginative discourse, along with economic and social circumstances, to limit any individual struggle for orientation within the passage of historic and personal time. The interzone of knowledge and dreams through which the two principal characters migrate is expressed in evocations of haunting and emptiness as domains of the modern industrial unconscious. This exploration is for the purpose of shining a light on the epistemological framework underlying the articulation of various discourses, or the history of systems of thought. In these inherited systems of thought, or *epistemes*, which are primarily unconscious, fact and value dichotomies do not hold sway. It is like Deweyan pragmatism that finds that "reality is a *denotative* term, a word used to designate indifferently everything that happens. Lies, dreams, insanities, deceptions, myths, theories are all of them just the events they specifically are."[37] The narrative has, in some measure, the organization of a dream.

Broadly, the narrative might be said to follow the tradition of the autobiographical allegory of descent into the underworld, itself a play on a simultaneous presence and absence, yet in a modern underworld of moral dissolution including government buildings and developing infrastructures that occur as troubling memories in the minds of the characters. The abyss in its depths is the empty space filled by colonial images and their mimicked inversions. This strategy compromises the so-called pure style with the "tainted truth of the other, the historical time spent in hell."[38] Jump cuts, recurring voices inserted at random into the narrative, repeated flashbacks, and alternating perspectives all function to undo any sense of a unitary fabric to the novel. Rather, composites of image and affect imply the perpetual swirling collision of unmoored collective mental representations. Masks are peeled off as secrets are unveiled, only to lead to further masks and a widening atmosphere of disorientation: "unlike me, she yearned for tropical climes, cruel suns, purple horizons. In her eyes, I was a symbol of all her hankerings."[39] The mask falls from Mustafa Sa'eed's face and he himself falls from the stage when he kills his wife: "Everything I did after I killed her was an apology, not for killing her, but for the lie that was my life."[40] At his trial he finds himself as yet another phantom when the defense lawyer argues that these "girls were not killed by Mustafa Sa'eed but the germ of a deadly disease that assailed them a thousand years ago."[41] Identities collapse into one another, the narrator saying of Mustafa Sa'eed that "My adversary is within and I needs must confront him. . . . I begin from where Mustafa Sa'eed had left off."[42] There is no single point in time to ground all others.

After having mocked and humiliated the narrator for the impractical and irrelevant character of his foreign doctoral degree, Mustafa Sa'eed's mask of a simple farmer is quite quickly knocked off when he exposes himself by drunkenly reciting a poem in high English during a drunken evening gathering. Or is it accidental at all? We are tempted to suppose that Mustafa Sa'eed's slip is an intentional bait intended to draw the narrator to him so he may, at his leisure, unveil his dark past in order to finally be discovered and recognized as perhaps a radical and original economic and social thinker, a challenger of received morality and an avenger of Africa and Islam, or a self-reformed man who found peace and ultimate truth in his native traditions only at the very end of his life. Or are these only the suppositions of the narrator as he becomes increasingly obsessed with and engrossed in every detail of Mustafa Sa'eed's life, particularly following his death by drowning one summer evening in a flash flood? The novel does not provide a definite answer to this question. Indeed, we do not even know for certain whether or not Mustafa Sa'eed is in fact dead, or whether he merely slipped away under the cover of a staged death to begin yet another life in his long series of mythically inspired regenerations. We only know that he leaves behind an enormous amount of records for posterity, suggesting an economy of accumulation in the early phases of global capitalism, and an attachment of significant value to the inheritance of this fragmented knowledge about his life. He turns himself in death, as in life, into an object of value.

We are even uncertain as to his very reality, so much does he at times seem to resemble a shadow of others' imaginations and prejudices. We are only certain of Mustafa Sa'eed's tremendous impact on the life of the narrator, and more forebodingly on that of Sa'eed's wife, who, touched by his contagion, proceeds to commit the second act of gruesome knife murder in the novel when she is forced by the entire community to remarry an old man against her will. This violent upshot of the legacy evokes vividly how "the germ of violence has entered the village and change has come about, perhaps brought by the stranger Sa'eed or by the residue of cultures in contact and of new ideas from the world outside the village."[43] As I have said, Sa'eed represents the outside. This germ, surely, is the haunting that permeates the novel itself. The predominance of artificial form, of idealized repressive form for timeless being as clung to in the narrator's imagination, is forced to yield to a return of history, or the crisis produced in the overall history of capitalism's global expansion. Likewise, the totalized notion of a progress of history or homogenized historical evolution is violently caught up with by the "inheritance of the dispossession of the world by a conquering Europe."[44] Within this context, Mustafa Sa'eed's own demand for difference and identity is a dialectical response bringing its own violence and antihumanism. It is such ideas in themselves, as a mimicking of Western modernity's Manichean precepts, which usher in the violence of the novel's end as a doubling of the earlier violence committed by Mustafa Sa'eed in his London days. His exaggerated masculinity in his conquest of the West contrasts with the femininity attributed to him during his life in the village as he passively "submits" to national tradition. Transformed by her marriage to him into a modern woman, his wife responds to the tensions of encompassing tradition through an act of extreme violence that unfortunately leaves nothing left to be negotiated either one way or the other. In this sense the narrative develops the idea of a middle way. Social, economic, and political conditions of change necessarily open struggle over the meaning of tradition, or the limits of thinkables and unthoughts, inevitably not least where issues of gender and social justice are concerned. In that these conditions of change were set in motion not by cultural contact but through the particular violence of the colonial project, it is imperative in engaging in these struggles not to reproduce the very logic of that historical experience.

These literary themes, captured vividly by Salih, are visible in Iran today. From the twentieth-century Iranian past, where the national movement under Reza Shah became twisted through a combination of ideological errors and political misfortunes into mirroring the repressive structures of the very colonial order it had set out to fight; to the dream of an Iranian Islamic purity untouched by Western modernity as envisioned by Fardid and successors and enthroned ideologically with the 1979 revolution; today, with the popular movement for democracy, the Iranian public embarks on a middle way between the inevitability of global modernity and the continuing life of Iranian traditions as two mutating aspects of Iranian national life.

In *Season of Migration*, we see the alternative to a middle way in inevitable fears of contagion and obsession with fixed boundaries. The central theme in the novel of a fear of contagion is the counterpart to a reproduction in the characters' modes of thought on the discursive binaries that accompanied the enterprise of colonial modernity. Or, the two principal characters as intellectuals, who are in relative positions of power and influence, renege on their responsibilities to their community in the face of a severely challenging future by either taking refuge in denial and languid dreams of paradise unchanged, or alternating between doctrines of romanticized heroic violence and veneration of a mythic past in the idealized person of the grandfather with the secret. These various ideological imaginaries are of course deeply interwoven, and indeed the separate person of the two characters is put into question. The ideological imaginaries, however much dialectically wedded to capitalism and schizophrenia, are harmful in their application in lived reality. In this way the entire village is forced to undergo a violently traumatic *as well as* permanent transformation at the hands of Mustafa Sa'eed's ghost. These are what might be called the dream or possibly magical realist aspects of the novel, buried as they are in a narrative that conveys a brutal and harrowing sense of social realism.

Ghosts explore the "nature and limits of the knowable."[45] Thereby metaphorically reflecting on the themes of identity, aim, and background as they define the structure of knowledge, Salih overcomes the limits of a thought tendency epitomized in the modernity of presence or the internal rational structure of the absolute as an epistemological dogma and end, the totality of reality through a work that is a meditation on the permanence and reality of absence and change. Salman Rushdie once commented that "the most important events in our life happen when we are not there." Although in *Season of Migration* nothing is identified as being fundamentally the most important, the world constructed in the narrative bears out this observation of reality in consistent fashion and thereby refutes the identity of the absolute subject. There can be no rational absolute beyond the pluralistic specificity of time through which we may aspire to gather already formed generalities as anything but pragmatic expedients to growth; they can never be final or fixed ends of meaning, roots, or history. Entangled inevitably in this account are the questions: Where is home? What is the controlling imagination? How to reckon with the nonexistence of a metaphysical hiding place? Salih's work attempts to reply to these questions nondogmatically and with the hope of a nonviolent path. It is a comparable path of hope and openness to change, anchored in a public democratic politics, that we see rising against fierce state opposition in Iran in recent times.

Salih's work uses a strategy of doubling, not unlike Conrad's *Heart of Darkness* or Celine's *Journey to the End of Night*, which both present their own meditations on the inextricability of Europe's colonial project and the innermost identity of an all-embracing global modernity. Both of them do so, at differing degrees, from within a European perspective. For Conrad it was Marlowe and Kurtz, for Celine, Bardamu and Robinson, for Salih it is the narrator and Mustafa Sa'eed. Yet the images of both a heart and an end suggest somehow an ultimate center or final stopping point, an absolute encounter, generally in the solitude and death of the individual person. Conversely, the images of both season and migration suggest at once transience and cycle. Salih's vision is grounded in the continuing and pluralistic life of the community, and precisely not the frozen or idealized community of a nostalgic imagination. This testifies to Salih's novel as very much a work of passage, a way, which confronts us finally with an open path and not the dead end of a mimetic black hole of either individual despair or a politics of authenticity. Just as every existence is an event, despair is not the essence of life but one of its moments. As Rushdie has argued, "one hour of darkness will not make us go blind." This comment harbors a deeper epistemological sense that seems to be one of the principal ideas in *Season of Migration to the North*. The work is then about learning and the value of knowledge as continuous growth.

Combined with this overarching narrative are two archetypal figures borrowed from myth and who, woven into the narrative, function to define the core ideas of the novel. The first figure is Narcissus, who, as a metaphor for identity, at once indicates doubling and pure image, as well as the illusionary love of a ghost which leads to death. This is the fate not only of the women who loved and died for Mustafa Sa'eed as an image of the Orient, but of the man himself as he perished in a desert flood pursuing the ghost of authentic traditional Sudanese life. Narcissus indicates a world of mirrors or glass, the fleeting and endless reproduction of identities that is late capitalism. The second figure, who skims the surface of the narrative in more visible flashes, is the figure of Othello. At Mustafa Sa'eed's trial, the defense lawyer insists that the women did not die because of him but because of a "disease that assailed them over a thousand years ago." He likely has in mind the collective misunderstandings and enmities that began with the early Arab conquests and later the Crusades. In hearing this, Mustafa Sa'eed feels robbed of his own personhood and agency, reduced to the vanishing substance of a dream: "It occurred to me that I should stand up and say to them: this is untrue, a fabrication. It was I who killed them. I am the desert of thirst. I am no Othello. I am a lie. Why don't you sentence me to be hanged and so kill the lie?"[46] Othello, similarly emblematic of a plague of misconceptions that have surrounded the East-West binary, stood between the cultures and faced the obstacles of entrenched discourse that shaped his behavior and choices, insecurities and paranoia, and resulted at last in the unjust murder of his wife and his own downfall.

It is the narrator who, following Mustafa Sa'eed's death, inherits custody of his sons, his wife, and the key to the permanently locked room in his house containing his secret. In his recognition of his love for the widow but his inability to decide to marry her even to rescue her from her unwanted suitor, and in spite of her open death threat, the narrator's indecisiveness contributes decisively to the final episode of bloody destruction. There is, prior to this, some resentment in the community at this inheritance that amounts to the question of who knew Mustafa Sa'eed best – or who was best prepared to cope with the legacy and the future of the outside that is very much *inside*. Unbeknownst to those who thought they knew him, only the narrator shares his secret and is therefore worthy to inherit the labor of reconstructing his identity from the enormous mess of fragments and clues he has left behind. Yet the narrator is himself increasingly haunted by the value of his own knowledge: "Thus Mustafa Sa'eed has, against my will, become a part of my world, a thought in my brain, a phantom that does not want to take itself off. And thus I too experience a remote feeling of fear, fear that it is just conceivable that simplicity is not everything."[47] He also has doubts about his grandfather, whose symbolism has already been detailed: "Is he really as I assert and as he appears to be? Is he above this chaos?"[48] Finally, he doubts the value of his own knowledge in relation to the life of the community: "When they laugh they say, ask forgiveness of God and when they weep they say, ask forgiveness of God. Just that. And I, what have I learnt?"[49]

These are doubts expressed over the work of memory: "These memory places function for the most part after the manner of reminders, offering in turn a support for failing memory, a struggle in the war against forgetting, even the silent plea of a dead memory."[50] Once again this deals with the question of the structure of knowledge. Inside Mustafa Sa'eed's secret room, the narrator finds a perfect reproduction of an English gentleman's living room, with antique fireplace and bookcases filled with only English books. It is another frozen moment or shrine to an ideal and imagined past, in its sterility forming the counterpart to the African room left behind in London where young English women were seduced on their way to death with exotic images of the mysterious Orient. It is in effect negative cultural reductionism that cannot face postcolonial Sudan as a part of global modernity and therefore a hybrid zone. As a form of knowledge, these two rooms exhibit the poisonous epistemic tendency of an end of the world or of history, a space free from the flow of time, a perfect world of either everything or nothing, pure in its cultural identity, and a kind of death in the absolute where memories are crystallized into ghosts and "the universe, with its past, present and future, was gathered into a single point before and after which nothing existed."[51] Both tormented by his fear that he too much resembles Mustafa Sa'eed and embittered by the death of the widow, the narrator decides to burn the room in a transforming activity apparently beyond meaning, value, and norm as he is lost in the flood of another man's violent memories. This act, by its absolute nature, expresses the tacit destructiveness and violence of ideologies of total change.

The final scene in the novel is perhaps the final moment of migration. The narrator enters the river naked in the dead of night with the presumable intention of either drowning himself or, more implausibly, reaching the other side. This act seems to again echo the life story of Mustafa Sa'eed, who himself died by drowning (the echo, too, recalls Narcissus in relation to Echo's passive love in the original myth). It seems almost as if by this act the narrator expresses an inner obsession with transcendence or going beyond in the form of forgetting, shown earlier in taking refuge in fantasy, and this is its ultimate moment of expression. Yet he stops right in the middle of the river, between the northern and southern shores. It is like a moment of transcending the ironic dedication in the notebook containing Mustafa Sa'eed's completely blank life story: "to those who see with one eye, speak with one tongue and see things as either black or white, either Eastern or Western."[52] In this situation the narrator makes what is perhaps the first real decision of his life when he decides that he wants to live. In so doing he sees that "it is not my concern whether or not life has meaning. Rather, I shall live because there are a few people I want to stay with for the longest possible time and because I have duties to discharge."[53] We see here an acknowledgment of the everyday world. In the final moment, in screaming for help, we see the narrator's concession at last that he is not alone, and never has been, that he is interdependent with others, and they with him, and so it is for communities of people everywhere beyond the mentally conceived figures of ontological enclosure that place a fetish for meaning or purity above the lives of actual people.

Salih's book has a great deal to offer in terms of the situation of modern Iran. His fascinating novel concerning experiences of colonization and intellectual desires to return home teaches us that after the colonial encounter, life has changed so greatly that even elementary notions such as home, native, us, and them cannot be defined with any clarity. Iran has learned through difficult experience that the starting point for all democratic political change is within the rich and diffuse realm of everyday life, where it is possible to build diverse coalitions on the ground and expand the democratic public space in alternatives to state-centered politics of ideological change from above. It is necessary to set up dialogue across societal divisions based on pragmatic principles of justice and truth, on the assumption that although conflict is an inherent part of social life, it need not be resolved through violence.

Season of Migration to the North presents two different narratives. First there is Sa'eed's desire to go back home and live an authentic life with his people, which proves to be an impossible dream. We see from this that authenticity can only work in two contexts: (1) At the level of discourse. Nativism is a powerful force that can mobilize masses when imagined as real and meaningful, and can be used to reject new ideas and change. (2) At the practical, everyday level, it may also work if one is willing to engage in massive violence and total denial of what happens in native everyday life, and if one is willing to employ the brutal use of physical force inspired by a distorted and corrupted imagination. Sa'eed, faced with the reality of women's role in his own culture, made the ethical decision to step out of his nativist world and break its perceived framework of ethical authority. Conversely, a good recent example of those who are willing to embrace death and destruction to uphold a nativist project were the Taliban in Afghanistan.

What is imagined as the authentic or native is of course not given or fixed by any agreed criteria in any community anywhere in the world. It is inevitably rather a representation of the imagination and only given genuine definition in the course of some real experience. Yet as a concept, *native* is only called for to be defined in the moment that a social or cultural project decides to build its defining principle around a definition of authenticity. It is therefore necessary in this scenario to engage in the imposition of a set of ideas and practices that entail the exclusion and denial of certain other ideas (including memories of identities and moral values) and practices. The fact is that open and democratic societies necessarily avoid the imposition of a narrative of authenticity, and although they may offer some general national narrative, they can never base social inclusion on acceptance of that principle. In the case of Iran, even the most moderate version of a nativist discourse of necessity involves excluding other possible nativist discourses. Those who define nativism in the context of Iran as a religious society may think that an Islamic nativist discourse offers protection against Western cultural hegemony. However, they often have a difficult time relating to other nativist discourses that, for example, privilege pre-Islamic Iranian national origin as being uniquely authentic to Iran. Any macro model of social change derived from nativism in any guise is clearly violent and problematic from its inception, the moment we give appropriate consideration to the multiple micro aspects of change or "life worlds."

3

Modernity beyond Nativism and Universalism

When contemporary Iranian political concepts, imaginatively derived from European political discourses, become frozen in their assumed meaning – the West, universal reason, tradition – it is often forgotten idealistically that those European populations over which state rulers sought to extend their control largely resisted, long and violently, in a process in which scientific reason was instrumentalized. The modern institutional forms of democratic political participation, often perceived forgetfully as "natural" to "Western culture," were the unintended consequence or byproduct of programs by European state makers to build armies, enforce conscription, maintain a tax base, cement coalitions, and thwart multiple moments of threat and rebellion from below. For many intellectuals in today's Iran, notions such as modernity, the West, universalism, tradition, and nativism are accepted as *given*, and therefore views on these important issues and concepts generally lack an appropriately specific historical and social context, or sense of the multicentered experimental significance of historical, political, and cultural evolutions. As a result, instead of seriously engaging the ongoing debates around these complex ideas, these influential Iranian intellectuals reduce their contributions to such simple binary notions as inside/outside, modern/tradition, and universal/local. One side of the debate is defined as Western, alien, and new, whereas the other is declared to be traditional, Iranian, and familiar, in a manner that is severely limited and inadequate to the task of developing forms of thought appropriate to existing social, cultural, and political conditions.

Today's Iran, after almost two centuries of experiences with the West and a particular national passage through modernity, lives in a world of ideas as much European as they are local, and the significance of this fact is that we now have a tradition of Iranian modernity and a specifically modern way of imagining our own traditions. This specifically Iranian and globally mediated modernity is reflected in the changing worldviews expressed among certain contemporary Iranian activists and thinkers, who go against the grain of an older essentialist worldview in Iranian political thought going back to important and ultimately harmful intellectual threads in the Constitutional Revolution (for example, Sayyid Hassan Taqizadeh's imagining of Western scientific modernity). A dawning recognition of the profound change that has taken place in Iranian intellectual culture is increasingly being expressed in the discourses of contemporary Iranian intellectuals who lived through and participated in the 1979 Iranian Revolution. We find this new worldview, which reflects the singularity of the modern Iranian experience mediated by global experiences, in the thought, for example, of Alavi Tabar. Only nineteen at the time of the revolution, he became a prominent journalist and leading member of the Iranian Reform Movement in the 1990s. He cites his experience of the revolution under the statist ideas of Shari'ati, and his subsequent involvement in organizing various intellectual and political groups, as fostering his strong commitment to free critical thinking and refusal to endorse a view of the sacred in politics.

The very concepts of *modernity* and *tradition* have, in themselves, their own multiple meanings and complex histories that represent varied and often different experiences. It therefore becomes the task for any serious study of Iranian modernity to critically examine what Iranians mean when they employ the often-overused terms *the West*, *modernity*, and so on. It is necessary, for this purpose, to understand and fully appreciate the complex, violent, and contradictory history of modernity in Europe. Too often Iranian intellectuals imagine the European counter-Enlightenment as if it were simply interchangeable with liberal modernity in England or radical Enlightenment in France or Germany. They borrow ideas from Locke and Marx and Nietzsche as if these figures and their ideas lacked any social or political contexts or histories. The varied European experiences did not pit modernizing elites against traditional landed authorities on behalf of the general population and its welfare, as the imaginary dichotomy of modernity/tradition would have it. Rather, great varieties of political entrepreneurs struggled in an expansive process over resources, populations, and territory, involving diverse class and institutional alliances, in order to meet the demands of survival within the dynamic interstate matrix. The concepts we now employ, such as modernity, reason, and tradition, grew out of the complex specificity of these struggles, with differing relations between religious and secular institutions defining diverse nation-making and political-development processes. These are reflected in the writings of Marx, Nietzsche, Locke, and others.

As for certain religious intellectuals, we see a tendency to advocate a more liberal and universal modernity while simultaneously insisting on defining their own cultural identity in nativist and local terms. When from within this contradictory framework their research reaches the inevitable impasse, they prefer to remain silent rather than acknowledge their contradictory theoretical disposition. Within the newer Islamic reformist generation exemplified particularly by Soroush, there is the theoretical impediment of embracing liberal democracy while insisting on a radical transformation in the existing understanding of Shiite theology. It seems very difficult for Soroush and his followers to understand that the development of modern democracy is linked to the creation and establishment of democratic institutions and not some radical change in the religious ideas held by Muslims. The action of calling for a radical revolutionary change in our religious knowledge is far more consistent with the very Hegelian or Heideggerian philosophical tradition that Soroush has made a career out of criticizing. It was Hegel who, in his preoccupation with the "spiritlessness of the age," became obsessed with *geist*, or absolute knowledge, or the "end of history," touching on religion and the state and consigning all particular perspectives on these cultures to the status of decadent, alienated, and broken, and thus ultimately damaging to the prospect of "progress." From this perspective of totality, all time is dominated by historical utilization, and the "end" is all that matters: the "end of history" as the attainment by the universal historical process of absolute identity. Existing "alienated" forms of religion and culture must be superseded in a revolutionary dialectical resolution of history into one absolute future. Ultimately, in the very moment that the projected totality or "conflict-free society" becomes empirical, it necessarily becomes totalitarian, refusing any difference or outside beyond itself. This is a very modernist idea of religion in the totalitarian vein, obsessed with finality or closure, insisting that a necessary adjunct of the perfected state is the radical overhaul and perfection of existing religious forms. Similarly, Heidegger insisted that traditional religions were inadequate to the task of reawakening a profound and authentic reconnection to the primordial sources of being and a rooted and meaningful social existence. Soroush's reflections on transformations of the religious mind, without realizing it, follow in this very modern tradition of seeking political salvation through the fostering of a radical, new, socially shared worldview.

Where the theoretical and practical task of constructing democratic modernity is concerned, very much in contrast to such "philosophies of history," what is of primary importance is the creation of viable democratic social institutions. A necessary aspect of this task is a respect for everyone's religious and cultural understanding, and therefore the process must not require that even the most traditional religious people change their thinking or beliefs in order to make democracy possible. Such an injunction grounded in a totality is, to the contrary, emphatically undemocratic. The Kian Circle in Iran, for example, of which Alavi Tabar was an active member, started as a debating society over questions of religion and modernity and evolved into a powerful force of activism in the democratic struggle of the Iranian Reform Movement. This organization, composed of religious individuals who adopt an essentially secular political view, is less concerned with transforming people's religious mentalities than with organizing new democratic institutional forms.

It was Hegel and later the counter-Enlightenment movement that rejected democracy as meaningless and lacking a moral core and insisted, as a remedy, on a completely new understanding of our time and of being. In this shared aspect we can call Davari and his followers a certain kind of religious intellectual who seeks to reconnect modernity with religion, itself ultimately a conservative project that seeks to impose uniformity and closure on forms of religious experience to cope with the fragmentation of what is believed to have been taken for granted as a "whole" at a more "innocent" period in history. It amounts ultimately to a refusal to recognize the "otherness" of others in a bid for security against the outpouring of radical energies that are the basic experience of modernity.

We note a growing tendency among certain Iranian intellectuals influenced by the Reform Movement to move beyond the endless fascination with modernity as a phenomenon somehow "out there." Mustafa Tajzadeh, for instance, a Muslim and member of the Reform Movement who served as an adviser to President Mohammad Khatemi, argues that the spirit of the movement is linked to a rising world consciousness of the value of democracy. The effect of moving beyond the dualistic and totalizing conceptions of modernity will be that many of the theories, ways of thinking, and notions that for many years have blinded Iranians in their dealings with the practical aspects of the contemporary condition will be exposed as a hindrance that is both irrelevant and useless:

1. Modernity is not a reality that is outside of the geographical, cultural, or even historical experience of Iran and Iranians. Iran and Iranians are and have been a part of the larger world of global modernity for a long time, and to suggest otherwise is to be blind to this evident reality. Many ideas, institutions, problems, and possibilities that Iranian society is in the midst of encountering are modern ideas and practices. To pretend that we have a choice of either entering the modern or seeking alternative paths is to commit a deep and unproductive intellectual denial, a utopian and romantic fantasy dangerous in its political implications.

2. On the other hand, modernity is not a single narrative about the European history of progress. There are many different expressions of modernity, and even the experience of European modernity is that of many narratives evolving through earlier European societies and their internal struggles to form modern democratic institutions. It is also the history of societies such as Iran that came to know and experience modernity through European colonialism and then became part of the global modern experience. Modernity is now a globally constituted reality, and Iran is placed squarely within it, despite any romantic fantasies of the periphery or the outside.

3. One cannot therefore define modernity as a mainly European phenomenon. The struggle to come to terms with modernity, including the embrace of democracy and the resistance to living in either an open society or an isolated and traditional one, all form part of our modern experience. The battle over ideas and visions is not the struggle between native traditions and outside forces. It is precisely such dualist interpretations that Dewey criticized at length in favor of more nuanced and specific sociological observations of modernity as such in its many situated and conflicting variations. Any battle over ideas is therefore a reflection of competing visions within a single modern society with ultimately global links.

It is unnecessary, for example, to plummet far beneath the surface of the main debates animating Iranian intellectual life in the wake of the 1979 revolution to trace their source to a broader discursive level of crisis in historical interpretation that entails negotiating the multiple dimensions of meaning in global modernity. Scarcely can such debates be mistaken for being purely a matter of some insular religious concern, let alone of one closed religion or culture to the exclusion of the world and ideas beyond. On the contrary: the obsessions of postrevolutionary Iran can be said to share in a conceptual transformation common to "East" and "West" in reflective hermeneutics that puts into question the very defining elements of nation, religion, and social meaning, in sum "modern identity" itself. Debates following the revolution were defined by the opposing views of the two unofficial regime intellectuals, Reza Davari and Abdolkarim Soroush. Soroush subsequently went into exile as a dissident intellectual and now lives mostly in the West. He was particularly important in introducing the ideas of Karl Popper and Thomas Kuhn into Iran (including *The Structure of Scientific Revolutions*). During the early years of the revolution, he defended the works of Habermas and Hayek against charges of being "impure" and "Western" and responsible for the corruption of the youth through "secular atheism." Davari has had an important role in introducing the nineteenth- and twentieth-century German metaphysical philosophy that has created its own dark wave in contemporary Islamic thought.

At the center of these debates is first the nature of "the West" and then the relative merits of positivism (for Soroush, following Popper) versus historicism (for Davari, inspired by Heidegger). Through these separate lenses, the issue of "the West" appears in strikingly different lights. Involving the exploration of philosophical and political questions, we hear in these exchanges the Islamic ideology as a new beginning grounded in problematic modern realities and reaching for answers in the more original and sometimes dangerous intellectual discourses of the twentieth century. The Islamist discourses that emerge are certainly conspicuously lacking the benefit of historical or theological precedent in either theory or practice in spite of vehement claims to identity with a venerated traditional ancestry that is more imagined than real.

A discussion of several key Iranian intellectuals who helped to shape developments of the late twentieth century leading up to and following the Iranian Revolution of 1979, and whose ideas continue to shape contemporary Iranian society and politics, offers a window to analysis of the different sources of the strongly anti-Western rhetoric that became the staple of the Iranian Islamist revolutionary discourse and of Islamism as an ideology more generally. Ironically, through this discussion, it is possible to demonstrate not only these intellectuals' intimacy with and borrowings from certain essential Western discourses of the twentieth century, but also the loose yet coherent existence of a broader movement of "authenticity" that is global and historical in character – in both "the East" and "the West." In this sense none of the thinkers in this chapter are "anti-Western" at all, in spite of what may be their fantasies to the contrary. Rather, they participate in a broader global movement that has at least as much background in "the West" itself through – speaking in very broad terms – a long fight between "cultural particularism" and "transcultural universalism" that has adopted nearly identical terms. We read it in Herder, Dilthey, Jünger, and Spengler, to say nothing of Yukio Mishima and Sayeb Qutb, and so many more in so many variations. To a considerable degree, modernity has been defined by this broad historical trend of opposition between "Enlightenment" and "counter-Enlightenment" that has been identified in some detail by, for example, Richard Wolin in his *The Seduction of Unreason*.

The actual scope and power of "counter-Enlightenment" as a coherent political and intellectual discourse, however, very often goes unrecognized in its non-Western manifestations. This is itself an aspect of the epistemological problem of Orientalism. Such expressions are routinely subsumed under familiar simplifying stereotypes based on dialectical binaries of modern/traditional, rational/irrational, and so forth, which themselves constitute in some measure the panoply of a steadily disintegrating "dominant discourse of modernity," through academia, schools, and the media, as a Eurocentric project. There is a serious mistake in short-sightedly attributing the flourishing of these discourses in Islamic societies to any innate hostility of "the Orient" to "the West"; their force is political rather than geographical in nature. As discourses expressing an unselfconscious "global movement," they boast a coherent and lofty intellectual pedigree and seductive as well as complex philosophical origins. These discourses exist above all as a long-standing and dispersed rebellion against the tradition of modern Enlightenment (particularly in its more totalizing theoretical and practical aspects) and its concomitant principle of secularism. It is a question of an alternative and particularly dangerous discourse of modernity. In place of a "universal" and secular truth, there is an equally modern championing and politicization of the "truth" in cultural tradition, or defense of a single overarching sociocultural meaning as both an ontology and a mode of political organization. This is especially the case in the powerful philosophical writings of Heidegger and the Nazi social revolution he later helped to bring about. It is in this way and by extension that these discourses and movements, although potentially populist, are inherently hostile to the very concept of formal democracy and pluralism, even on the level of principle.

Davari is a professor of philosophy, is a member of the Iranian Academy of Sciences, and was until recently the editor of the journal *Nameh Farhang*, organ of the Ministry of Culture and Islamic Guidance. Influenced by a Hegelian philosophy of history, Davari conceives the West in essentialist terms as a "totality" or "united whole." Identifying the principal legacies of the West as "humanism" and "modernity," he writes that the West "is a way of thinking and a historical practice which started in Europe more or less four hundred years ago, and has since expanded more or less universally. The West portrays the demise of the holy truth and the rise of humanity which views itself as the sole possessor and focus of the universe." In this view, the West is conceived as an absolute other to be set dialectically against an authentic Islamic identity in a precise reverse reproduction of the classical Orientalist episteme. In an apocalyptic following of Heidegger, he proceeds to explain how "western civilization has reached its termination point" in a technological nihilism. Therefore, we hear still another echoing of the "narrative of despair." For Davari, Heidegger is the "great sage of our time" and the "pioneer of future philosophy." In the wake of the rupture in Iranian thought initiated through Fardid, then, we see one of the most influential Iranian thinkers creating a striking combination of dialectical aggression and hermeneutical reinterpretation with a profound debt to the darker aspects of German idealism and phenomenology in the name of affirming the "true" Islam.

Yet Soroush, who now lives in the U.S. and was a researcher at the Iranian Academy of Philosophy, for his part argues that the "unified and totalizing Hegelian construct" is meaningless in its envisioning of the West as a simple object to be either accepted or rejected. He asks, "Where do you draw the boundaries of the west?" throwing into relief the blurry distinction between geographic reality and phantasms of the imagination where the East/West binary is concerned. The same antidogmatic line of thought is extended to Islam, as Soroush argues that "I do not believe that a religious government like the Islamic Republic of Iran has (or should have) the intention of converting the whole world to Islam and Islamic government. The first step should be to promote and respect religious thought (of whatever kind) around the world." In this, there is a fundamentally differing interpretation of the basic inner mission of Islam as a religion, but above all as a modern political construct, and one in which the aim is intercultural dialogue, rather than the militant protection of an abstractly conceived essential identity.

This points to a larger problem that has often cracked modern political thought down the middle: is social freedom a question of an imposed universal consensus of spiritual belief, as Heidegger would argue; is it a realization of a historically unified and reconciled "conflict free" society, as Hegel thought; or does modern political liberty depend, as Dewey argued, on the continual renewal of debate instigated by multiple experiences and points of view as at once the means and the end of liberty itself? Dewey wrote that "reflection occurs only in situations qualified by uncertainty, alternatives, questioning, search, hypotheses, tentative trials which test the worth of thinking." He therefore deplored "objects constituted once and for all by thought."[1] We can say broadly that Hegel presents a dialectical position, Heidegger a hermeneutical one, and Dewey an alternative to both in a "conceptual pluralism" that rejects that there can be "somehow fixed in advance, a single 'real,' a single 'literal' sense of 'exist' (or) 'identity.'"[2] In the primary discourses of postrevolutionary Iran, we can see variations on these questions at work intermingled deeply with the Orientalist imagination and leading to a continuous interpretation and reinterpretation concerning the proper boundaries that define the nation, religion, social experience, self, and other, in a hermeneutical dismantling of tradition that ranges from an echoing of the Machiavellian "two moods" affirmation of perpetual tension in difference to hopes for a restored Heideggerian "nearness to being." Today, with the Reform Movement gaining momentum in Iran, we see an ever greater number of intellectuals articulating a discourse that values democracy and openness as the primary value for political organization – with calls for new beginnings on the mental horizon in neither secular nor religious terms.

Hermeneutics as a critical method begins in principle with the premise that there can be no presuppositionless knowledge or pure access to reality. The famous hermeneutical "circle," then, is the idea that we always begin from inside an understanding that is probably in large part unconscious, and that we cannot be somehow "objective" outsiders or a knowing "subject." This was an ideal of epistemological purity or pure transparency that Dostoyevski ridiculed in his image of the glass house in *Notes from the Underground*, and to which he opposed the sagacious, timeless, and impenetrable wisdom of the Russian Orthodox Church. Rather, for hermeneutics the world is already filled with meanings given by each tradition. Any knowledge begins from within some tradition and interprets that tradition in the context of moving time and in relation to itself or other traditions, but never from any "absolute beyond." Thinking along such lines, we quite quickly see the complex difficulty in

making any neat separation between traditions, to the degree that there
can be said to be any such borderlines at all. One is tempted to follow
the path of Dara Shikoh (1627–58), whose seminal contribution to the
composite culture of India included *Majma'ul Bahrayn* (*Mingling of the
Two Oceans*), which shows that there are a great number of similarities
between the two religions of Hinduism and Islam. Yet in the context
of claims to power within the modern nation-state and international
power imbalance, an essentialized wall often becomes the anchor for
a hermeneutics of authenticity, at the opposite end of falling into the
fashionable abyss of a bottomless regress of interpretations as we see in
Derrida. The abyss amounts to nonaction coupled with cynical dismissal
of everything behind a mask of revolutionary nihilism. The wall amounts
to a breed of violent totalitarian politics intended to protect an imagined pure identity from the supposed nihilism of "Western" modernity.
Hegemonic narratives of modernity rising in the colonial era found their
own strongest expression, in turn, in dialectical forms of reasoning so
dogmatic in their transcendental claims as to exclude even any idea of the
"hermeneutical turn" as it was later to be launched with revolutionary
consequences, most notably by Heidegger.

The origins of the hermeneutic tradition are essentially religious and
coincide with the theorization of the exegesis on biblical texts by Protestant theologians. The discursive tradition emerged with the crisis in
religious authority and identity triggered by the political and doctrinal
shattering of western Christendom in the Reformation. Since the nineteenth century, hermeneutics has been taken in charge by philosophy
and rethought outside of the domain of the sacred texts. It became an
influential theory of meaning and comprehension that posed problems
concerning the interpretation of literary texts. In the nineteenth century,
the theoreticians of hermeneutics, Schleiermacher and Dilthey, described
understanding as a process of reconstruction by the reader of the original
intention of the author. From this point of view, in which a metaphysical
essentialism lingers, the text is at bottom the expression of this intention.
This theory therefore postulates a determined meaning to existence, as it
is based on a belief in a preexisting meaning in the text, with the process
of interpretation being only its rediscovery.

Radically alternative conceptions were later evolved by Heidegger and
Gadamer that posed the problem of the temporal distance that separates us from the meaning of texts. The introduction of the problem
of time undoes the static essentialisms of metaphysical certainty. From
this point of view there is no "floor" to understanding the text, and

so interpretation is nothing but the development and rectification of a received understanding. There is only tradition to refer to, itself an evolving phenomenon in which any interpretation is already implicated. No pane of glass divides us from the truth "object." The difference between the meaning that results from interpretation and the meaning interpreted is destined to be abolished in the course of the process itself. Truth is thereby historical in character and potentially multiple, mounting an attack against essentialism by way of an alternative to the singular and dialectical subjectivity of Hegelian historical "universal" truth – itself a highly creative effort to reckon with the flux of modernity – with its far older discursive and metaphysical ancestry. As a tradition, hermeneutics appears by comparison to be relatively recent; yet it is tradition capable of superimposing itself over the enormous vista of the past by way of a claim to represent the true "underground" tradition that had at some point gone astray. It was Nietzsche who opened this gate through the showing the interactions of paradigmatic historical alternatives in *The Birth of Tragedy.*

In the context of modern politics, hermeneutics enters a strange coupling with the nation-state, a notoriously dialectical institution. Dialectic basically searches for the truth through a method of juxtaposing of opposites and seeking to transcend their contradictions. From Plato through Hegel and Marx, dialectic has served many functions and taken on different meanings. For Plato, the dialectic led by way of building concept on concept to an ontological level beyond consciousness, beyond mere appearance and sensation, to the absolute and transcendent Idea of the Good. It therefore represented a road to true consciousness in opposition to the supposedly illusionary character of mere opinion and common sense. A pure object of truth, by means of dialectic, was thus enshrined in a mysterious Beyond with obvious elitist overtones. Hegel exploited this metaphysical tendency in the modern context when he argued that "It is in fact in the life of a people or a nation that the *Notion* of self-conscious Reason's actualization... has its complete reality."[3] This deeply rooted defining tendency in Western thought is what Dewey made a target of fundamental critique when he argued that

it is the intricate mixture of the stable and the precarious, the fixed and the unpredictably novel, the assured and the uncertain, in existence which sets mankind upon that love of wisdom which forms philosophy. Yet too commonly, although in a great variety of technical modes, the result of the search is converted into a metaphysics which denies or conceals from acknowledgement the very characters of existence which initiated it, and which gave significance to its conclusions.

or "that striking division into a superior true realm of being and lower illusionary, insignificant or phenomenal realm which characterizes metaphysical systems." This debate, in significant ways, establishes what is at stake in the political and intellectual struggles taking place in Iranian society today.

Experiences of war and national mobilization, as Iran experienced after the revolution, are themselves tinged with an ideologically dialectical quality in the promises they extend. Just as Mazzini in the early nineteenth century asserted that only the violence of national determination would pave the way to eternal peace, and the United States was united as a nation by the Civil War, this dialectical logic can confront states with threats to their very survival (Kurdistan) or centuries of struggle (Armenia, Ukraine). Yet the aspiration to resolve conflict and achieve self -consciousness nonviolently remains the highest ideal where a democratic politics is the aim. Dewey's conceptual pluralism provides a more valuable route with its openness than the dialectical way with its tacitly totalizing end. Whereas in the modern rationalist tradition initiated by Descartes dialectic was condemned, as it also was later by Kant, as an illusionary foundation for true knowledge, it was Hegel who gave the dialectic new life and meaning as the movement of thought in accordance with being or Absolute Spirit itself. He most notably extended this to a metaphysically conceived teleological History. Instead of an essentialism that floats above as Forms and thus ignores the traces of time, Hegel conceived all time itself as being the inevitable movement toward the fulfillment of one great essentialism to be witnessed at a later date. Through the dialectical overcoming of contradictions, a higher and superior unity, or Absolute Knowledge, would be attained in the historical "process" itself. Through the subsequent works of Marx, Sartre, and Bachelard, among many others, the profound effects of dialectical thought on twentieth-century thinking and political experience are well known.

Dialectic expresses a Universalist ideal linked to Enlightenment, given expression in nationalist, Marxist, and liberal discourses in which difference is essentially united under a larger concept. This political tendency is embodied most notably in the French Republican assimilationist ideal. At worst, it means a totalizing suppression of difference in the name of either "Reason" or some other absolute category. But as the example of Aristotle shows, dialectic can equally function as a simple tool. Hermeneutics, on the other hand, begins from the premise of difference and, through radical reinterpretation of received tradition, endeavors to create a space for dialogue without necessarily resolving difference into a larger and "ultimate" whole somehow "beyond." Yet, as we see with Heidegger and Shari'ati, hermeneutics can be given an ontological sanction that makes it dangerously totalizing. Soroush and the Algerian thinker Arkoun, in still another example, also use hermeneutics and with the expressed intention of avoiding the pitfall of such totalizing dogma and to address issues such as, in the case of Arkoun, the "violence-sacred-truth" triangle of the three religions of the Book.

Arkoun considers mimetic rivalry in claims to an absolute truth as a source of violence in both religious and secular modern thought as an "anthropological triangle of sacralized violence." Rather than seeking a unity through an absolute, his project aims to redefine and expand the boundaries of received cultural and religious identity through dialogue at the frontiers of the "unthought." In the context of monotheism, Arkoun writes that "we need to create an intellectual and cultural framework in which all historical, sociological, anthropological and psychological presentations of the revealed religions can be integrated into a system of thought and evolving knowledge."[4] Along similar hermeneutical lines, Soroush has argued that

> believers generally conceive religion as something holy and sacred, as something constant. One cannot speak of change or evolution in religious knowledge. They seize on the idea of fixity. Yet as I have showed in my work, we must make the distinction between religion on the one hand and religious interpretation on the other. Those who insist on the idea of fixity are ignorant of the history of Islam as well as other religions. Islam is a series of interpretations of Islam just as Christianity is a series of interpretations. Because these interpretations are historic, the element of historicity is present. . . . We must go to history and, from there, return to the Qu'ran and the Hadith in order to put interpretation in its proper historical context.[5]

In rejecting the notion of some fundamental ontological anchor in hermeneutical interpretation, these thinkers are much closer to Dewey's "conceptual pluralism" than Heidegger's more widely contemplated project of "fundamental ontology." They seek to undo the unconscious epistemic walls that have accrued from diverse historical experiences, particularly of colonialism and the construction of modern nation-states linked to the Israeli crisis, in the Middle East. Heidegger, on the other hand, sought essentially to consolidate such barriers against the fracturing of Germany's unique "soul" in the context of Germany's confrontation with "Western" modernity.

Arkoun seeks precisely to undo this "West-other" dualism: "Through my critique, I would like to bring contemporary reason to reflect differently than it does on the world of cultures, and not in opposing one western culture to others which are neither modern nor evolved."[6] Yet in the Iranian context of Cold War–era struggles for national independence and revolutionary political upheaval, the dominant wave in intellectual thought was carried by the Heideggerian variant on hermeneutical thought. At this level we can see how a spontaneous discourse of anti-Westernism did not simply ferment, but rather an already existing Western discourse met with a receptive ear among struggling Iranian intellectuals – and ultimately, the masses for and to whom they reconstituted and disseminated it – just as certain other Western discourses (nationalism, liberalism, Marxism) were falling decidedly out of favor as a result of definite events (the Azerbaijani oil crisis, the 1953 coup d'état). The rising influence of the discourse of authenticity occurred in the form of its being received piecemeal by word of mouth and translation, taken apart and reassembled in accordance with local circumstances and the needs of the moment. It never existed in any pure form, needless to say, and proved its effectiveness as an idea complex by way of the powerful axes of politicization it presented in a familiar world of rapid and unequal modernization from above, urbanization and destruction of traditional modes of life, domination by foreign interests, and the existence of a vicious and autocratic regime that refused to share power even with its narrow margin of potential supporters among the population.

We might argue, with Benzine, that this Islamist discourse forms part of a second, albeit totalitarian, current of Islamic reformism at work in the contemporary world:

On the one hand the current attached to the thought of Hassan al-Banna or of the Pakistani journalist Abu Ala Mawdudi (1903–1979), founder of Jama'at-i islami ("the Reunification of Islam"), the current we can qualify as Islamist because it always seeks the increase of Islamic presence and power in political and social organization and the state. On the other hand there is the current we could call critical Islam, and in which the first great figures are the Indian poet and philosopher Muhammed Iqbal (1877–1938) and the Egyptian Ali Abderraziq (1888–1966).

Social Contexts of Enlightenment

How and to what extent are national modernities possible? If one is to go beyond the philosophical-metaphysical approach to modernity stemming from dichotomizing theories of enlightenment to consign questions concerning geographical origin, singular/plural, authentic/universal essence to the marginal status of an ideological conflict, then one may begin to broach more important questions such as: what are the historical experiences and social contexts within which different theories of enlightenment evolved and, in the Iranian case, what are the historical, social, and cultural ideas, institutions, and practices by which an enlightenment project may be fruitfully realized in Iran today?

There are also other national modernities that are more relevant to the Iranian case. In thinking about constructing an Iranian national enlightenment project, we may reflect beyond merely the French, English, and American traditions and look also to the Japanese and Indian cases for consideration of modernity's multiple possible forms. In beginning to think of articulating an Iranian enlightenment project, I propose the following issues for discussion and debate:

Critique of Iranian Traditions

This is one of the most important theoretical challenges for those who are interested in a reflective and democratic enlightenment project for Iran. It is particularly challenging because there are already several established approaches that are widely accepted, and a new theory must problematize them to make room for new possible lines of thinking.

> To suggest a need for a national enlightenment in Iran is to indicate a new and different mode of thinking about Iranian history, culture, and traditions. This new mode of thinking will make it possible to create a clear distance from, or critical understanding of, Iranian heritage and tradition while nevertheless refusing the metaphysical violence of engaging in any total destruction of the past. A democratic enlightenment in the Iranian context requires a purview both critical and imaginative, one hopeful and inclusive, to foster an understanding of Iranian cultural heritage that is prepared to blend various aspects as well as reject others. On this, I agree with Richard Rorty's argument in *Achieving Our Country*. As important as it is to point to the history of injustice, oppression, and inhumanities that are a part of the very long history of Iran, it is also crucial to explore and make visible the ideas, values, and structures that have helped to create, legitimize, or maintain the other side of Iranian history in a democratic and humanitarian vision for the future. Iran needs to reconcile its future-oriented vision with what has been the good or the humanitarian side of Iranian past traditions. We find such a tendency articulated powerfully in the critique of absolutist epistemology in the writings of Dewey, and the same ideas expressed in the vivid historical narratives and practical reflections of Nehru.

The discourse of a radical beginning or the idea of a total break from everyday life as it exists now combined with the promise of a utopian future may strike us superficially as more attractive and intellectually imaginative. However, theories that follow the new beginning philosophy privilege certain romantic images (such as rootedness and liberating identities, or total freedom) over the real possibility of a democratic society. Because utopian projects appear more liberating and meaningful and to offer solutions to every kind of human suffering, a democratic vision can hardly compete in terms of the vivid demands of religious, secular, or nationalist lines of imagination. It is only when these imaginative visions are evaluated in their sociological contexts – that is, when they become the reality of the nightmare made flesh – that democratic projects are revealed to be clearly more suited to any social setting where humanity and human beings aspire to live a better life on sociopolitical, ethical, and spiritual levels.

Therefore, in a democratic approach to Iranian traditions, one is always hopeful of finding ideas and structures that may assist in the future betterment of the society. The goal is less to condemn the past and close the door to possible positive moments than to find valuable and hopeful ideas and make the link to future democratic possibilities.

It is therefore important that the language and discourse of Iranian enlightenment be critical, but also inspiring and capable of imagining the past and its traditions as moments of hope. It is necessary to conceive contemporary Iranian history as part of the overall human struggle for constructing an honorable and good society on the broadest possible basis. It is also important not to confuse a critical or genealogical approach to the past with totalizing subversive sensibilities, the politics of despair, and utopian/prophetic theories. The goal here is not to transform everything as it now exists and to come up with a new beginning. In each case it is to help to create a democratic society with the active involvement of those people who are the existing citizens.

A good case is the Constitutional Revolution of 1905. The current revisionist writings would have us believe that the revolution for a constitution was fundamentally flawed. The charge is often made that its leaders, ideas, and visions were all problematic from its origin, and some even blame the Constitutional Revolution for the struggle on every level within which Iran continues to be locked. For the purpose of contributing clarity to the current political and cultural/intellectual crisis in Iran, a sociological critique of the Constitutional Revolution will point out both the shortcomings of this movement and its positive experiences. There

is much that is positive and may be pointed to: one of the most important and lasting institutional structures, for example, is the separation of
powers, the role of the legislators, limits on executive power, the role of
the press, the redefinition of subjects to citizens. All of these are essential
democratic infrastructures that have survived and exist in today's Iran.
The fact that these institutions have been weakened and undermined by
autocratic states does not lessen their importance to the past, present, and
future of Iran.

It is in light of these reflections that a call is made for a more nuanced
and pluralistic view of social phenomena in general, beyond the dichotomous and viselike grip of old modernist certainties still locked down in
the competing ideological factions of the Cold War. The question is not,
for example, whether Gandhi was a modernist or a traditionalist, a com-
promised modernist, or either a secular or a religious activist. These affiliations cannot be realistically or practically conceived as simply opposed
categories and necessarily interpenetrate and mix in a numberless variety
of formations that are each more or less specific unto themselves, calling
for a situated reading of events, activists, and worldviews.

An instructive case, once again, is that of Soroush. Returning to Iran
after the 1979 Islamic Revolution, he was given a chair in the depart-
ment of Islamic culture at the Tehran University. After the closing of the
universities, he became a member of the Assembly of councilors of the
cultural revolution. He described the period in this way: "The time was
characterized by a great intellectual ferment, a period of great political
and ideological liberties. Intellectuals were 'bombarded' with questions
and incited to engage in ideological duels." Soroush considered the "eigh-
teen years which followed the revolution as being a period of constant
intellectual combat." These intellectual upheavals inevitably contained a
strong religious dimension, at once transforming in the mix of cultural
and social ideas. Benzine writes that "All through these years, (Soroush)
tried to clarify at the same time his own relation to religion and religiousness, and the relation of religion to social and political institutions."
Soroush thus engaged in fertile studies of Islamic philosophy and Western social sciences, working on the ideas of such philosophers as Winch,
Habermas, and Hayek, as well as Motahari and Ibn Khaldoun. In doing
so he inevitably came up against the narrow-mindedness of prevailing
political power as, throughout the early years following the revolution,
the social and human sciences were accused of being "impure," "Western," and responsible for the corruption of the youth through "secular
atheism." Affirming that the social and human sciences were equally as

important as the natural sciences, Soroush referred to the "competitive nature" of science and knowledge. Subsequently, employing the methodology of scientific philosophy, he "progressively broached the philosophy of religion, and began to extend the same concept of competition to religious knowledge." He equally extended his intellectual efforts to history, ethics, science, and modern theology.

Even though Soroush is presently in exile, his influence on the thought of young people in Iran has been enormous. Yet without preaching any dogmatic doctrine, Soroush's long intellectual career has been principally a raising of questions. In a hermeneutical frame, he has asked: Why do different scholars reach entirely different interpretations of the same holy text? Why do the same verses produce different interpretations in the history of Islam between, for example, the *mou'tazilites* and the *ash'arites*? In a political context, how does the Sufi ideology of fleeing the world from the same textual source as an ideology of political and material domination in the hands of Ali Shari'ati or Mehdi Bazargan? Why do certain interpretations appear within a specific historic time and not others? These are questions Soroush discussed in weekly debating groups with university students, inspiring many written works on these questions. The powerful continuing life of Soroush's ideas and questions in today's Islamic Republic and many other countries are surely a reflection of the fact that his line of thought addresses the realities of people's lived experiences in their full complexity, far away from any simplistic and totalitarian dogmas of "purity," or "East" and "West," or "modern" and "traditional," and perhaps beyond the "secular" and "religious" dichotomy itself.

Certainly, we may therefore say that nativism is at most a fantasy in the minds of certain statesmen and intellectuals and very far from the realities of everyday life in any social context. As for universalism, any notion of this must be tempered by the following considerations as expressed by Arkoun: "We are leaving the dualist framework of knowledge where reason is opposed to imagination, history to myth, truth to falsehood, good to evil, reason to faith, etc. We are adopting a pluralistic rationality, in transformation, and welcoming." The thinkers and activists in this study work at these frontiers. Whether it is in an effort to seal them, as with Heidegger, or to expand them and invite further questioning at the borders, as with Dewey, all of the different horizons and angles point to a growing space where only courageous and open debate can take us beyond old dogmas in their various intellectual and political expressions and create a politics grounded in everyday realities and experience.

4

Heidegger and Iran

The Dark Side of Being and Belonging

> It is a Heidegger's saying that we become part of what we know and there-
> fore, the only hope for us to be saved from the disease of Westoxification
> and the contemporary sickening modernity is to understand the true face
> and spirit of the west.
>
> Ali Shari'ati[1]

In a contemporary Iran where the institutions of the public sphere struggle
for their very survival and Iranians yearn for a democratic life, many intellectuals are vigorously prescribing an epistemological revolution. Why is
this? At the center of these calls stands the cherished figure of Martin
Heidegger, who also happens to have been the leading philosopher of the
National Socialist movement in the early 1930s. What is the significance
of the Heideggerian philosophical project that such important and influential thinkers as Ahmad Fardid, Jalal Al-e Ahmad, Ali Shari'ati, Dariush
Shayegan, and many more recent Iranian intellectuals, in one way or
another, are so influenced by it? And why, despite the bitter experience
of the past years, do so many still find it viable and important today?

In this chapter we consider and try to map out the nature and the implications of Heidegger's influence in some detail, based on a reading of the
seminal work *Being and Time* as well as several other key writings and
recent studies of the thinker and his legacy. The essay also includes a presentation of several key Iranian intellectuals who helped to shape developments of the late twentieth century leading up to and following the
Iranian Revolution of 1979, and whose ideas continue to shape contemporary Iranian society and politics. An analysis of the different sources of
their strongly anti-Western rhetoric will ironically demonstrate not only

their intimacy with and borrowings from certain essential Western discourses of the twentieth century, but also the loose yet coherent existence of a broader movement of "authenticity" that is global and historical in character – in both the "East" and the "West." In this sense these thinkers are not "anti-Western" at all, but give renewed articulation to an existing historical discourse that is political rather than geographical in nature. This movement, which boasts a high intellectual pedigree and seductive as well as complex philosophical origins, is above all a rebellion against the tradition of modern Enlightenment and its concomitant principle of secularism. This rebellion is mounted in the name of an equally modern championing and politicization of the fundamental truth in cultural tradition, or of the demand for an overarching sociocultural meaning for society as such. Such discourses and movements are in this way openly and basically hostile to democracy, which in principle permits multiple contesting points of view and identities.

This consideration motivates the approach to Heidegger's thought in this study. We are interested in *Being and Time* not in its narrowly philosophical sense but rather in terms of its more extended social and political reach. It is therefore necessary to provide a sketch of the historical lineage in which Heidegger's work both extended and radically revitalized an already existing political tradition of discourse. Heidegger's thought is principally a variation on a long discursive tradition critical of the Universalist and secular-democratic claims of Western modernity. Richard Wolin's genealogical study of the Counter-Enlightenment begins with the "new breed of anti-philosophe (which) emerged" at the time of the French Revolution "to contest the epistemological and political heresies proposed by the Party of Reason." The anti-philosophes, including Joseph de Maistre and Antoine de Rivarol, relied "mainly on theological arguments" and "cautioned against the spirit of critical inquiry" while emphasizing "the need to preserve order at all costs." They believed "that any challenge to (the) unquestioned primacy (of altar and throne) threatened to undermine the entire social edifice" and that "men and women were fundamentally incapable of self-governance."[2] Maistre "sought to defend the particularity of historical traditions against the universalizing claims of Enlightenment humanism, which had culminated in the Declaration of the Rights of Man and Citizen of August 20, 1789."[3] He argued for a hierarchical and spiritual ordering of society based on the principle that "what we ought not to know is more important than what we ought to know."[4] The French Revolution itself was "an act of divine vengeance visited upon France for her Enlightenment-driven apostasies" and underlined "the futility of all human efforts to endow history with intelligibility and meaning." He therefore rejected the Enlightenment faith in the power of reason to model human society and lifted his interpretation of the events from the level of the historical to that of the theological. Subjective agency is therefore a chimera: "It is not men who lead the Revolution, it is the Revolution that employs men."[5] Wolin writes that "If one is interested in discerning the main lines of the right-wing critique of democracy – a tradition that would culminate in the visceral antiliberalism of European fascism – their writings remain an indispensable key."[6]

Later, the "very different, yet complementary, critiques of metaphysical objectivism proffered by two nineteenth-century thinkers, Kierkegaard and Nietzsche, stand as crucial harbingers of Heidegger's own philosophical program."[7] Friedrich Nietzsche, with his radical attack on Western thought and Christian morality, shared the conviction of the anti-philosophes that Europe was experiencing a "reigning spiritual crisis." His works were intended as "declarations of war" against this condition of decline.[8] Nietzsche believed that an essential element in the decline was the leveling effects of democracy, a system that spawned mediocrity. Greatness was the province of the elite, and his own role as a prophet or savior was envisioned within this political context: "The new philosopher can arise only in conjunction with a ruling caste, as its highest spiritualization. Great politics, rule of the earth, are at hand."[9] Nietzsche's thought, although sharing the conviction of modernity as a spiritual decline with the anti-philosophes, introduced a new element of envisioning radical transformation in the future. Conversely, "Maistre and his contemporaries (had been) horrified by the spectre of radical change." Later still, the fascists understood

that, in an age of total war, a point of no return had been reached: there could be no going back to the tradition bound cocoon of the *ancien régime*. They elected to combat the values of the French Revolution with revolutionary means: violence, war, and total mobilization. Thereby, they ushered in an alternative vision of modernity, one that was meant to supersede the standpoint of the philosophes and the political champions of 1789.[10]

Heidegger's thought, in some measure, made a profound philosophical contribution to this worldview. It is therefore disturbing to consider that his thought also "develops a framework that fundamentally revolutionizes our understanding of traditional philosophical problems and subject matter."[11]

It is within the broad discursive context of this "alternative vision of modernity" that Heidegger's thought, as well as its influence on significant Iranian intellectuals and social movements may be fruitfully understood. Heidegger, too, under the influence of such discourses, deplored democracy as the system of a more general historical decline and dreamed of restoring a higher and deeper cultural meaning to both politics and society. He declared modern democracy to be a "moribund semblance of a culture."[12] Liberalism promotes "the slavery of 'contingency.'"[13] In a grander philosophical vision of human destiny, however, politics were for him something of a minor detail. A tension existed between his concern with the "decline of the West" and the particular national destiny of Germany. Both concerns perceived modernity, as a soulless objectifying universal, to be the principal culprit needing to be reckoned with. The tacit nationalist thrust in his thought proved to be his downfall when he enthusiastically aligned himself with the National Socialist Revolution in 1933. Heidegger's seemingly extreme swing from an apolitical philosophical disposition to committed Nazi activism can be explained in terms of his belonging to the tradition of the German mandarin intelligentsia, whose attitude "ranged from a die-hard apoliticism – which sought refuge from the turmoil of contemporary historical reality in the realm of traditional Germanic cultural ideals – to a jingoistic affirmation of German militarism."[14] His thought at this time, and generally in successive variations, can be understood in the broader context of the "antimodernist critique of post traditional societies." The "antimodernist attitude of the German mandarin intelligentsia" is distinguished by the "contrast between *Kultur* and *Zivilization*, where the former term connotes the sublimity of spiritual cultivation and the latter signifies the superficial materialism of the decadent capitalist West."[15] With regard to the political implications of this worldview, Wolin writes: "what is of especial importance about the uncompromising anti-Westernism of the mandarin intelligentsia – and here, Heidegger is merely a typical case in point – is that the rejection of capitalism as an economic ethos rapidly translated into a dismissal of Western political values *simpliciter*: liberalism, individualism, and democracy were all dismissed as alien to the German spirit."[16] It is against the background of radical social dislocation effected by rapid modernization and the crisis of World War I and its aftermath that we need to understand *Being and Time*: "*Being and Time* is a study in 'fundamental ontology,' 'hermeneutical phenomenology,' *Existenzphilosophie*, etc., but it is also emphatically something else: an attempt, based on a re-posing of the 'question of Being,' to suggest a path of deliverance from the contemporary cultural crisis – the 'decline of the West.' "[17] This social crisis was understood by Heidegger and contemporaries in his intellectual *milieu* as a primarily spiritual crisis: "By the early 1920's, (German academics) were deeply convinced that they were living through a profound crisis, a 'crisis of culture', of 'learning', of 'values', or of the 'spirit.' "[18] Wolin therefore writes: "perhaps in order to be fully appreciated as a philosophical treatise, *Being and Time* must simultaneously be understood as a *historical document* – as a product of determinate historical conditions and of a specific intellectual historical lineage."[19] It is against the background of this European lineage, and its subsequent expression in new form in many non-Western societies which have faced similar experiences of sociopolitical and cultural crisis, that we undertake our examination of Heidegger's *Being and Time*. Our interest in doing so is grounded in a concern with the prospects for achieving a democratic modernity in contemporary Iran.

On a political level, Heidegger's thought concerns the reconfiguration of modernity within the national context. Yet its suggestion for doing so is grounded in a totalizing truth claim stemming, albeit in reconfigured form, from a tradition in the remote past. For Heidegger and those of his generation, so "thoroughgoing seemed the bankruptcy of all inherited belief-structures that only a transformation of values that was radical and total seemed worth entertaining."[20] The contradictory tension between these two tendencies creates a simultaneous call for a total change and absolute authority in tradition. Our critique of Heidegger forms part of a broader critique of movements and discourses that portray modernity, both its promise and its peril, in the manner of a totalizing vision. This is in one way ironic, as *Being and Time* has often been welcomed as a break from the "logocentric" hold of the traditional understanding of Western modernity, which heralded a "hermeneutic turn" in philosophical discourses by placing new emphasis on difference and multiplicity. Yet, as we shall show, Heidegger's avowed concern with resisting the homogeneous grasp of a decadent "Western" metaphysics indeed disguised its own potentially lethal obsession with a single spiritual purity.

In the Iranian context, what almost all proponents of a Heideggerian project share is their deep hostility toward what is an essentialized notion of the "West." To be sure, this idea of the "West" represents less a geographical space than a cultural construction: secular, universal, and morally unstable, it stands as the determined foe of the "truth" in tradition and of being and belonging, both of which it routinely undermines to render "man" a homeless and hopeless creature lost in the confused turmoil of change without existential moorings. Insofar as Heidegger offers a radical critique of secular Enlightenment, he speaks to these preoccupations. His vision offers an alternative to secular modernity in a mysterious, semireligious, and revolutionary utopian "new beginning," and a total displacement of modern everyday life coupled with the promise of an authentic community rooted in being. This radical conservative critique of the "West" opens several important cultural spaces:

1. Those concerned with "spiritual" and religious sensibilities find in Heidegger's critique of secular modernity a reaffirmation of their own "cultural" or "moral" views and tradition. In the Iranian context, Henri Corbin's reinterpretation of Shi'i Islam represents a Heideggerian version of Shi'ism as the "spiritual" version of Islam. Shari'ati embraced both Heidegger and Corbin and constructed an ideological version of Shi'i Islam that in large part paved the way theoretically for the revolution of 1979.

2. Heidegger's project has also offered a philosophical refuge for those who want to construct "nativist" ideologies and confront "Western modernity" as a universal project that has no tolerance for "local" cultural or moral ideas and practices. In this discourse the "West" becomes the antithesis of any "national" aspirations. Many forms of extreme nationalism, from racial to ethnic and religious variations, find a Heideggerian project very attractive. In the Iranian context, the discourse of "Westoxication" articulated by Al-e Ahmad comes directly from Fardid's interpretation of Heidegger and achieved massive influence both at the time of publication and in the decades that followed leading to the present.

Needless to say, not all intellectuals who admire Heidegger's work are either right-wing Islamists or extreme nationalists seeking a philosophical justification in the philosopher's ideas. And yet: Heidegger's well-known hostility to democracy, combined with his aim of retrieving the "pure source" of being, produced a vision in which the formal freedoms of democratic modernity necessarily yield to the promise of a meaningful collective guidance under a single conception of being. This vision has proven seductive both to radical intellectuals on the left and religious-minded intellectuals from the conservative wing of contemporary Iranian politics. By completely rejecting both modernity and Enlightenment, Heideggerian philosophy opens the possibility of new and perhaps more liberating social and cultural forms. This is something that intellectuals in general find attractive and interesting. However, by proposing some kind of "return" to the sources or roots of authentic being, and a total and all-encompassing "tradition" to be derived from this endeavor, Heidegger's project becomes appealing to *unequivocally modern* revolutionary conservatives of all kinds, from radical Islamists to fascists.

1. Heidegger, the Ambiguous Heritage of the "West," and the Problem of "Inauthenticity"

Heidegger's relation to "the West" was of course complex and ambivalent. On one level, he felt himself entrusted by "being" to retrieve the original and forgotten origins of authentic Hellenic-Western culture in a fallen world of nihilism and technological frenzy. In this sense, he apparently viewed himself in the role of championing the cause of the "authentic" Western tradition. On the other hand, he identified Germany as the "chosen" nation "in the middle" between the soulless rationalism of "Western" capitalism and "Eastern" communism, each caught in the grip of the same metaphysical disease – which may be said to include much of what Heidegger disliked about the Enlightenment. This relation to the West is at first sight contradictory, unless we understand the peculiar logic of Heidegger's standpoint against the more general background of the historicist and counter-Enlightenment movement of authenticity, to which Heidegger's own work contributed enormously.

Being and Time presents, in one way, a peculiar and highly original view of the history of the West. It is a tacitly essentialized view, with much to say about secularism, universalism, being and belonging, and the concept of revelation as a basis for social action. The view that is presented is one of decline, and therefore a strong element of pessimism pervades the work, in spite of a perpetually implied promise – or possibility – of a great change to come. Initially, we detail the complex concept of historical decline that runs through *Being and Time*, and then the inevitable counterconcept of authentic historical existence.

Unsurprisingly, history functions as a key concept in *Being and Time*. The problematic character, or "inauthentic historicity," of the relation of modernity to cultural histories operates at the heart of the fundamental "question of the meaning of being." Heidegger writes, "it is inevitable that inquiry into being . . . is itself characterized by historicity."[21] "Inauthentic historicity" is constituted by the combination of modern everyday life and the scientific-technological worldview, which together suspend Western man in a condition of "rootlessness" that is self-perpetuating and ever-expanding to the rest of the world. This view is summed up thus: "the ontological character of its own being is remote from Da-sein because of the dominance of its entangled understanding of being (being as objective presence)."[22] "Entanglement" refers to an absorption in modern everyday life, and "objective presence" refers to the Cartesian and modern scientific worldview. For Heidegger this was in essence a metaphysical problem, yet one with a necessary and inseparable social and political dimension.

The fundamental problem revolves around the true nature of the past and the relation of that past to our future as a public and private world:

Whether explicitly or not, (Da-sein) *is* its past. It is its own past not only in such a way that its past, as it were, pushes itself along "behind" it, and that it possesses what is past as a property that is still objectively present and at times has an effect on it. Da-sein "is" its past in the manner of *its* being which, roughly expressed, on each occasion "occurs" out of its future.[23]

This implies that the past is an essential part of us, and shapes our future, rather than something behind us that can be cut off in the manner envisioned by the French Revolution. Yet it is possible to fall into a state of alienation in relation to this past.

Distressingly, modern people are cut off from this past in a way that is unprecedentedly harmful. In modern society, we live an "inauthentic historical existence (which is) burdened with the legacy of a 'past' that has become unrecognizable to it." This historical existence, although alienated by the experience of modernity, consequently "looks for what is modern."[24] In doing so, it is blind to the latent and mysterious power of the historical past: "in inauthentic historicity the primordial stretching along of fate is concealed." In a storm of the superficial, the living historical heritage in its depth and power is neglected and forgotten: "while awaiting the next new thing, (it) has already forgotten what is old." Modern society, severed from its authentic heritage, is "blind toward possibilities" and "incapable of retrieving what has been."[25] The importance imparted to "possibilities" indicates that Heidegger's philosophy is promoting an alternative *and rooted* framework for social action. Meanwhile, the modern capitalist social life is simply "driven about by its 'affairs.'"[26] In this deracinated social setting, "everything is haunted by the *enigma of being.*"[27] This "enigma" is the challenge taken up by Heidegger in *Being and Time*. In his view, the answer will amount to not merely a new intellectual perspective but rather a "new beginning" in human history.

The claim that modern society is alienated from tradition is certainly not unique to Heidegger or to the specific intellectual background of

Counter-Enlightenment against which the philosopher moved and drew inspiration. Karl Marx and Max Weber, as two distinguished examples, have articulated a similar insight. The claim, however, that modern society is therefore "inauthentic" is very specific to the tradition of Counter-Enlightenment, and Heidegger reconstructed it with an unprecedented complexity, vividness, and force. Wolin has identified a "confusion of levels of philosophical analysis that afflicts the relation between the 'ontological' and the 'existential' dimensions" of *Being and Time*. He describes these two levels and their confusion in this way:

First, the claim that traditional philosophy, as a result of its inordinate preoccupation with the nature of "entities" or "beings," has perennially bypassed the more fundamental or "primordial" question concerning the *nature of Being in general*. One might refer to this as the "ontological" dimension of Heidegger's work. Second, the contention that the "being" that offers privileged access to the realm of ontological inquiry – human being, which Heidegger dubs "Da-sein" – is neither *res cogitans*, nor a "transcendental ego," nor an "intentional consciousness," but, first and foremost, an *embodied* subjectivity: a *Being-in-the-world* that is subject to a prescientific forestructure of practical and social relations. One might refer to this as the "existential" dimension of Heidegger's inquiry.[28]

Within this conflation of a *sociological* and a *philosophical* problematic, modern Western society is declared to be, in a totalizing way, "inauthentic." Hence, "the self is initially and for the most part inauthentic, the they-self. Being-in-the-world is always already entangled."[29] This is a decidedly social and contemporary condition: "(the self) understands itself in terms of the possibilities of existence that 'circulate'[30] in the actual 'average' public interpretedness of Da-sein today."[31] Yet *Being and Time* is fundamentally an attack on the traditional representational theory of perception, which invests the idea of truth as correspondence and self as a subject, and on the basis of this "objectifying" metaphysic, the West is declared to be in the grip of a long historical and spiritual decline. Heidegger argues that the original meanings of Greek ontology have been passed down and perverted through a historical tradition that, in its intimate metaphysical link with everyday life, becomes increasingly deracinated over time.

Michael Inwood has succinctly captured this circular and mystical vision of history: "What started life as Plato's idea has degenerated into our modern *Vorstellung*, or representation." This decline touches all aspects of Western existence: "philosophy has declined since the Greeks along with more or less everything else." A link is alleged to exist between metaphysics and everyday life: "This happens with everyday talk as well."

Rooted social meaning is advanced as the remedy, to be achieved through a reconnection with the original Greek experience that first gave birth to the original ontological concept: "It is the Greeks and their 'first beginning' of Western history that mainly interest Heidegger, though the early Germans compete for his favour.... It is the flash of illumination that he wants to recover or "repeat'... perhaps it will help us to prepare for a new flash of illumination that will halt our spiritual decline: the 'other beginning.'"[32] The concept of "repetition" grounds the possibility of an authentic alternative and salvation from this decline. The image of a "flash" and "other beginning" suggests the apocalyptic suddenness and totality of the change that is envisioned. In Heidegger's hope for salvation and change, there was almost a faith in magic words: "Essential words are actions that happen in those moments when the lightening flash of a great illumination passes through the world." Therefore, the greatness of the fallen origins is contained in the very language of ancient Greece, which harbors within itself "the creative force of the people which, in its poets, thinkers, statesmen and artists, performed the greatest assault on the whole of beyng that has ever happened in western history."[33] The enormous importance attributed to the power of language explains why, in Heidegger's view, philosophy has an essential role in bringing about this fundamental change. The reference to statesmen indicates its political edge. Although *Being and Time* is far from an explicit political program, there is something definite in the vision of the world it conveys that lends itself very readily to a deeply problematic kind of politics in the modern context.

This vision of a salvation from "inauthenticity" is fantastic and imaginative in its dimensions. Yet its implications extend to real life politics. "Being" in this account is the hidden spiritual life of the world that may or may not take on institutional form, depending on the authenticity of our relationship to it. Whether it is a question of what we make of it, or of what it makes of us, seems to change throughout Heidegger's philosophical career as his faith in human agency evaporates following the bitter disillusionment of the Nazi years. In either case, Heidegger's obsession with a "return" was inevitably also an obsession with the creation of corresponding social institutions. In this context *Being and Time* centers the concept of a radical return to the pure origins through the combination of the philosophical language it invents and the authentic action – ultimately collective in character – that it aims to unleash.

Heidegger's critique of modern society as "inauthentic" amounts to a critique of "empty" cosmopolitanism. He called this condition "nihilism." On a philosophical level, it amounted to this: "To forget Being and to cultivate only beings – that is nihilism."[34] The "beingness of beings as a whole is conceived as the being-represented of the producible and explainable."[35] This is the eventual outcome of the even longer historical decline in addition to both the legacy of Enlightenment and the scientific-industrial order it has engendered. In this setting "technology" threatens to turn the universe itself into a stockpile of resources "in which everything presents itself as uniformly 'intelligible' and controllable."[36] Heidegger thus promoted a "return" to Being. On a social level, the condition "makes us wholly incapable of even understanding that such a return is necessary (and) uproots the historicity of Da-sein to such a degree that it only takes an interest in the manifold forms of possible types, directions, and standpoints of philosophizing in the most remote and strangest cultures, and with this interest tries to veil its own groundlessness." Inauthenticity is a preoccupation with other cultures on the superficial level *of knowledge* and a forgetting of one's own in genuine *lived* depth. Indeed, the abundance of knowledge was a symptom and cause of nihilism: "in spite of all historical interest and zeal for a philologically 'objective' interpretation, Da-sein no longer understands the most elementary conditions which alone make a positive return to the past possible – in the sense of its productive appropriation."[37] In Heidegger's view, the past must therefore exist as a productive force. Meanwhile, modern social life forms an obstacle to authentic modes of life: the "movement of plunging into and within the groundlessness of inauthentic being in the they constantly tears understanding away from projecting authentic possibilities." "Inauthentic" possibilities are characterized as an experience of "restlessness and excitement from continual novelty and changing encounters," driven by a "curiosity" which "reveals a new kind of being of everyday Da-sein, one in which it constantly uproots itself."[38] This "new kind of being" is too fast to take root: its tendencies "make sure that what is done in a general and new way is outdated as soon as it emerges before the public."[39] It "drives one to uninhibited 'busyness'" and the "opinion (arises) that understanding the most foreign cultures and 'synthesizing' them with our own may lead to the thorough and first genuine enlightenment of Da-sein about itself."[40] This passage presents a crack at the universal claims of Enlightenment in terms of objective knowledge. The central message of the book is, on the most basic level, that the "West" has strayed from the appropriate relation to being, and is now riven with rootlessness and inauthenticity as a result.

In Heidegger's account of "inauthenticity," Wolin has pointed out that we can "identify an interlacing of (*Being and Time*'s) *philosophical* and *ideological* components." He writes, "the content and structure of the 'existential analytic' – the presentation of the constituent features of Da-sein's Being-in-the-world – would be unthinkable without both moments, ideological as well as philosophical." We can recognize how "the self-conscious radicalism of Heidegger's philosophical project – its indictment of 2500 previous years of Western philosophy, which has been tainted by a deficient understanding of Being – is incomprehensible apart from the deflation of European cultural confidence following World War I." He therefore calls for "attentiveness to those aspects of its thematic structure that have internalized constitutive moments of the conservative revolutionary critique of modernity."[41] This "*conservative revolutionary world-view* that became so influential among the German mandarin intelligentsia in the middle of the late 1920s" also, "in many crucial respects, laid the intellectual foundations for Hitler's rise to power."[42] Although we do not find biological racism in Heidegger's philosophy, the strong preoccupation with *ontological truth* and resisting the *leveling effects* of a soulless cosmopolitanism attests to the existence of this ideological affinity.

The counterconcept of "authentic" historical existence as envisioned by Heidegger does nothing to allay such concerns. He argued that "according to our human experience and history, everything essential and great has arisen only out of the fact that man had a home and was rooted in a tradition."[43] Accordingly, in *Being and Time,* intimacy with being is entirely dependent on intimacy with the subtle and undetectable essence of one's own cultural and social background, and this constitutes "worldliness." The "universalism" implied in "scientific" "objective presence" falls short of the primordial reach of "handiness" that brings us closer to being.[44] This handiness, in turn, "always already occurs on the basis of a familiarity with the world."[45] Heidegger writes:

When we just look at things "theoretically," we lack an understanding of handiness. But association which makes use of things is not blind, it has its own way of seeing which guides our operations and gives them their specific thingly quality. Our association with useful things is subordinate to the manifold of references of the "in-order-to." The kind of seeing of this accommodation to things is called *circumspection.*[46]

This evocation of primordial everyday modes of practice that precede any theoretical knowledge on the one hand constitutes Heidegger's interesting affirmation of pragmatism in the world of everyday affairs. We find a quite similar point made in Michael Polanyi's *Personal Knowledge*, a critique of the fact/value dichotomy in the hegemonic ideology of science, when he argues that a "skilful performance is achieved by the observance of a set of rules which are not known as such to the person following them."[47] He offers a swimmer or a cyclist as examples, extending the point to the activities of everyday life. However, Heidegger's suggestion of an unconscious and localized practical mode of existence that is "closer to being" than abstract cognition can only imply the primacy of cultural particularism as "the way to truth in being." Whereas Polanyi's similar point remains at the existential level, Heidegger extends it into the murkier realm of the ontological. For Heidegger, the simple fact that one knows one's way around in a native environment, native language, and native culture receives ontological rather than merely existential privilege. Such "unconscious knowledge" is given the sanction of having a link to the "primordial phenomenon of truth," of which the "traditional concept of truth" (or representation) is a simple derivative.[48]

Such a view raises questions but is not in itself necessarily menacing. It might be said to favor "traditional, organic, precapitalist forms of life" over modern scientific knowledge and the industrial world of production that depends upon it for a base. However, when we read that modern "average everydayness" is only "the way of fleeing and forgetting (being)," it becomes clear that something more sinister is afoot.[49] The "inauthenticity" of modern everyday life is characterized by Heidegger in this way: "This averageness, which prescribes what can and may be ventured, watches over every exception which thrusts itself to the fore. Every priority is noiselessly squashed. Overnight, everything primordial is flattened down as something long since known. Everything gained by a struggle becomes something to be manipulated. Every mystery loses its power."[50] It is modern everyday life itself that ensnares and stifles the primordial force of authenticity in being. To this totalizing condemnation, Heidegger adds: "entangled, everyday being-toward-death is a constant flight from death." It serves "to veil completely (Da-sein's) ownmost nonrelational possibility."[51] It is the nonrelational, or "pure," core of ontological identity that Heidegger hopes to emancipate from the restraints of modern public life. We thus enter the discourse of authenticity opposed to the entire material life and institutional complex of modern life.

Heidegger's concept of an "authentic" existence, in contrast to the "inauthenticity" of modern everydayness, is far from a recommendation to return peaceably to premodern lifestyles and cultural norms. Rather, his concept of "authenticity" embraces those *heroic* values reflecting "the quasi-apocalyptic, anti-modernist sentiment of the German intellectual elite" at the time. Wolin has described the core tendencies of this view:

> The conservative revolutionaries were thoroughgoing believers in the (Nietzschean) rites of "active nihilism": bourgeois values of commerce, materialism, security, constitutionalism, intellectualism, and toleration, which were already on the decline, needed to be given a final push. Only then could a new series of *heroic* values emerge, based on the pseudo-Nietzschean concepts of will, power, struggle, and destiny.[52]

Heidegger's proposed new "truth basis" is inextricably interwoven with these heroic values. He describes the authentic counterpart to inauthentic everydayness in this way: "*Authentic* being-toward-death can*not evade* its ownmost nonrelational possibility or *cover* it *over* in this flight and *reinterpret* it for the common sense of the they."[53]

It is necessary to grasp Heidegger's central concept of "primordiality" in these terms. There is a paradoxical reverence for an *imagined* tradition stretching back to an ancient distance in time combined with, as Wolin has remarked, "the idea of a total break from the past" or "active nihilism."[54] Heidegger believed deeply in the importance of heritage: "If everything 'good' is a matter of heritage and if the character of 'goodness' lies in making authentic existence possible, then handing down a heritage is always constituted in resoluteness."[55] The social and political constitution of an "authentic" relation to being necessarily demands the existence of a strong tradition. Heidegger defines "resoluteness" as constituting "the *loyalty* of existence to its own self," in which "loyalty is at the same time a possible reverence for the sole authority that a free existence can have, for the possibilities of existence that can be retrieved."[56] Heidegger is here opposing the rootlessness of modernity to the guidance of traditional heritage. He did not want to see the cultural past as something neutralized and preserved in a museum display case, but wanted it to have a living relation *of power* to the present social world and most importantly to that of the future. It is unambiguous that "resoluteness" is advanced as a truth claim: "the phenomenon of resoluteness" leads to "the primordial *truth* of existence."[57]

Yet, as Wolin has noted, when we inquire as to the *basis* for "resoluteness" in *Being and Time*. we are only told: "*Only* the resolve itself can answer this. . . . Resoluteness is certain of itself only in a resolution."[58] Wolin has identified this as a variant of the "decisionist" legal philosophy conceived by the German political philosopher and jurist Carl Schmitt in the 1920s. He writes:

"Decisionism" provides a quasi-heroic alternative to the abyss of "meaningless-ness" that threatens to overwhelm a Dasein permanently awash in radical his-torical flux....For once the inauthenticity of all traditional social norms has been existentially unmasked, the only remaining basis for moral orientation is a *decision ex nihilo*, a *radical assertion of the will*; a will, moreover, that is pure and unrestrained by the impediments of social convention.[59]

Such a foreboding of a total vacuity of fixed meaning is nevertheless coupled with an appeal to what is supposedly an ancient tradition. Hei-degger very likely experienced the foreboding of a meaningless universe. As Winfried Franzen wrote: "Heidegger's *Being and Time* was written at a time when the first of the great world catastrophes had, more than ever before, shaken the confidence of the (Western-scientific) heritage that began with the Greeks."[60] Yet Heidegger wanted emphatically *not* to be "rootless" and to find a way out of the crisis of modern rootlessness. Therefore, he asserted, it is only the historically dominant tradition that renders contemporary existence "inauthentic," while the "authentic" and "primordial phenomenon of truth," or "*aletheia*," is waiting to be resur-rected from its submergence under many historical layers of "inauthentic" interpretation. Heidegger insisted that there was a "*necessary* interpre-tation of what the oldest tradition of ancient philosophy primordially surmised and even understood in a pre-phenomenological way." Against both the dominant metaphysical tradition and its supposed polluting effects on everyday life, he wrote that "it is the business of philosophy to protect the *power of the most elemental words* in which Da-sein expresses itself from being flattened by the common understanding to the point of unintelligibility."[61]

These projects to retrieve "authenticity" and "roots," as it were, from underground, were not intended to be confined to academia but necessar-ily took on a world-historical significance. Heidegger wrote: "Authentic being-toward-death, that is, the finitude of temporality, is the concealed ground of the historicity of Da-sein." Historicity is the "authentic retrieve of a possibility that has been."[62] This regarded the future: "Da-sein can *be* authentically having-been only because it is futural . . . having been arises from the future."[63] . In this way Heidegger conceived the ancient past as making a claim upon the "lived lives" of the future within the frame-work of an overarching tradition, in opposition to the "arbitrariness" and "slavery of 'contingency'" that is modern democracy. Thus, despite an absence of specific reference to institutions in Heidegger's work, and an overriding preoccupation with the power of words, the message concerns the monopolization of political and ethical relationships on the basis of the supreme ontological truth of these words.

2. The Problem of Authenticity and Roots as "Primordiality"

Heidegger's response to the "enigma of being," so far, is that democracy and cosmopolitanism are expressions of spiritual decline, inauthenticity, and rootlessness, coupled with a totalizing appeal for salvation based on a combination of imagined tradition and heroic values of "active nihilism." At the same time, there is the claim that the dominant Western tradition is inauthentic, and that the presently buried "authentic" one must be restored to its proper place. All of these major themes resurface in the Islamic ideology that took hold in the Iranian public imagination in the decades leading up to the 1979 revolution through the works of Al-e Ahmad, Fardid, Shari'ati, and others.

The fundamental aim of *Being and Time* is "to expose the horizon for the most primordial interpretation of being."[64] The "primordial truth of existence" is opposed to the traditional metaphysical conception of the abstract universal idea. Such universal ideas, which are inauthentic, come from a sphere of abstract reflection, whereas primordiality comes from the ground of existential authenticity. There is a nihilistic core to this idea, combined with heroic values: "The nothingness primordially dominant in the being of Da-sein is revealed to it in authentic being-toward-death."[65] *Being and Time* aims to attain this "primordial truth of existence" through a "destruction" of the dominant metaphysical tradition, which conceals beneath its "inauthentic" shell the original Greek "flash of illumination that (Heidegger) wants to recover or 'repeat.'" The aim of *Being and Time* is less the attainment of a new intellectual perspective than the recapturing of a lost historical *experience*: "This destruction is based upon the original experiences in which the first and subsequently guiding determinations of being were gained."[66] The "destructive" method is the first of the two principal methodological axes that drive the main argument of *Being and Time*. We may say that if the tradition has become a dead husk, severed from the roots that may sustain authentic life, Heidegger's project is to tear away the rottenness in order that the buried soul may "repeat" itself in our contemporary historical moment.

The second methodological axis is "phenomenology." Heidegger's "phenomenology" is based on the conviction that "What is ontically nearest and familiar is ontologically the farthest, unrecognized and constantly overlooked in its ontological significance."[67] He writes: "a phenomena can be concealed. And precisely because phenomena are initially and for the most part not given phenomenology is needed. Being covered up is the counterconcept to 'phenomenon.'"[68] These assertions undermine the celebrated claim that *Being and Time* dispensed with hidden metaphysical abstractions in favor of concreteness. Heidegger did indeed argue that: "The being of beings can least of all be something 'behind which' something else stands, something that 'does not appear.'"[69] This rejection of Kantian *noumena* is set in the context of a fundamental nihilism in *Being and Time* that is expressed succinctly in the claim that the human essence, or "being-guilty," is "uncanniness, primordially thrown being-in-the-world, as not-at-home, the naked 'that' in the nothingness of the world."[70] Nevertheless, the entire argument in *Being and Time* is afflicted by another sense of a hidden reality in "primordial roots." The philosophical framework therefore does not transcend what Richard Rorty has identified as a worried preoccupation with "hidden realities":

> To worry in this way, you need to take seriously the question whether our descriptions of reality may not be all too human, all too influenced by our hopes and fears. It helps to anguish about whether Reality (and therefore Truth itself) may not stand aloof, beyond the reach of the sentences in which we formulate our beliefs. You must be prepared to distinguish, at least in principle, between beliefs which embody Truth and beliefs which are merely good to steer by.[71]

In *Being and Time* Heidegger merely transfers the essentialist separation between mind and the external world to that of "authentic" and "inauthentic" existence. In doing so Heidegger does not dispense with the claim of a totalizing "Truth": "primordial and authentic truth must guarantee the understanding of the being of Da-sein and of being in general."[72] The ontological priority of this "hidden reality" is made explicit: "phenomena" is defined as "something that does *not* show itself initially and for the most part, something that is *concealed*, in contrast to what initially and for the most part shows itself, indeed in such a way that it constitutes its meaning and ground."[73]

The presence of a hidden and independent "authentic" reality is explained in terms of the "concealing" powers of the dominant metaphysical tradition and "inauthentic" modes of being in modern everyday

life. This assertion lies at the very heart of Heidegger's central methodological axis of "phenomenology":

the thesis only suggested at the beginning: *The being that we ourselves always are
is ontologically farthest from us* (has now been demonstrated). The reason for this
lies in care itself. Entangled being-together-with-the-'world' initially taken care
of, guided the everyday interpretation of Da-sein, and covered over ontically the
authentic being of Da-sein, thus denying the appropriate basis for an ontology
oriented toward this being... freeing the primordial being of Da-sein must be
wrested from Da-sein *in opposition* to the entangled (ie: everyday), ontic, and
ontological tendency of interpretation.[74]

Heidegger continuously reiterates the "necessity" for a fundamental
divide between the "inauthentic" truths of the dominant tradition and
the "Truth" of being which he endeavors to "wrest" from the human
existential situation that is the focus of his investigation. Being, he insists,
"will require its own conceptualization, which again is essentially distinct from the concepts in which beings receive their determination of
meaning."[75] This division is all important, amounting to a philosophical
carte blanche for Heidegger as he creates/unearths a new/ancient world
of thought. The natural consequence of this conviction on Heidegger's
part is a rejection of reasoned argument with regard to this "primordial
truth." He therefore writes that "traditional logic which is itself rooted
in ancient ontology... cannot be applied to being."[76] Nor is "primordial
truth" obliged to submit to the scrutiny of any received "inauthentic" analytical tradition: "it should not at all be our task to satisfy the demands
of any established discipline."[77] Heidegger insists that such "indefinabil-
ity... does not dispense with the question of (being's) meaning but forces
it upon us."[78] Heidegger's philosophical framework, intent on restoring existential roots and a sense of belonging to modern existence, is an
avowedly anti-intellectual project. It is set up, rather, in terms of "revelation." His "primordial truth" concerns an *experience of authenticity*
rather than a system of knowledge: "*Being* guilty is more primordial than
any *knowing* about it."[79] Throughout, Heidegger's intellectual framework continues to express an avowed hostility to "everyday life:" "*The
they does not permit the courage to have* Angst *about death.*"[80] Therefore, in a way consistent with the privileging of "direct experience" and
"heroic values" over "intellect" or "common sense," access to "primordial truth" becomes a matter of "courage" rather than understanding.

   The "revelation" involves the conception of "authentic roots" or
"primordial truth" in *Being and Time* that can therefore very well be

understood as a *vitalist* critique of modernity. Wolin has written that such a philosophy:

represents the prospect of an existential transformation of life in its routinized everydayness, its elevation to a higher plane. The norm must be destroyed insofar as it represents the reign of the merely "conceptual," the "abstract," the "average." Under such conditions, the substance of life itself, its pulsating fluidity, is prevented from coming to the fore. The cardinal virtue of the sovereign decision, therefore, is that it *explodes* the routinization to which life is subjected.[81]

In *Being and Time* "primordial roots" are the fusion of decisionism and the human essence or "being-guilty." The "primordial truth" is an *experience* of being in proximity with death: "Being anxious discloses, primordially and directly, the world as world."[82] Yet this experience is only the precondition or potentiality for "authenticity" and not yet its realization. As Heidegger writes: the "primordial potentiality-of-being of Da-sein (is) being-guilty."[83] It is necessary to make a "decision" out of the experience of this void that is the human essence. This fusion, which rises above chance and accident, Heidegger calls "fate":

Existing fatefully in resoluteness handing itself down, Da-sein is disclosed as being-in-the-world for the "coming" of "fortunate" circumstances and for the cruelty of chance. Fate does not first originate with the collision of circumstances and events. Even an irresolute person is driven by them, more so than one who has chosen, and yet he can "have" no fate. When Da-sein, anticipating, lets death become powerful in itself, as free for death it understands itself in its own *higher power*, the power of its finite freedom, and takes over the *powerlessness* of being abandoned to itself in that freedom, which always only *is* in having chosen the choice.[84]

This existential "choice" forms the pinnacle of "authentic" existence in Heidegger's *Being and Time*. As noted before, this is the "decisionist" moment at the heart of the treatise. Yet of crucial importance is that this "authentic decision" is not made by an individual consciousness as such. It is necessarily made within the larger framework of a living historical tradition: "Authentic existential understanding is so far from extricating itself from traditional interpretedness that it always grasps its chosen possibility in resolution from that interpretation and in opposition to it, and yet again for it."[85] This passage expresses the very interesting idea that every living tradition is without closure and is perpetually expanding with fresh interpretation. Yet this claim is made in the context of Heidegger's revolt against the dominant tradition of modernity. He is not espousing a cultural relativism or a purely open-ended and anarchic appreciation of meaning. On the contrary: Heidegger believed passionately that "according to our human experience and history, everything essential and great has arisen only out of the fact that man had a home and was rooted in a tradition."[86] It was the strength of this belief that motivated his life-long search for *the* "meaning of the unity that belongs to the totality of being of all beings."[87] In *Being and Time*, this meaning is conveyed as a moment of "authentic" action that, out of the strength of inherited tradition, grounds the advent of continuity for that tradition as "fate" by way of *radically conservative* new forms.

Heidegger's preoccupation with "fate" as rising above the contingency of existence is of course opposed to modernity and democracy as sites of "soulless" disorder. The "moment" of "authenticity" has the explicit function of overcoming these "inauthentic" and "rootless" traditions: "the temporality of authentic historicity . . . *undoes* the making present of the today and the habituation to the conventionalities of the they."[88] Modern everydayness is only a necessary point of departure for analysis in order to overcome "inauthenticity" and reach the "authentic" essence

All ontological inquiries into phenomena such as guilt, conscience, and death must start from what everyday Da-sein "says" about them. Because its kind of being is entangled, the way Da-sein gets interpreted is for the most part *inauthentically* "oriented" and does not get at the "essence," since the primordially appropriate ontological line of questioning remains alien to it.[89]

This "decision," as is consistent with a philosophy of "vitalism," is ultimately concerned with *action* rather than ideas: Authentic "being-toward-death" "brings one without illusions to the resoluteness of 'acting.'" The initial brush with death is the awakening, which "frees for death the possibility of *gaining power over* the *existence* of Da-sein and of basically dispersing every fugitive covering over."[90] The dross of everydayness having been thereby swept away, the ground is cleared for what can only be called a revelation: "Resolute, Da-sein has brought itself back out of falling prey (everydayness) in order to be all the more authentically 'there' for the disclosed situation of the 'Moment.'"[91] It is out of this "Moment" that a higher and deeper goal is born to revitalize and extend the *spiritual and political* power of the "absolute" tradition that Heidegger aimed to foster with the "question of being": "Only being free *for* death gives Da-sein its absolute goal and pushes existence into its finitude."[92] Heidegger was not simply affirming any tradition, but aiming to create *the* absolute authentic tradition. This preoccupation with an "absolute goal" of course echoes Nietzsche's own writings on the need to harness the received historical accumulation of *religious energy* to the end of creating fantastic new social and political forms with higher ends than mere democracy or everyday life:

the fight against Plato or, to speak more clearly and for "the people," the fight against the Christian-ecclesiastical pressure of millennia – for Christianity is Platonism for "the people" – has created in Europe a magnificent tension of the spirit the like of which had never yet existed on earth: with so tense a bow we can now shoot for the most distant goals . . . we who are neither Jesuits nor democrats, nor even German enough, we *good Europeans* and free, *very* free spirits – we still feel it, the whole need of the spirit and the whole tension of its bow. And perhaps also the arrow, the task, and – who knows? – the *goal*.[93]

Heidegger's *Being and Time*, in less fluid and seductive language, endeavored to lay the groundwork for the creation of such goals: "the existentially more primordial interpretation also discloses *possibilities* of a more primordial existential understanding."[94] Elsewhere, more bluntly, he announced: "We call for the goal that should be posited for man in and for his history."[95] This appeal, according to Heidegger, was made in the name of the "oldest" tradition of thinking, which had been unjustly dethroned by "representation" or "accordance": "we encounter an old – though not the oldest – tradition of thinking, according to which truth is the accordance."[96] As we have seen, this "oldest" tradition, or *aletheia*, is closer to religious thought in its embrace of mysticism and refusal of reason, and remote from most core religious values in its embrace of a modern apocalyptic and nihilistic ideology.

Based on this reading, we see that *Being and Time* envisioned a hidden depth of "authentic" experience of being *as such* covered over by a historical accumulation of "inauthentic" conventions that further contribute to a condition of historical decline. By aiming to recapture an "authentic" experience of being from its remote burial in the past, Heidegger hoped to reestablish the dominance of the "authentic" tradition over the human existential situation. The "question of the meaning of being as such" is surely a topic that hovers on the frontier between the philosophical and the theological. Unsurprisingly, Heidegger broaches it more by way of suggestion than by any definite answer. In the process, however, he manages to intertwine ideological and philosophical currents that enshrine a powerfully paradigmatic conception of a clandestinely grounded essence of history as invisibly competing truth claims, with an apocalyptic flavor of radical moments of overall transformation. He accomplished this in the spirit of his own concern with the fate of the unique German "soul" in the context of "soulless" liberal and communist "universalism," global technology, and leveling cosmopolitanism. The paradigmatic idea complex in *Being and Time* found great appeal among many intellectuals struggling against the oppressive "Westernizing" regime of the Shah in the decades prior to the Iranian Revolution, and oppositional discourses took form around it to what was ultimately detrimental effect. In the following section we attempt to sketch the political implications for Heidegger's philosophy, particularly with regard to secular democracy.

3. A Regime of the Authentic and the Problem of Secularism

Heidegger dreamed of returning to a "great beginning." He explained the "great beginning" in this way: "The primordial disclosure of being as a whole, the question concerning beings as such, and the beginning of Western history are the same."[97] This is by any standard an inflated and totalizing conception of the beginning of Western history. Believing deeply that this "great beginning" could be "repeated" in the context of a long-standing historical decline of the West, or modern society, he posed the question:

The history of truth, of lighting up and transformation and grounding of truth's essence, has only rare and widely separated moments. For long periods this essence seems solidified, since only the truths determined by it are sought and cultivated. . . . Do we stand at the end of such a long period of hardening of the essence of truth and then on the brink of a new moment in its clandestine history?[98]

This view of a "clandestine" history accords with Heidegger's "decisionist" philosophy. He wrote: "The rare and simple decisions of history arise from the way the original essence of truth essentially unfolds."[99] The "leveling" modern period, in its preoccupation with materialism and objective knowledge, embodied decline because "being" was "forgotten": "Precisely in the leveling and planing of this omniscience, this mere knowing, the openedness of beings gets flattened out into the apparent nothingness of what is no longer a matter of indifference, but forgotten."[100] Being was for Heidegger a spiritual concern that embodied "a concealed essential ground of man, and in such a manner that the experience transposes us in advance into the originally essential domain of truth."[101] Heidegger certainly aimed to resurrect the link between human existence and being, but not in such a way as to render being accessible to human knowledge. He made it clear that, on the contrary, a healthy relation to being accepts as a precept that being is inaccessible to human knowledge: hat conserves letting-be in this relatedness to concealing? Nothing less than the concealing of what is concealed as a whole, of beings as such, ie; the mystery; not a particular mystery regarding this or that, but rather the one mystery – that, in general, mystery holds sway throughout man's Da-sein."[102] In this preoccupation with the "forgotten," or historical decline, and the need for "remembrance" of what we cannot and must not know, Heidegger is in fact expressing a religious discourse that calls on modern people to bear *witness*. A spiritually healthy society must exist in perpetual cognizance of the mystery of being: "Wherever the conceal-ment of beings as a whole is conceded only as a limit that occasionally announces itself, concealing as a fundamental occurrence has sunk into forgottenness."[103] In order to be perpetually cognizant of being, and not merely so in random moments, a structure is necessary to impose the act of witness: "Only when the strangeness of beings oppresses us does it arouse and evoke wonder."[104] Heidegger believed that in the neglect of such an act of witness, "man goes wrong as regards the essential genuine-ness of his standards." As a result, "beings are covered up and distorted" and "semblance comes to power." This "inauthentic" condition of for-getfulness results in the arrogance of humanism: "(Man) is all the more mistaken the more exclusively he takes himself, as subject, to be the stan-dard for all."[105] There is a philosophical corollary to this arrogance in metaphysics: "Metaphysics regards (its) truth as the imperishable and the eternal, which can never be founded on the transitoriness and fragility that belong to man's essence."[106] This, then, explains the problem of "for-getfulness" in Heidegger: because humanity lives in time, it is forgetful and therefore goes astray. Heidegger did not simply wish to alert human-ity to the "wonder" of being, but to build the institutions necessary for sustaining this relation of "wonder" as an enshrined collective practice. This is to say, to give meaning to life, and if necessary by force. A new esoteric philosophy and hierarchical order is required whereby "instead of furnishing representations and concepts, (mankind) experiences and tests itself as a transformation of its relatedness to Being."[107] The "repe-tition" of the "great beginning" is the order envisioned by Heidegger to fulfill this purpose. This is to be set in motion, as we have seen, by way of the equally religious notion of revelation or the "Moment."

We should not be surprised by the pervasive religious concern that saturates Heidegger's work. Some impression of his life experiences may illuminate the formation of this thinker who was at once passionately religious and socially radical, and willing to court murderously violent political ideologies in the name of a third way between capitalism and communism. Heidegger's life may be summed up almost as a series of regenerations. In his early youth he was a devout Catholic from a strictly religious background. His father was a sexton at the local church. He was lifted to the eminence of a university career from the conservatively religious farmlands of southern-central Germany through a series of scholarships funded by the church. In his early twenties his first publications appeared in *Der Akademiker*, an ultraconservative Catholic journal, and he spoke out against the dangers of "modernism" to the timeless wisdom of Catholic institutions and theological truth. Yet in 1919, at thirty, he broke traumatically with the Catholic Church and converted to Protestantism based on a personal and philosophical transformation of the previous two years. This was immediately following the Great War, which had cost 16 million lives, and the Bolshevik Revolution in Russia. The Hohenzollern dynasty of 1701 to 1918 had met its final end in Germany and a socialist republic had been proclaimed, followed by the outbreak of virtual civil war. Heidegger himself had spent four months on the Western Front and been involved in preparing poison gas attacks on U.S. soldiers. Yet in his letter to the Catholic priest, Heidegger made reference to none of these cataclysmic events. Leaving them in silence, he described his religious transformation as if it had occurred in a sealed vacuum. In his letter he does not actually renounce his Catholic faith, but vows to proceed with attempting to retrieve the hidden inner meaning of Christianity through a phenomenology of religion. Surely the separation in his mind between religious concern and sociohistorical circumstance was not as clear as this letter would suggest, and the apoliticism was itself ideological. The preoccupation with a "great beginning" through "revelation," with the importance of witness, and with the dangers of modernism surely testifies to this.

The combination of a religious passion rooted in his upbringing, his "radical conservative" ideology absorbed from his social milieu, and his somewhat fantastic and phantasmic visions of reality as a philosopher unfortunately rendered him susceptible for a time to believing the political ascendancy of the National Socialist state was indeed the "great beginning" he had dreamed of. Heidegger himself was quick to reveal the possible collusion of his main ideas in *Being and Time* and key aspects of Nazi ideology after the National Socialist Revolution took power in 1933. It is perverse that a book of such near sublime complexity should lend itself to a totalitarian regime bent on racial purity through genocide and the military domination and enslavement of Europe in the name of a new German master race. Without belittling Heidegger's philosophical achievement, it is necessary to concede that important elements in his thought sadly lend themselves to such a calling, and to understand why. To be sure, the somewhat eccentric and fanciful ideas about a "great beginning" with which this section opened are difficult to immediately reconcile with images of the horrors inflicted on so many by Nazism during World War 2. In this chapter we are concerned with what we identified at the opening of this essay as the loose yet coherent existence of a broadly international movement of authenticity. Where this is concerned, Heidegger's revolutionary philosophical framework is anything but a harmless idea, and his damning fling with Nazi ideology is only one instance compared to an intellectual afterlife through his works that in its capacity to inspire movements of authenticity is far from exhausted.

In *Being and Time*, as noted before, philosophical and ideological themes are inextricably interwoven. The concept of the "situation" is considerably charged with political significance. A central philosophical argument in *Being and Time* is that Da-sein does not first somehow exist and *then* move – as if there were somehow an ideal copy, in the Platonic sense, outside of the world – but that Da-sein is itself movement. This is more or less the claim of "facticity," or being-already-in-the-world, by which existence is an ungraspable and continuous flow of action without perfect precedent or otherworldly counterpart. "Falling prey" is movement, and a general preoccupation is announced with the "enigma" of "movement." Yet the philosophical investigation slides into a dubious ideology when this anti-metaphysical stance unfolds in the claim of an ontological primacy for momentary decision and action, as it were, sprung from the void, over any established universal principle or ideal. This points, very problematically, to a philosophy of the will, or of the will in the grip of a higher power, as the basis for a radical and "authentic" social reconstruction. This is a point made in the concept of "situation," or "fate," as the moment of authentic experience and action vis-à-vis being:

> Far removed from any objectively present mixture of the circumstances and accidents encountered, situation *is* only through and in resoluteness.... *For the they, however, situation is essentially closed off....* Resoluteness brings the being of the there to the existence of its situation.... This makes it quite clear that the call of conscience does not dangle an empty ideal of existence before us when it summons us to our potentiality-of-being, but *calls forth to the situation.*[108]

Situation, then, is a privileged moment of inspiration sent from being. It is not an abstract "ideal" accessible to anyone and everyone. Situation, linked to "resoluteness," is inaccessible to the mass in their dreary and cowardly mediocrity, but opens itself to those special men who hear the "call of conscience" summoning them from the nothingness of being: "We shall call the eminent, authentic disclosedness attested in Da-sein itself by its conscience – the *reticent projecting oneself upon one's ownmost being-guilty which is ready for* Angst – *resoluteness.*"[109] This is clearly a strong image of authentic action taking place under some kind of inspiration. If *Being and Time* sets up modern society as a case of long-term degeneration and promotes a radical rebirth, it offers moments of decision seized in the rapture of an encounter with being as the only possible road to authentic transformation. Yet it is uncertain whether it is actually a philosophy that privileges the will. Rather, it seems that being itself selects a vanguard from among the population in order to bring about its vindication. If Heidegger's later works certainly erased human will in favor of being, in *Being and Time* there is still a muddle between them. It is clear that human practice affects our relation to being, for there is "a necessary connection of being and understanding, although perhaps concealed in its primordial grounds" (*understanding* must be understood as practice rather than cognition).[110] Yet whether the volition in fact resides with being or human beings themselves, the unbridled tyranny implicit in this centering of volition as a political category is unmistakable. Moreover, the inevitable institutional forms these social transformations must take suggest a politics of charisma in which "authentic" leaders take the helm. In these ways, the religious concern expressed in the problem of a need to bear witness finds its program of action in the nihilism of the "situation."

The combination of religious concern and the "situation" as a course of action appeals to the authority of "heritage." Authentic existence combines the future, a naked and "heroic" confrontation with our eventual death that dispels any dreamy ideals, with the past, a spontaneous flooding of inspiration from among a gallery of dead heroes: the "authentic retrieve of a possibility that has been," for which Da-sein must "choose its heroes," or heritage. This is certainly a long leap from the philosophically conceived practical orientation of Da-sein with regard to temporality in everydayness, and moves us into the strongly ideological current of *Being and Time* that appeals to each of our primal experiences and is hence subjectivist within a constraining framework of traditional order. With this movement from the philosophically original analysis of everydayness to the ideologically charged "authentic temporality," modern and rootless everydayness is declared to be inauthentic. The subjectivist world of anxiety, death, and moments of vision is declared the possible ground for the realization of an authentic and rooted future social collective:

"The fateful destiny of Da-sein in and with its 'generation' constitutes the complete, authentic occurrence of Da-sein."[111] The "completion" of "authenticity," then, necessarily involves the social collective as a whole in unity with the aforementioned "absolute goal." The legacy of the past is fused with tomorrow's world in "anticipatory resoluteness," or "authentic temporality," in which "Da-sein can *be* authentically having-been only because it is futural . . . having been arises from the future."[112] To sustain such a condition of collective "authenticity" over any period of time is inconceivable without something like a totalitarian institutional foundation. In *Being and Time*, then, we find a quite romantic and fantastic imagining of a great past or original beginning making an absolute claim on the *social and political* future in opposition to the moribund existence of the "inauthentic" present. This is why it is forward-looking and utopian, seeking an alternative modernity rather than a "retreat" into the past.

The nihilistic vitalism as well as elitism expressed in the concept of the "situation," the insistence on the need to establish a hierarchical and unified collective with its moorings in a mystified tradition of antiquity, are given their radical edge in an atmosphere of "aesthetic modernism" – the fascination with limit situations and extremes. In the spirit of Nietzsche's *Zarathustra*, in which the lion and the child unite a fascination for destruction with a passion for creating monumental orders and symbols of power, these paradoxical impulses motivate the radicalism of *Being and Time* rather than any radical aims of the traditional Left – human rights or social equality – which, of course, Heidegger held only in the deepest contempt. If, as Isaiah Berlin has claimed, the roots of fascism are in the European Counter-Enlightenment, Heidegger's *Being and Time* occupies a unique and important place in this particular stream of modern political thought.

Underlying this whole framework is the concept of primordiality. Heidegger wrote that "the origin of something is the source of its essence."[113] Origin, or original experience, or the darkness of instinct and the unconscious, or indeed the penultimate origin and unmoved mover in God, which will offer the highest guidance, restores the power of myth and social cohesion to frail, rootless, and inauthentic modernity. This obsession was very visible in Heidegger's life. By way of his conversion to Protestantism, Heidegger was enabled to become the teaching assistant of Edmond Husserl, who was delighted by the conversion but recalled the "difficult inner struggles" that accompanied the "radical changes in (his) basic religious convictions."[114] In this way Heidegger's first regeneration took place. It was only two weeks after his letter to the Catholic priest announcing his break with his Catholic background. He began his ground-shaking lecture course at Freiburg University in 1919, amid Germany's postwar social chaos and struggle, as a radical phenomenologist passionately calling for a "return to the authentic origins of the spirit" through immersion in the concrete practical experiences of real life. We thus glimpse in these lectures the intertwining of the ontological and the existential themes that would dominate *Being and Time*. Kierkegaard, Luther, Pascal, and ultimately Augustine became his main sources of inspiration. He embarked on an intensive study of the "factical experience of life" of the New Testament communities in order to "recover authentic Christian experience."[115] It seems he was persistently digging for authentic origins and investigating spiritual ground.

This problem as a political preoccupation for Heidegger is most obvious in his discussions of aesthetics: art has a "founding function" in relation to the historical life of a people. Heidegger dismissed "contemporary literature" as "largely destructive," lacking a relation to being or the historical life of a people.[116] The scientific worldview, modern literature, and modern everyday life share a single metaphysical groundlessness in "nihilism" – that is, they are detached from the command of a specific cultural tradition, or the "absolute" tradition of the "absolute goal." This reveals the criteria of candidacy for Heidegger's ultimate aims. Although the appeal is to identity or raw life as opposed to principles, and to direct and momentary experience rather than argumentation, the ultimate goal is to create a uniform and shared meaning for society as a whole. The living pulse of being is accessed only by way of living out a specific tradition. In the "history of being," Heidegger therefore celebrated the Greek temple as a defining cultural paradigm that publicly displayed the dimensions of being's essential meaning and therefore life's possibilities. He wrote: "It is the temple-work that first fits together and at the same time gathers around itself the unity of those paths and relations in which birth and death, disaster and blessing, victory and disgrace, endurance and decline acquire the shape of destiny for human being."[117] This was similarly the case with the medieval cathedral, which showed the dimensions of salvation and damnation. Heidegger dreamed of a center of *values* and *meaning*. In the degenerated nihilism of the scientific modern age, such a center is lacking: "To forget Being and to cultivate only beings – that is nihilism."[118] Everything is reduced to a mere thing for calculated manipulation without any essential background. The calling of art should be to rescue us from this estrangement from being and produce "truth," in

Heidegger's quasi-religious and highly political sense of the word: "The essence of truth is, in itself, the primal strife in which that open center is won within which beings stand and from which they set themselves back into themselves."[119] More explicitly still, Heidegger wrote: "(One) way in which truth occurs is the act which founds a political state."[120] Such a criterion of truth seems at best, particularly considering the world-view of the state to which Heidegger swore his allegiance, dangerously misguided. Underlying such an idea of truth is, again, the philosophy of "decisionism." Thus, "whether art will decline into an 'instrument of cultural policy,' or will set the truth (in)to (the) work once more is a matter for 'decision'; the outcome is uncertain."[121]

In a radical reconceptualization of truth, Heidegger decided that everyday life was a circle and a text that had to be read to locate its hidden and authentic possibilities. There was no doubt in Heidegger's mind at this time that philosophy was involved in a struggle over "truth" that would decide whether it "shall live or die."[122] He insisted that the "overall dominance and primacy of the *theoretical*" was to blame for "messing up the real problematic." Traditional philosophical metaphysics, with its objectivism, was sucking dry "lived life," and thus he conceived the hermeneutical circle as a radical phenomenological remedy and alternative truth basis: "When you live in the firsthand world, everything comes at you loaded with meaning, all over the place and all the time, everything is enworlded, 'world happens.'"[123] Implicitly this asserted that human experience, including religious experience, is never in need of either scientific or analytical proof to be "true." This alternative truth basis clearly aims to encompass life as a whole – or existence – in contrast to the limits of mere epistemological theory. Yet in spite of this explosion of metatheoretical passions during the Weimar years, and the antimodernist edge of the philosophy he was espousing, Heidegger remained staunchly apolitical in these years right up until the eve of his infamously enthusiastic political embrace of Nazism in 1933.

The crowning moment of this second regeneration as a radical phenomenologist was, of course, the publication of *Being and Time* in 1927 and its revolutionary effect on an entire generation of German scholars. According to Gadamer, who following Heidegger achieved significant philosophical fame and considerable influence in his own right, the treatise "effectively communicated to a wide public something of the new spirit that had engulfed philosophy as a result of the convulsions of World War I."[124] We can recognize the creeping social pessimism of the society that surrounded him in his flamboyantly totalizing condemnation of Western history in its near entirety as a decline. Yet *Being and Time* was not intended, primarily, as a political work. Heidegger had his sights set on a far loftier plateau of human reality. If *Being and Time*'s indictments of political modernity are somewhat tacit, both Heidegger's public statements and actions under the Third Reich express these convictions unambiguously. In this time the purportedly a priori and universal existential human structures of *Being and Time* were contracted to a specifically German mode of being, intended to give greatness and strength to the "German spirit."[125] We thus see *Being and Time* put to use in the Rectoral Address of 1933, "The Self Determination of the German University." This was his third regeneration as a committed Nazi activist. In this time Heidegger himself declared the existence of an essential connection between his political actions and the philosophical core of the treatise via the concept of historicity. In a conversation with Karl Löwith, Heidegger claimed this concept was the "basis of his political 'engagement.'"[126]

Although there is nothing like the biological racism of Nazi ideology in *Being and Time*, there is certainly something like a total and all-encompassing ontology of authentic primordiality championed over the false laws and customs of democratic modern mass society. This is apparent in both the bemoaning of the "they," as it happens against an industrial background and the vehement insistence throughout *Being and Time* on the deluded, blind, and harmful nature of popular understanding as an expression of this "they." He characterized abandonment by being as "a world-darkening and earth-destruction in the sense of *speed*, of *calculation*, of the claim of the *mass*."[127] In opposition to mass politics and popular religion, there is a hunger for the resurrection of mysterious and ancient traditions. There is evidence that around 1928 Heidegger may have become personally atheistic. Certainly, by the 1930s, and heavily influenced by Nietzsche, Heidegger considered Christianity to be a "decadent falling away from the primordiality of Greek experience." In this scenario Plato represented the "beginning of the metaphysical oblivion of being."[128]

In Heidegger's final regeneration following World War 2, we find a return to a stubbornly silent apoliticism coupled with a new mysticism that renounces the very possibility of any effective political action while asserting that "only a god can save us" in our abandonment by being. The fundamental preoccupation with the problem, if not the politics, of "authenticity" remains intact throughout Heidegger's series of regenerations. Relinquishing his hopes for the possibility of engendering the "other beginning" by force of violence, he became mesmerized and lost in contemplation of numberless unique and perishing worlds: "World-withdrawal and world-decay can never be undone."[129]

This yearning for an experience of higher guidance and restoration of myth to effect social cohesion is necessarily a prelude to the goal of an "authentic" regime of unconditional "spiritual" command in the modern context. This brings us to serious problems around the issue of secularism. In these ideas of an historic decline based on a lost primordial essence, and one that must be recaptured to create an institutionally centered and unified social meaning, we see an imagined territory that is potentially ideal for those concerned with both the "religious" and the "nativist" problems of secular modernity. The idea is self evidently the antithesis of anything like "multiculturalism." It is also antisecular. Heidegger's critique of modern religion is that it exists inside individuals and churches, but not in the world. He wrote:

the era is defined by god's failure to arrive, by the "default of god." But (this default) does not deny that the Christian relationship lives on in individuals and in churches. The default of god means that no god any longer gathers men and things unto himself, visibly and unequivocally, and by such gathering, disposes of the world's history and men's sojourn in it.[130]

The enclosure of both physical and mental social space within a single religious universe, which would eliminate the distressing experience of continuous change and explain everything, is lacking.

If the Enlightenment put reason to use toward the aim of illuminating human existence as such where dogma or superstition had long obscured it, Heidegger would reconstitute a spiritual heritage and authority beyond sight and reach of logical argument. This step – which is clearly a step away from humanism and into a mysterious terrain – is needed to purify the "ontological understanding" that is presently degenerated. If the Enlightenment was concerned with the extension of human autonomy, Heidegger is here concerned with the revival of an unconditional "spiritual" authority to oversee the boundaries of human action. It is declared categorically that the "ontological understanding" by its very nature "deprives Da-sein of its own leadership in questioning and choosing." Free will would appear to be irrelevant; it is only the proper access to primordial truth by which to be guided that holds importance in the transformation envisioned. Central to Heidegger's vision is the concept of "guidance," or "authentic guidance," beyond individual will and intellect. This guidance necessarily comes from the past, as "retrieve," in the form of "authentic tradition." Thus, we read that: "Resoluteness

constitutes the *loyalty* of existence to its own self. As resoluteness ready
for *Angst*, loyalty is at the same time a possible reverence for the sole
authority that a free existence can have, for the possibilities of existence
that can be retrieved." Yet this "authentic tradition" is a decidedly modern project. Just as Ernst Bertram summarized Nietzsche's career as an
"Attempt at a Mythology," we may say that *Being and Time* functions
as a complex philosophical framework for the production of essentialist
national myths in the modern context. There is a curious notion of identity contained in this notion of loyalty – one that eludes the constraints
of logic or principle – and for which a free existence is the equivalent of
servitude to an unnamed mystery extending out of the past. It echoes the
Nietzschean ideal in which "What is essential (is that) there should be
obedience over a long period of time and in a *single* direction." Heidegger's historicity is grounded in the understanding that such an authority
is necessary for a healthy spiritual public life. The clear absolute primacy
intended for the "meaning of the unity that belongs to the totality of being
of all beings" almost certainly ensures a political formation in which formal liberal freedoms disappear into irrelevance under the fanciful promise
of a rooted experience of being.

4. The Islamic Ideology in Iran

An analysis of the core ideas of the following seminal Iranian intellectuals
shows how so-called anti-Western intellectuals can be very open to Western ideas: the pre-revolutionary thinkers, Al-e Ahmad, Ahmad Fardid, Ali
Shari'ati, Dariush Shayegan, and the postrevolutionary debates between
Reza Davari and Abdolkarim Soroush.[131] Not only are they open to
Western intellectuals, but they share a discourse in common with them
to which they contribute significantly in their turn. These thinkers, all
of them key in the evolution of modern political Islam for Iran, very
directly breathe the atmosphere of a Heideggerian universe as well as
various other sources from the mainstream of twentieth-century Western
intellectual culture and political thought.

   Initially I will lay out the principal concepts and key sources by which
the "movement" exists as a living ideology independently of those individuals who adopt it for their own purposes within a specific sociohistorical conjuncture. The key points are as follows: there is the desire to
reconfigure modernity in the national context (as nativism, according to
Mehrzad Boroujerdi's analysis, or as a discourse of authenticity, which I
named it in my own work, or as a variant of nationalism). This localized

reconfiguration of modernity is conceived as a radical movement forward, not a return, and moreover as a creative re-rendering of tradition, or even as the invention (in some manner) of a new one. The genealogy of such a movement in Iranian intellectual thought and political culture has its roots in the strong Western tradition of counter-Enlightenment leading through Maistre and Herder to Nietzsche and Heidegger, as well as Spengler, Jünger, and Schmitt. This counter-Enlightenment tendency has received a related but considerably different articulation in the genealogically interwoven ideas of French poststructuralism, including Foucault, Baudrillard, and Deleuze. In addition, the flowering of this intellectual movement in the Iranian context drew inspiration from the highly pessimistic prognosis ventured by the cream of the West's own intellectual literati, including Sartre, Camus, Ionesco, Beckett, and others. These popular Western authors represented the West as undergoing a terminal spiritual crisis with only the bleakest of ends in sight. Third, the movement for authenticity in Iran freely borrowed concepts from the traditional left and Third Worldist ideas and conceived itself in terms of a project of radical social reconstruction that aimed to establish just social relations by way of (in many cases) a classless society. Yet above all, the credit for the fermentation of radical anti-Western ideas, without which the movement of authenticity would likely never have taken root, must be given to the specific experience of "Western modernity" endured under the modernizing, secular, and Western-backed Pahlavi state of the Shah. This state was violently forced into being through a military coup in 1953 and terminated a decade of hopeful democratic experimentation. It was subsequently experienced as the imposition of an "alien outside" on the Iranian people's own aspirations to create a modern and democratic society. It was this above all that engendered a hatred for and mistrust of the "West" as such, and only on this basis was the stage set for the embrace of radical anti-Western philosophies – as a "solution" – coming ironically in part from the ideological nomenclature of the West itself and ultimately evolving into a tidal wave of mass politics oriented around a complex and severely misguided idea of Iranian authenticity.

The most important figure in introducing the "German philosophy" to Iran, particularly Heideggerian historicism and ideas on authenticity, was Fardid. Fardid (1912–94), who was educated in Germany and France, served from the 1950s on as Iran's leading authority on the philosophy of Heidegger. By the 1960s he was appointed professor of philosophy at Tehran University, where he taught such courses as the history of modern philosophy (from Bacon to Kant) and history of modern and contemporary philosophy (from Kant to the present). Fardid reconceived the Orient-West binarism – itself a spatial and cultural configuration produced by modern political discourses around the enterprise of Western colonialism – in terms of Heidegger's concept of the essence of truth as historical.

As noted before, Heidegger had proposed this idea of a clandestinely grounded essence of history as invisibly competing truth claims in view of his own concern with the fate of the unique German "soul" in the context of "soulless" liberal and communist "universalism," global technology, and leveling cosmopolitanism. For Heidegger, the current regime of truth was an objectifying nihilism centered on beings to the exclusion of being and taking the form of global technological mastery. Somewhat in line with this, Fardid maintained that the historical destiny of the contemporary world is that of the "West" (and like Heidegger, with hopes for impending change):

the present age throughout the world is the age of civilizational traditions and not cultural memoirs. All Islamic countries and indeed all oriental nations, without exception, are situated in a phase of history in which, contrary to their Western counterparts, they can no longer be in possession of their own historical trust. This is due to the fact that since the eighteenth century, Western culture has metamorphosed into the (dominant, in Heideggerian terms) historical tradition or civilization.[132]

This passage at once evokes the classically antimodernist attitude of the German mandarin intelligentsia in contrasting local *Kultur* and universal *Zivilisation*, as well as identifying the Enlightenment as the onset of the present state of decline. There is also a lamenting of the loss of cultural heritage in the modern world. Up to this point, the German reactionary modernist argument is reproduced term for term. But Fardid twists the received metaphysic of German cultural nationalism to the Iranian religious context in which, he says, "the moon of reality has risen while the sun of truth has gone into eclipse." The frame of reference takes a giant step out of Europe and into Asia and shifts the ontologically sanctioned dogmatism of Heideggerian "being" to an Islamic "truth." In this scenario, scientific facts (reality) overwhelm truth (religion), in a "history of (western) philosophy (which is) a centrifugal motion away from the essential Truth."[133] Yet in spite of the important modifications, this idea complex very much echoes the entire Heideggerian preoccupation with the "fall from being" on the road to a culturally groundless future of mere scientific manipulation. It similarly reproduces the critique of Western history in its totality as a spiritual decline. There is even a rival historicist reading of the "fall from being." The "authentic ecclesiastical thought of the Orient (originally) engendered Greek cosmologism and cosmocentrism," which led through the "theocentrism" of the Middle Ages and finally the "anthropocentrism" of the "Modern Age." In the Middle Ages "God" was understood based on "Greek cosmological and metaphysical thought" and not on "true religious thought." With Renaissance humanism, humanity was made the focus of ethics and politics to the exclusion of "the true spiritual essence."[134] In a refashioning of Heidegger's account of the Western decline from and need to retrieve the original Greek experience of "being," Fardid relocates the original and authentic spiritual experience of humanity in a nebulous Orient/Islam. In effect, Fardid's modifications transfer the role of the "spiritual nation in the middle" from Germany to Iran, within the same problematic of Cold War encirclement and secular "universal" modernity. In this predicament it is necessary to abandon *Gharb* (the West) as both an ontology and a way of life. Curiously, in order to do so, it is first necessary to discover the "essence of the West" as a prerequisite for once more retrieving the true Islamic self. This is of course not unlike Heidegger's idea of a bridge home to being through a deconstruction of the dominant tradition. The terms of the need for a socially grounded spiritual obedience have changed, but the need remains the determining idea. In Fardid's re-rendering of the Orient-West binary and Heideggerian historicism, the Orient represents the essence of the holy books and divine revelation, which has been concealed under a succession of Western mantles leading to the technological anthropocentrism of the Modern Age. In this construction of West and Orient as bearing opposing essences, with the Orient harboring the ontologically legitimate truth capable of overcoming the technological nihilism engendered by the West, Fardid's *gharbzadegi* ("Westoxication") is the interlude between the self and being on the path to renewed Islamic self-realization.

It is remarkable that such an obscure amalgamation of Heideggerian metaphysics, variations on the familiar Orientalist binarism, and transfiguring of Iranian Shi'i theology should have provided the secret spring for the most radical book to appear in Iran in the 1960s, one that helped considerably to alter the country's future. Yet it was directly from Fardid's analysis of Heidegger that Al-e Ahmad derived and developed his concept of "Westoxication." This idea revolutionized the thinking of his entire generation by offering a "nativist" alternative to the previously dominant "universalist" ideology of the Left. As one prominent writer and literary critic, Reza Baraheni, wrote: "Al-e Ahmad's *Gharbzadegi* is the first Eastern essay to make clear the situation of the East vis-à-vis the West – the colonialist West – and it may be the first Iranian essay to have social value on a world level."[135] This makes clear that the essay was received as a message suited for the anti-imperialist struggles of the time, yet now in terms of an ontological reconstruction and reversal of the East-West binary with Shi'i Islam as the force of revolutionary authenticity and social change, aiming to overcome the empty nihilism of encroaching Western modernity. Al-e Ahmad himself had undergone a lifetime of personal transformations before reaching his verdict on "Westoxication," and this trajectory shows the nature of his fundamental aim. He had been a Marxist in the Tudeh party, yet became disillusioned with the party's subservience to the Soviet Union during the Azerbaijani oil crisis of 1947; a nationalist under Mosaddeq prior to the devastation of the 1953 coup; and a Sartrean existentialist prior to his life-changing realization that only Islam – which he had criticized in his earlier fictional works as an opium of the people – offered the one genuine possibility of a locally authentic ideology truly capable of mobilizing the broad mass of Iranian people toward a revolutionary end. Even though Al-e Ahmad apparently skimmed his knowledge of Heidegger from his relationship with Fardid, his central ideas are remarkably faithful in carrying the main precepts of the Heideggerian project through into a discourse of Shi'i Iranian Islamic authenticity.

Westoxication (1962), which dominated the Iranian intellectual panorama of the 1960s, perhaps played the founding role in the effort to articulate a local, Islamic modernity as a blueprint for revolutionary social change in Iran. This discourse must be understood against a background of successive experiences of disillusionment with "Western" and "universal" philosophies of liberation, for both the particular author in question and the general society that received his work. It rearticulated the dilemma of Iranian intellectuals – which had previously been understood in terms of a "universal" struggle for human emancipation through liberal, nationalist, and Marxist discourses – in terms of an essential choice between cultural authenticity, or "return to the self," and subservience to the West, or "rootlessness." "Westoxication" is defined as "the aggregate of events in the life, culture, civilization, and mode of thought of a people having no supporting tradition, no historical continuity, and no gradient of transformation."[136] This so-called disease, already afflicting the West itself – as Al-e Ahmad had learned from Eugene Ionesco, Ingmar

Bergman, Jean Paul Sartre, and Vladimir Nabokov, among others – was now being inflicted on Iran by the modernizing regime of the Shah. There is an ambiguity to this in that the "West" is conceived simultaneously in the role of a victim of this "disease" and that of an outward aggressor on account of suffering from it. This is a disease of the soul, and Iran is urged to resist a similar fate. Al-e Ahmad's work, which concerned itself with the general problem of "modern man's search for a soul," produced the basic vocabulary of the Islamic ideology that was to dominate the future of Iranian politics. If the terms of the "disease" echo the descriptions of modern man's plight in Heidegger's *Being and Time* – an "inauthentic historical existence . . . burdened with the legacy of a 'past' that has become unrecognizable to it" – this is not merely a matter of coincidence. The radical intellectuals of Iranian authenticity discussed here may very well be described as being among "Heidegger's children."

As a thinker, Al-e Ahmad may have been unsystematic, but he displayed a sharp insight in his selection of concepts from far and wide to begin the process of dressing modernity in a semblance of continuity with local Shi'i tradition. We can therefore say that what projected itself as a championing and recovery of the "true" Iranian culture via the works of Al-e Ahmad was not particularly indigenous at all – on the contrary, it made use of a complex framework grounded in previous intellectual revolts against a cosmopolitan and secular modernity, and staged its own revolt on much the same grounds.

Al-e Ahmad himself was certainly aware of his debt to this particular trend in German philosophy. In the preface to *Westoxication* he indicates his intellectual debt to Ernst Jünger, whose work he translated into Persian, and whose ideas had also deeply influenced Heidegger. He wrote: "Jünger and I were both exploring more or less the same subject, but from two view points. We were addressing the same question, but in two languages."[137] In this way the Gharbzadegi discourse was similar to the German "reactionary modernist" movement (as Jeffrey Herf identified it) with its longing for the preservation of a unique German cultural identity. For Al-e Ahmad the critique of Gharbzadegi also expressed a yearning for an "authentic" Islamic identity and in this way embodied far more the plight of a modern intellectual lost in the labyrinth of modern experience than any return to a traditional Islam – where, in any event, concepts such as the "self" do not play a focal role. Rather than anything like a "return" to indigenous culture, we see one self-conscious option that confronts the modern intellectual in any number of social situations. This is an option, however, that in its radical concern with politicizing the problem of shared social meaning poses a direct threat to the pluralism of institutions that are secular democratic in nature.

Between his two major works, *On the Service and Treason of the Intellectuals* and *Occidentosis,* Al-e Ahmad traced the roots of Gharbzadegi to mid-nineteenth-century intellectual movements in Iran that promoted ideas of secularism, social progress, and Western-oriented political systems, and elaborated the global symptoms of the disease as "mechanosis." Mechanosis is the compound of nihilism and technological frenzy that grew indigenously within the "West" and extended itself like a plague to the world as a whole. In an echoing of Heidegger's remark that "from a metaphysical point of view, Russia and America are the same (in their) dreary technological frenzy (and) unrestricted organization of the average man," Al-e Ahmad warned that "now all of these 'isms' and ideologies are roads leading to the sublime realm of mechanization." There is the same reductive metaphysics, based on a Heideggerian historicist reading, to explain the entire complex of international political events. Yet unlike Heidegger, who saw Germany caught "in a great pincers" as "the nation in the center" and "the most metaphysical of nations," Al-e Ahmad envisioned a world divided into two opposing halves in a different sense: "the beat of progress is in that ascending part of the world, and the pulse of stagnation is in this moribund part of the world."[138] In this way, he adapted Heidegger's peculiarly anti-Western German stance to the situation of the Third World as a whole. This further developed and gave concrete political expression to ideas that had been only vague and tacit in Fardid. Against this bleak background "we (Iranians) have been unable to preserve our own historico-cultural character in the face of the machine and its fateful onslaught." Like Heidegger, he conceives the attack of the "machine" as being on the intangible yet essential reality of a nation's soul: (Mechanosis is the) "murderer of beauty and poetry, spirit and humanity."[139] This combination of Third Worldism with a Heideggerian critique of technological nihilism, transposed onto a radically reconstructed Shi'i Islamic revivalism, is far less representative of any traditional religious discourse than of the array of counter-Enlightenment ideologies that it conceals.

Meanwhile there is also, in a paradoxical mirroring of another Heideggerian obsession, the preoccupation with preserving "tradition" as a living power and avoiding its transformation into a dead relic from an exotic past by the forces of Western modernity. Thus, Al-e Ahmad writes: "I, as an Asian or African, am supposed to preserve my manners, culture, music, religion, and so forth untouched, like an unearthed relic, so that the gentlemen can find and excavate them, so they can display them in a museum and say, 'Yet another example of primitive life.'"[140] Yet the "tradition" he in fact endeavors to keep alive is more an imaginative ideological construction than anything like traditional Iranian Shi'ism and is intended to overcome the challenge of prevailing modernity by way of transfiguring it according to a higher spiritual command.

Certainly it must be understood that Al-e Ahmad intended from the outset to transfigure modernity and not abolish it. While advocating a reconfiguration of modernity within the national context, he emphatically never advocated the rejection of technological modernity, saying: "I am not speaking of rejecting the machine or of banishing it, as the utopians of the early nineteenth century sought to do. . . . It is a question of how to encounter the machine and technology."[141] It is rather a matter, for him, of wedding modernity as a totality to a foundation in local Shi'i Islam. There is a strong foundationalist preoccupation in Al-e Ahmad's discourse. If the West itself spawned nihilistic mechanosis, as we are given to understand – "the god technology had for years exercised absolute rule over Europe mounted on the throne of its banks and stock exchanges, and it no longer tolerated any other god, laughing in the face of every tradition and ideology" – then the only remedy for the onset of mechanosis in Iran (and similarly besieged countries) is the subordination of technology to the power of authentic traditional Iranian culture.[142] This entire line of thinking implies a subterranean metaphysical life to technology, in a Heideggerian vein, beyond the simple Weberian or Marxist claim that modernity effects the melting into air of all solid traditions. He writes: "Although the (West) who created the machine now cries out that it is stifling him, we not only fail to repudiate the garb of the machine tenders, we pride ourselves on it."[143] This "garb" is Western culture and ideology: "That is how the Iranian intellectual has gradually turned into a root which is not planted in the soil of this land. And he always has his eyes on Europe, and always dreams of escaping there."[144] At this point we see the division set in place between the culturally authentic and inauthentic (gharbzadegi), with some Iranians inevitably falling outside of the line that is to be drawn. Al-e Ahmad demands rhetorically: "Must we remain the mere consumers we are today or are we to shut our doors to the machine and technology and retreat into the depths of our ancient ways, or is there a third possibility?"[145] Again, here, we feel a Heideggerian presence as a call is made to abandon futile hopes of a return to more tranquil times in "old" traditions, but rather to reconfigure tradition that it may master and lead modernity forward along a locally authentic path as a "third way" beyond the "soulless" predicament of the present. A local solution is needed in order to win the future, to "break (the machine) into harness like a draft animal . . . and impress it with the human will."[146]

It was the rather un-Islamic conception of the self as plagued by a loneliness requiring the heroic oblivion of great sacrifice that gave his discourse an additional Heideggerian edge. In his later account of his trip to Mecca on Hajj, we see his work proceed in its endeavor to build subversive purpose into traditional structures. He arrives at a revelation concerning the place of the individual as fodder for the power of mass faith and cultural identification:

This self, if it doesn't exist as a particle working to build a society, is absolutely nothing. It is not even a "self." It is that piece of rubbish or particle of dust, except (and a thousand exceptions) when it exists in the context of a great faith, or a great fear. Then it becomes the builder of everything from pyramids to the Great Wall of China, and even China itself.[147]

This equation of "faith" and "fear" as ontological movers for mankind could very well spring from Heidegger's analysis of "anxiety" as a fundamental mode of ontological disclosure and a key to taking authentic collective action beyond the stifling vacuity of the "they," or modern mass society. Al-e Ahmad's revitalized Shi'i Islam seems to offer a similar way out from the impasse of dull and stifling meaninglessness that is secular modern society.

If Al-e Ahmad was the most influential intellectual figure of the 1960s, then Shari'ati (1933–77) dominated the 1970s and gave a more thorough and sophisticated articulation to his predecessor's ideas. If Al-e Ahmad conceived the basic criticism of secularism and modernism that was to dominate Iranian politics in the decades to come, it was Shari'ati who fully articulated Shi'i Islam as a modern revolutionary ideology. Although Shari'ati died shortly before the revolution broke out, he was one of its most celebrated figures and continued to dominate political debate in Iran well after the revolution was over. Shari'ati was politicized first by his father, who was a political Muslim, and later during his studies in France during the politically radical and volatile years of the 1960s.

Shari'ati articulated a brand of Islamic discourse that reflected the needs of a society undergoing an extreme degree of transformation, but in which most people felt deeply alienated from a process that they saw as going severely wrong. By his hermeneutical reading of the Shi'i Islamic tradition, Shari'ati created a precedent and an all-compelling obligation for a social revolutionary in the Islamic context. Yet this reconfigured model of Shi'ism necessarily rested on an intellectual separation between the debased inauthentic and the higher authentic – a politically ontological frame of reference. His reading of the tradition unambiguously split Shi'i Islam into a subterranean authentic tradition, which is called on to overthrow the tyrannical injustice of any powers that be, as well as to oppose the dominant yet inauthentic strain of the tradition that lingers in the mire of passivity and conservatism. He therefore gave full expression to the concept, already tacit in Al-e Ahmad, of contemporary Shi'i Islam as divided between dominant and subterranean, as well as inauthentic and authentic historical currents. It is a historical metaphysics. This plastic and interpretive vision of ancient traditions, with antecedents in Nietzsche and especially Heidegger, substitutes the granite outer shell of received spiritual wisdom for a limitless ground to be dug up and uncovered by design. In this way Shari'ati's Islamic ideology served modern means with a foreground disguise of venerable traditional authority. Shari'ati's Islamic ideology insisted on religious grounds that in order to be a good Muslim one must fight to overthrow the existing social order, and condemned both secular radicals and conservative clerics within the religious establishment who might oppose his revolutionary plans.

This Islamic Ideology was replete with skillfully blurred contradictions that accelerated its inner dynamism. Although claiming to be grounded in the authentic traditional religious culture of Iran, and condemning "alien" ideologies, it borrowed its categories freely from Marxism while insisting those categories had been Islamic to begin with. At the same time it reproduced the Heideggerian vision of a world situation in which spiritual social existence lay in the deadly shadow of materialist ideas and social forms:

Both these social systems, capitalism and communism, though they differ in outward configuration, regard man as an economic animal.... Humanity is every day more condemned to alienation, more drowned in this mad maelstrom of compulsive speed. Not only is there no longer leisure for growth in human values, moral greatness, and spiritual aptitudes (but it has also) caused traditional moral values to decline and disappear as well.[148]

According to this passage, historical reality is divided into two layers. On the surface layer, which is false, the rival world systems only appear to be antagonists, whereas on the deeper and concealed level of metaphysical truth, they are in fact one. In this declaration of an ontological equivalence

in the opposing world systems, there is a promise of restored moral purpose and social belonging in the "authentic" Islamic alternative. The soul,
equated not only with cultural heritage but also with social inclusion and
higher meaning, is said to be threatened by these converging embodiments
of modern nihilism. In this context, only an ideology that is ontologically
grounded – and no mere free-floating intellectual construction – can adequately challenge and overturn the growing ascendancy of nihilism in
the modern world. Rather than politics being a question of options, it
is one of authenticity. The result in Shari'ati's vision is a collapsing of
"culture" (the masses), "ideology," and "God" into one unified force.
"God" – or the Heideggerian substitute "Being" – is extremely important
for granting singular and ultimate authority to the mass movement. Also
similarly to Heidegger, there is the yearning for a shared and unifying
purpose to society as a whole, as opposed to what Shari'ati called "irresponsible and directionless liberalism," the "plaything of contesting social
forces."[149] The precondition for a modern utopia is the resurrection of a
lost primordial nature that has lain dormant throughout a long period of
decline:

We are clearly standing on the frontier between two eras, one where both Western
civilization and Communist ideology have failed to liberate humanity, drawing
it instead into disaster and causing the new spirit to recoil in disillusionment;
and where humanity in search of deliverance will try a new road and take a
new direction, and will liberate its essential nature. Over this dark and dispirited
world, it will set a holy lamp like a new sun; by its light, the man alienated
from himself will perceive anew his primordial nature, rediscover himself, and
clearly see the path of salvation. Islam will play a major role in this new life
and movement.[150]

This strongly utopian blend of Qu'ranic images with a Heideggerian sense
of impending apocalypse and spiritual rebirth, leading to a classless society, is very far from any return to pure Islamic sources. Rather, it presents
an elaborate dialogue between an unconventional Shi'ism and numerous
Western systems of philosophical thought. Above all, this dialogue is
guided by the conclusion that what Iran needs is a modern community.
Shari'ati, then, "revived" Islamic tendencies that perhaps never existed,
but spoke to people's contemporary needs in modernizing Iran through
a traditional-symbolic language. Such an achievement fitted his own self-
image as a modern Shi'i ideologue of the future, fighting for technological
advancement and national independence. This is why he disparaged conservative clerics and Islamic doctrines that he considered "backwards
looking."

Shari'ati's vision of an alternative future modernity for Iran is troubling. The major critique of modernity in his work is the attack on what he
called "the materialist cosmos," where "man turns out to be an object."
In contrast, Islam shows "a fundamental bond, an existential relation
(between man and the world), in regarding the two as arising from 'a single (sublime) origin'."[151] This reproduces nearly term for term the central
philosophy of Heidegger, who also felt a pervading religious background,
had slipped away and left people atomized from the ontological bond to
their community. Shari'ati's purpose, then, was to bring this bond explicitly into the everyday political lives of Iranians, as a recovery of the ideal
and unified Islamic society. He aimed to overcome the cultural rootlessness in everyday life inflicted by modern existence. Thinking along these
lines, he depicted Iran's domination by the West less in a political or
economic sense and more in terms of Western infestation within Iranian
society. Once again, then, it was necessary to divide contemporary society
between the authentic and the inauthentic, or *Gharbzadegi*.

This affinity of Heidegger's thought with his own was of course not
lost on Shari'ati. He openly expressed his admiration for Heidegger as
a "religious" thinker in contrast to the otherwise atheistic disposition
of many prominent philosophers in the West: "Today, in philosophy,
Heidegger does not speak in the (atheistic) terms of Hegel and Feuer-
bach. . . . Heidegger is searching for Christ in humanity, and Planck is
searching for God in the world of physics."[152] If we conceive a lost ideal
age, there is little hope of bringing it to rebirth unless we adopt a peculiar
view of history. This is the view of history presented tacitly in Heidegger's
Being and Time and very much in his later works. It is a somewhat more
cyclical vision in which opposing tendencies compete, often invisibly, to
occupy a tangible surface of reality that permits the domination of the
historical era in question by one of the various currents of tradition. It is
not history as facts but as a reconstruction of the self based on named currents. Certainly Nietzsche conceived such a vision in his *Birth of Tragedy*,
between the Apollonian and Dionysian. The opposing tendencies in such
historic visions represent a single culture, and this is why a single tradition
can be radically transfigured beyond any semblance of its "original" self
based on multiple variations and yet remain faithful to an "essence." It
is after all modernity that sets every tradition afloat with many colors,
and such historicist visions respond to this experience. Postmodernism,
in certain respects, tried to embrace such a vision without identifying any
moment of closure and ended up lost in a kind of epistemological and
ethical relativism. In order to stem the potentially infinite proliferation

of interpretations, it is only necessary to insist on the authenticity of a single interpretation of tradition over all others, and to consign the rest to a historical detour, into decadence and decline. This is a political act, and an emphatically modern one.

The seductive appeal of Heidegger has played itself out against the broader background of tensions between the allure of "authenticity" and the contradictory complexities of modernity as a social project in Iran. The political space opened up by Heideggerian philosophy is fraught with the dangers of authoritarianism and cultural particularism. Heidegger sought to provide a single ontological foundation to grant spiritual stability to the disorder of modern society. This idea can only prove harmful in a society such as Iran in its endeavor to build a democratic national modernity. Democratic modernity cannot base itself on any single epistemological, ontological, or moral assumption; it is by definition a pluralistic and pragmatic ethical project that is both limited and continuously evolving through degrees of imperfection. It therefore calls for a humble and specific approach, restricted within measured limits, rather than any total change modeled on the "true" meaning of "being," or any other absolute religious or philosophical projection inspired by the existential crisis of traditional "roots." Such total and abstract critiques in fact prove disastrous in practice and invariably usher in tragedy in place of whatever hazy and romanticized ideal or utopia they might have promised at the outset. The tragic unfolding of political events around modern totalizing discourses of "authenticity," in both their German national manifestation and their Islamic incarnation, have provided unforgettable testimony to this fact.

Therefore, any politics based on authenticity, we will contend, is both totalizing and intolerant and excludes the possibility of democratic social organization in the name of "higher" collective meaning. A politics of authenticity is elitist in practice, in spite of its populist rhetoric and the mesmerizing depth of attraction it frequently holds for intellectuals of many stripes. On the other hand, a democratic modernity is able to include the quest for meaning as well as religious and philosophical ideas into its larger project.

5

Democracy and Religion in the Thought of John Dewey[1]

The logic and nature of modernity as a subject of historical, sociological, and philosophical study has been submitted to multiple fundamental controversies following the World Wars and decolonization, and these debates persist into our current moment of post–Cold War "globalization." At stake in these debates is an epistemological dilemma with scientific and political resonance: the fact that in post-traditional societies there can be no single set of truths for understanding the world. There is often an unsettling religious edge to these controversies. In the previous chapter, we saw how the influential thinker Martin Heidegger interpreted the break from traditional forms of authority as a general decline, and so invested history with a Messianic hope celebrating a unity of will and condemning democratic secularism as an instance of nihilism.

Among the numerous theories that have attempted to either defend or dismantle the hegemonic discourses of Western modernity, the philosophy of American Pragmatism as articulated by Charles Pierce, William James, and, particularly, John Dewey has been considerably and unfortunately underestimated in the importance of its contribution to these debates occurring at the center of contemporary social transformations at an international level. Unlike Heidegger, Dewey was enthusiastic about the potential significance of declining traditional authority for cultures and social norms. Interpreting the situation as an opening for new and more creative ways of imagining social life, Dewey envisioned modernity as a road to more ethical and democratic forms of community. In this way he affirmed the democratic heritage of Enlightenment. He also embraced the achievements of modern science, while being critical of a dominant metaphysical narrative of science that, since the Enlightenment,

manifested itself in movements proclaiming a new universal truth – such
as Positivism and Rationalism. He described the thought of Auguste
Comte as the "division into a superior true realm of being and a lower
illusory, insignificant or phenomenal realm."[2] This critique was in turn
grounded in Dewey's own highly original and unconventional worldview
in which traditional metaphysical and supernatural notions of ultimate
reality are rejected in favor of a centerless environment of multiple histories – a view with considerable epistemic and political consequences.
Dewey was above all a thinker of the pluralistic consequences of modernity. He thought in terms of multiple singularities in an unfinished universe, with both science and everyday life conceived in terms of a notion of
disunity. In this chapter we focus on Dewey's contribution to the debate
on the politics of secularism, particularly with regard to the question of
modernity and facets of religious life.

Dewey developed a systematic pragmatism addressing the central questions of epistemology, metaphysics, ethics, and esthetics. Within this complex philosophy, a nuanced and many-sided understanding of modernity
emerges. In his rejection of dualisms, Dewey questioned not only the dualism of mind and body but also that of fact and value, means and ends,
thought and action, organism and environment, man and nature, individual and society. To him, Western historical epistemology amounted
to a great wall separating an imaginary and completed higher value or
pure being from the ongoing and forever unfinished multiple realities
of everyday lived experience, and hence sustained a socially elitist and
antidemocratic paradigm that was closed within its own imaginary walls.
The name he most often gave it was the "antecedent," implying a total
and fixed prior reality that had only to be accessed beyond the limits
of ordinary experience – by knowledge experts. Pragmatism, he argued,
"does not insist upon antecedent phenomena but upon consequent phenomena; not upon the precedents but upon the possibilities of action."
Its "consideration of the future takes us to the conception of a universe
whose evolution is not finished."[3] He viewed the "antecedent" in terms of
the surviving legacy of European feudalism with its aristocratic sublima-
tions, or "Being," but believed that modern "social forces have driven into
bankruptcy absolutistic and static dogmas as authorities for the conduct
of life."[4] He saw in such dogmas a vain and futile attempt to deny contingency, accident, and the human place among the world's myriad natural
life forms. For Dewey, the "essentially unreligious attitude is that which
attributes human achievement and purpose to man in isolation from the
world of physical nature and his fellows." He called for "a just sense of

nature as the whole of which we are parts."[5] Thus, Dewey, championing immanence and pluralism against abstractions and absolutes, also evoked a "religious attitude" in his reconceptualization of modernity's possible future.

In seeking to open up and expand philosophical discourse, Dewey argued that "idealized matrices for moral reasoning oversimplify the richness and complexity of moral experience *as lived*."[6] Like Heidegger, he shifted his investigations from an epistemic to an existential plane of reflection. Dewey sought the resources for resolving human conflicts and problems strictly within the limits of everyday life, based on his concept of immanence or deliberative democracy. He opposed the faith in abstraction that defined not merely the Western philosophical tradition but Heidegger's attempt to break away from it. Dewey urged direct social research involving as many participants as possible, rather than the solitary philosophical hunt for the final moral bedrock permitting subsequent freedom from thought in the reign of the absolute.

The pluralistic tendency extended to his conception of knowledge. Dewey conceived knowledge as "a product of the cooperative and communicative operations of human beings living together."[7] Philosophy was for him "a critical organ" for linking and "making reciprocally intelligible voices speaking provincial tongues," or a means to dialogue.[8] Its aims were necessarily provisional. Knowledge for Dewey was social, evolving, and active, embodying the flows of distinct worlds rather than the linear march of history toward a single end: "(instead of) setting out individually to construct a foundational, perspective-independent truth, in science or morals, communal dialogue between diverse perspectives allows us to develop flexible, well-tested points of view."[9] Rejecting the Cartesian rational subjectivity as the potential master of reality, he redefined the individual: "what an individual actually *is* in his life-experience depends upon the nature and movement of associated life."[10]

Against the conventional subject-object epistemology that seeks to reduce scientific method permanently to a fixed rule, Dewey's conception of everyday life encompassed the living community in its shifting environments rather than merely the reflecting individual. For him, the beginning and end of value in human life occurs through the dynamic activity of the community. Hence the importance of reckoning with existing institutions: "The aims of philanthropists, of Florence Nightingale, of Howard, of Wilberforce, of Peabody, have not been idle dreams. They have modified institutions. Aims and ideals, do not exist simply in 'mind'; they exist in character, in personality and action."[11] Dewey therefore wrote that the "problem of the relation between social relations and institutions that are dominant at a particular time is the most intricate problem presented to social inquiry."[12] It follows that he was deeply involved in the social issues of his day, from reform of American schools to matters of national and international politics. Dewey also spent time in Japan, China, and Turkey, as well as Mexico, where he chaired the inquiry into Stalinist lies about Trotsky.

Accordingly, Dewey's philosophy was oriented around committed social action. In rejecting the subjectivist premise of modern philosophy, he argued that "an individual is self sufficient in that kind of thinking that involves no action."[13] Conversely, his concept of "Intelligence, as distinct from the older conception of reason, is inherently involved in action."[14] This action is necessarily collective and generates meaning, a state in which "cause-effect has been transformed into one of means-consequence."[15] At the reflexive level of social experience, knowledge is not the discovery of a fixed existence so much as the relative choice among alternative existences.

This entails that "what needs to be challenged is the belief that principles, rules, and the systems they comprise must constitute the tethering center of either ethical theory or practice."[16] The idea of such a fixed center is the product of an imagined dichotomy between the closed world of pure reason and the manifold of ordinary experience. Dewey's worldview "de-centers production of closed systems" based on such abstract rationality in favor of "reasoning (which is) inherently social, embodied, and historically situated."[17] Dewey considered it a mistake to create a dichotomy between science, philosophy, and the "practical and personal."[18] The element of personal participation – inevitably from multiple perspectives – is indispensable for the advance of knowledge. Hence the religious or imaginative element of identity is linked to knowledge in the hope for transformation. Dewey wrote that the "connection between imagination and the harmonizing of the self is closer than is usually thought. The idea of the whole, whether of the whole personal being or of the world, is an imaginative, not a literal, idea. The limited world of our observation and reflection becomes the Universe only through imaginative extension."[19] Traditional monotheistic religious systems and Hegelian historicism present such real imaginary entities, but make claims of being linked to absolute truth to the exclusion of other systems.

This "personal knowledge" worldview where no center prevails has significant pluralist repercussions. Dewey viewed epistemology as a preoccupation with the "nature, possibility and limits of knowledge in general" and an "attempt to reach conclusions regarding the ultimate nature of reality from the answers given to such questions." In his view, such lines of thought are tacitly totalizing, corresponding to "a center or subject which is outside the course of natural existence, and set over against it."[20] Without the epistemic concept of "foundational principles" as the single *aim* of thought, the "significant distinction is no longer between the knower and the world; it is between different ways of being in and of the movement of things."[21] It follows that the dynamics of differing historical universalisms, from Islam to Kantianism, should be valued "for the meanings and shades of meanings they have brought to light rather than for the store of ultimate truths they have ascertained."[22]

American Pragmatism may be understood in part as a far-reaching critique of the received epistemic paradigm of modernity as articulated through the historical Enlightenments of France, Great Britain, and the United States. Dewey was essentially critical of the dualist subject-object epistemic paradigm in Western philosophy and the corresponding conception of truth as a fixed "object of knowledge." Affirming immanence, he opposed the "phenomenon defined by something outside of experience, instead of being defined by its relation within experience."[23] He argued that "like knowledge itself, truth is an experienced relation of things, and it has no meaning outside of that relation."[24] From this point of view "truth" can never be identified uniquely with a single object or essence, let alone a timeless principle: it is manifold, dispersed, and changing. Dewey therefore, like Heidegger, embraced the intellectual precept of temporality: "a mind that has opened itself up to experience . . . knows its own littleness and impotencies; it knows that its wishes and acknowledgements are not final measures of the universe whether in knowledge or in conduct, and hence are, in the end, transient."[25] In opposition to "real essences, hidden forms, and occult faculties," Dewey called for the "transfer of interest from the permanent to the changing" and the "expulsion of fixed first and final causes."[26] He opposed fixed metaphysical principles to critical genealogical researches: "Philosophy foreswears inquiry after absolute origins and absolute finalities in order to explore specific values and the specific conditions which generate them."[27]

In this sense Pragmatism shares important ground with so-called poststructuralist and postmodernist critiques stemming from Continental philosophy and with origins in the discourses of Friedrich Nietzsche in the nineteenth century and Heidegger in the twentieth. Yet Pragmatism is also marked by important differences from poststructuralist discourses. Dewey rejected absolute metaphysical discourses of modern science as the single "true perspective," but he also firmly identified science and reason with the potential improvement of specific human situations. Dewey did not embrace a metaphysical ideal of Progress as the scientific remodeling of reality on the road to completed perfection, but he certainly saw the value of scientific and democratic achievements in specific local and global contexts. Finally, just as he did not hold a metaphysical belief in Progress as an inevitable purpose, neither did he indulge in the opposite narrative of a general overall historical decline. These differences have important consequences at the political level for any democratic project.

To continue the comparison: for Heidegger the chief task of philosophy was to retrieve the original experience of being, in a process of "healing" or making whole.[28] His writing aimed to recapture the force of the most elementary words of primordial being by cutting through the dead routine of words as they are used in everyday common discourse in modern society. He wrote that common sense is "deaf to the language of philosophy" and "blind to what philosophy sets before its essential vision."[29] Heidegger accordingly conceived being in the manner of a lost essence needing to be retrieved against the onslaught of a modernism committed to universal progress by way of the continuous and often brutal revolutionizing of existence. In his opposition to universal projects that aim to actualize a promised future, Heidegger sought to return focus to being rather than becoming. Asserting that being appears only within a boundary, he deplored the universalizing process that eroded boundaries of place and thereby uprooted local traditions, customs, and beliefs (i.e., temporality). This affirmation of being over becoming privileged the local over the global, the national over the international, and place over space. Hence a radical critique of modernity grounded in the legitimacy of an "authentic" essence of being became the core of Heidegger's philosophical doctrine.

Heidegger took a despairing vision of the modern age whose essence he saw in technological frenzy and this despair alternated between a deep pessimism about any possibility of change and a revolutionary fury to bring about total change. In his call for a reinstatement of a core cultural paradigm to renew a collective spiritual life, he insisted that the social world be determined in the image of the "authentic" poetic philosophy. The calling of philosophy was not therefore to function as an instrument to achieve social justice for the greatest number, as the legacy of the French Revolution would have it. Rather, in his political phase, Heidegger urged that philosophy be wedded to an authoritarian and elitist politics, hostile to everyday life, in a radical bid to restore order to the expanding chaos and nihilism of Western modernity in the name of creating higher "authentic" values.

This story testifies to the political danger of Heidegger's radically essentialist revolt against modernity, with its extreme imbalance in favor of an aesthetic of national myth opposing rationality and a traditional stasis of being set against modernization. His uncompromisingly "either/or" stance ultimately amounted to a double of all the totalizing tendencies of Western modernity that he deplored, yet with these worst aspects amplified. He contributed to the creation of one of the most totalizing modern ideological tendencies in authenticity discourse.

Dewey confronted issues similar to those of Heidegger, such as the inhumanity of grand utopian social projects or "meta-narratives" that ravage the present for the sake of a purported imaginary future, and related tensions of place versus space, local versus global, and rationality versus religion and myth. Yet he proposed a way of thinking that achieved a far greater balance and intimacy between these opposing poles that have haunted and disturbed modernity as a growing international phenomenon from its earliest days until the present. Dewey articulated something closer to a middle way between the "comprehending universal" and the "recalcitrant particular."[30] Unlike Heidegger, Dewey achieved a simultaneous appreciation for being and becoming in his worldview, by proposing a role for philosophy as critically addressing social customs and institutions by way of pragmatic values in which the means should justify the end ("Means-consequences constitute a single undivided situation"[31]) – that is, the present moment of being is not overlooked or disdained in the name of a "great future," while the calling of philosophy is nevertheless to actively contribute to the steady advance or becoming of social freedoms. Dewey considered the problem of "the distinction between the instrumental and the final adopted (to be so) far reaching that it may be said to be *the* problem of experience."[32]

That Dewey saw the centrality of this issue is shown in his recognition that the "problem of restoring integration and cooperation between man's beliefs about the world in which he lives and values and purposes that should direct his conduct is the deepest problem of modern life."[33] He wrote that "the most far reaching question of all criticism (is) the relationship between existence and value."[34] This implies, firstly, an existential understanding. Dewey argues that "experience means primarily not knowledge, but ways of doing and suffering."[35] He recognized that "Man needs the earth in order to walk, the sea to swim or sail, the air to fly (and that) of necessity he acts within a world (to which) he must in some measure adapt himself as one part of nature to other parts."[36] We do not find in Dewey the metaphysical anthropocentrism by which humanity is somehow destined, by virtue of its sheer importance, to master nature, the earth, or history.

The consequence, secondly, is an epistemic modesty. Dewey rejected the model of knowledge as coercion, that is, as absolute. He argued that knowledge is not "coerced adaptation of part to part" (the uniform line), but a "search for meaning with respect to acts to be performed" (context specific).[37] He recognized the deep entanglement of fact and value in ordinary language and life: "Common sense . . . is innocent of any rigid demarcation between knowledge on one side and belief, conduct and esthetic appreciation on the other. . . . It takes striving, purposing, inquiring, wanting, the life of 'practice,' to be as much facts of nature as are the themes of scientific discourse."[38] Scientific knowledge can help to make adequate judgments but does not "break the tie" between human and environment in the manner of an all-powerful instrument. It rather "modifies the particular interactions that come within its reach, because it is itself a modification . . . subject to the same requirement of intelligence as any other natural occurrence" (i.e., there is no final knowledge beyond criticism, including criticism).[39]

This entails, thirdly, a concept of practical knowledge as reflexivity. There is no simple dualism between knowledge and reality, and no final truth will ever overhaul existing reality in a single sweep. Dewey argued that "the realm of meanings is wider than that of true-and-false meanings." He rejected the absolutist notion that "truth has a claim to enter everywhere," and argued that "poetic" and "moral meanings . . . are matters of richness and freedom of meanings, rather than truth."[40] The attempt to destroy traditional cultural meanings in some fervor of modern scientific enthusiasm was, for Dewey, an entirely mistaken and ideological action with no scientific basis. Hierarchic social structures grounded in traditional beliefs should be dismantled because of their unjust consequences, but not because their beliefs are "untrue." Embodied practices within a culture or religion might have an important value in themselves, as "attitudes that lend deep and enduring support to the processes of living."[41] Traditions "should be evaluated not as candidates for a commensurable moral concept but as instruments for ameliorating moral life."[42]

Last, because human actors can never acquire the complete knowledge required to guide all decisions, the element of uncertainty will always entail multiple possible perspectives in an objective world of ever-changing situations. Dewey argued that "in the end what is unseen decides what happens in the seen" and "when all is said and done, the fundamentally hazardous character of the world is not seriously modified, much less eliminated."[43] He rejected an antecedent "theory of knowledge which makes it necessary to deny the validity of moral ideas" because he affirmed their creative autonomy in the face of ongoing change and uncertainty: "all moral judgments are about changes to be made."[44]

As a result of these four beliefs, Dewey anchored his hope in the power of ordinary people applying intelligence (i.e., science and common sense) within the context of everyday life. Dewey contended that in institutions of law, "subject-matters of everyday experience are *trans*formed" but not "imposed" from "on high or from any external or *a priori* source."[45] The molecular roots of power and meaning are creatively contained within the workings of the everyday world – giving the world of ordinary life an immense potential power. This conception of deliberative democracy makes any single grand conception of modernity untenable. Modernity is composed of multiple singularities in which tradition is not a static stage of past historical development but a dynamic dimension of existing social life. Dewey argued that "The choice is not between a moral authority outside custom and one within it (but) between adopting more or less intelligent and significant customs."[46] This requires "intelligence," which always occurs from within a social and cultural background involving "the particular human environment(s), on which we depend, with its language(s), traditions, and institutions."[47] This view presents a departure from the dominant tradition of liberal Enlightenment as well as any radical "anti-Enlightenment" politics of being, taking into account both the importance of liberal freedoms/institutions and the genuine existential concerns that motivate the discourse of roots.

Dewey revolted against the epistemic foundationalism of Enlightenment, but not its democratic heritage. Although his view of democracy "certainly builds on the democratic strain in the Enlightenment," his concept of "deliberative democracy" and how it "could work is not an eighteenth-century one." Putnam identifies the central difference in the core feature of the eighteenth-century Enlightenment, "the valorization of reason, which was present in different forms in Plato and the Enlightenment." He writes: "Dewey does not, in fact, like the term 'reason' very much (certainly not 'Reason' with a capital 'R'), preferring to speak of the application of *intelligence* to problems, and the change in terminology is symptomatic of a deep criticism of traditional philosophy." This is so because " 'Reason,' in the traditional sense, was, above all, a faculty by means of which human beings were supposed to be able to arrive at one or another set of immutable truths."[48] This "Reason is in a word *pure,* structured and operating independently of the practical pressures of living."[49] For Dewey, "reason has a real, though limited, function, and a creative, constructive function."[50] Because there is no "pure truth" grounded in an antecedent or higher reality, reason must have "a practical rather than an epistemological function" as an "organ of modification in traditions and institutions."[51] In this light, structure is an ongoing process and reason is a temporally variable notion in which, "(as) lived, inquiry is story-structured."[52] This transformation of the role of reason points to a necessary immanence and pluralism in its inevitably more modest functioning: "To deny this qualitative heterogeneity (in the name of conclusions about the ultimate nature of reality) is to reduce the struggles and difficulties of life, its comedies and tragedies, to illusion: the nonbeing of the Greeks or to its modern counterpart, the 'subjective'".[53] At the same time Dewey argued that ideas and beliefs have important consequences precisely because the future is not made: "in a world where the future is not a mere word, where theories, general notions, rational ideas have consequences for action, reason necessarily has a constructive function (yet with) only a secondary interest in comparison with the reality of facts."[54]

Democracy is for Dewey never a final reality, governed by antecedently fixed metaphysical principles, but both a goal and a means. It cannot be merely identified with a mechanical system. Its creation does not involve identifying "antecedent" ultimate foundations (cultural, political), but the temporal setting in motion of a democratic organizing principle. There is no "purpose ruling social events" or "predetermined goal," but a specific "problematic situation" presenting "*alternative* possible ends."[55] The road to democracy involves inquiry into "the *efficacy* of different conceptions of *procedure*" (means), not "the question of an alleged intrinsic truth or falsity." The "plurality of alternatives is the effective means of rendering inquiry more extensive (sufficient) and more flexible."[56] Dewey envisions the multiplication rather than the reduction of possible perspectives, in viewing democracy as an ongoing means-end social process having no concern with claims to final truth.

In the rapid continuity of evolutionary or generational change that characterizes modernity, the best thoughts and actions of the entire community are required in order to perpetually reconstruct equilibrium. The community itself sets the conditions for this recovery within a variety of democratic institutional frameworks. Dewey's worldview privileges democracy as a process of inclusion and participation over any other theoretical or philosophical principle, including ontology or epistemology. This is why we do not find in Dewey a case for an epistemological revolution, a notion that in practice has often meant the violent imposition from above by the developing state of a perverse vision of "Westernization" in defiance of the general population (as in Ataturk's Turkey or Mohammed Reza Shah's Iran).

Dewey saw the significance of West-centric barriers within the modern tradition of Enlightenment. The democratic vision of radical immanence at the core of his philosophy offers a conceptual openness to modernity that paves the way to the possibility of what Mohammed Arkoun has described as "integrating into the same critical and cognitive movement, the trajectories of reason historically linked to non-"Western" contexts for the production of meaning."⁵⁷ Dewey envisioned a road beyond these West-centric barriers. He wrote that "it shows a deplorable deadness of imagination to suppose that philosophy will indefinitely revolve within the scope of the problems and systems that two thousand years of European philosophy have bequeathed to us" and that, accordingly, "the whole of Western European history is a provincial episode."⁵⁸

Today, the heart and soul of modernity is being defined in the social and political struggles of the so-called Third World, where variants of modernist and poststructuralist discourse have interacted powerfully with local situations. An especially striking and historically paradigmatic example would be Heidegger's considerable influence on the Iranian Revolution of 1979. The appeal of Heidegger played on the static dualist conceptions of tradition/modernity that prevailed throughout the early twentieth-century Iranian developmental experience. The end result was the imagined antithesis of democracy and tradition. There are also traces of a Heideggerian dualist worldview in the otherwise complex writings of Indian scholars Partha Chatterjee and Ashis Nandy, both highly influential in India and abroad since the post-Nehruvian consensus, in the central claim that the secular democratic nation-state is "derivative" and the National Movement that brought it into being based on inauthentic precepts. The Enlightenment, "Western" science, and modernity are held to be inauthentic, whereas true anticolonialism lies in rejecting the Western thematic (ways of thinking). Meanwhile, the site of lost Indian authenticity is held to be located in "community."⁵⁹ As an alternative framework, Dewey Pragmatism presents an important and far more nuanced potential contribution to contemporary debates on modernity as a secular and democratic project, with particular focus on his theories of a distinction between "religion" and the "religious." Dewey believed in the democratic possibilities of traditional culture and religion and argued for "restoring to the common man that which in the name of religion, of philosophy, of art and morality, has been embezzled from the common store and appropriated to sectarian and class use."[60]

Among the most striking examples of Dewey's influence in the twentieth-century politics of Third World nation making was his formative influence on the Dalit (untouchable) movement in pre- and particularly post-Independence India under the leadership of Bhrimrao Ramji Ambedkar (1891–1956). This radical grassroots democratic movement shows many of the aspects of Dewey's philosophy as detailed previously. Ambedkar was born into a poor Dalit family in Maharashtra and spent much of his life struggling against the injustices of the traditional Hindu caste system. He spent three years in the United States as a graduate student at Columbia University, where he was deeply influenced by Dewey's courses as well as by the Social Gospel Movement in liberal Protestant circles. Ambedkar's wife later remarked that her husband "happily imitated John Dewey's distinctive class room mannerism – thirty years after he sat in his classes."[61]

On his return to India, Ambedkar undertook a series of struggles on behalf of the Dalit community using civil disobedience tactics. He was active in the Indian national independence movement and was a chief architect of the post-independence Indian Constitution of 1949. In drafting the Constitution, Ambedkar combined Indian and Western political influences. His contribution was based on a study of *Sangha* practice among early Indian Buddhist communities, which had incorporated voting by ballot and rules of debate in their political process. At the same time, Ambedkar integrated Western-inspired civil liberties including freedom of religion, equal rights for women, affirmative action for disadvantaged castes, and the outlawing of discrimination. We thus see openness in Ambedkar's attitude to political practice in his willingness to draw from domestic Indian as well as Western intellectual traditions in the construction of an Indian modernity that expanded and enriched the global political tradition of secular democratic Enlightenment.

In the 1950s, Ambedkar, along with half a million followers, converted to Buddhism based on a hybridization of Dewey's concept of scientific temper and the teachings of the Buddha in a challenge to the traditional Hindu metaphysics of caste. In articulating this hybrid philosophy, he used Deweyan concepts such as fallibility, claiming "to treat all ideas as working hypotheses to be tested by the consequences they produce." Ambedkar also drew on the Deweyan concept of "intelligence," writing that "the path of all passion and all virtue . . . must be subject to the test of *prajna* or intelligence." As early as the 1930s, Ambedkar had framed the argument of one of his more influential books around the Deweyan call to "forego the quest for certainty, absolute knowledge or the ultimate Truth of Being." He employed the Deweyan concept of "criticism of criticism," writing that "everything must be open to re-examination and reconsideration, whenever grounds for re-examination and reconsideration arise." Finally, he also rearticulated the Deweyan concept of distinguishing the "religious" from "religion," arguing for a "religion of principles" against a "religion of rules." In conceiving his ideas, he also linked his discourse to existing heterodox, anti-Vedic, and materialist sects that had long existed on the margins of Hinduism.[62] All of these lines of thought reflect a Deweyan conception of democratic modernity: the critical reconstruction of inherited cultural values and social ethics that draws from and transforms existing traditions along democratic lines without seeking rupture or finality, which draws from multiple sources with a unified concept of means-ends tending to nonviolent democratic values and seeks the critical integration of scientific understanding with existing cultural patterns.

This Deweyan practice presents an alternative to the French Revolutionary paradigm in which a violent moment of absolute rupture severs the traditional past from the present in the birth of modernity, with the totalizing claims to a new knowledge this moment involves. It was the French Revolutionary model that mainly inspired Ataturk's authoritarian modernization program, and he in turn provided the inspiration for the Shah of Iran. Both envisioned modernity as a closed and completed project to be imposed from above on a culturally backward population, creating the predictable religious backlash that found such valuable conceptual resources in Heidegger's worldview. Dewey's work expresses a vision of modernity that is open ended and cannot be reduced to either a "materialistically" conceived "science" or to a social ontology of "roots and authenticity." His vision of modernity presents a new conception of democratic practice and struggle that transcends many of the basic tenets of conventional liberal Enlightenment, yet without falling into the dangerous pit of attacking liberal institutions as such. In Dewey's thought, we find an appeal for a more radical notion of a democratic life, through his focus on the social nature of knowledge and imagination, the importance of a connection to community and history, and in the radical critique of "foundationalism" that he ventures in the name of what Putnam has called "conceptual pluralism."

Conceptual pluralism is a critique of totalizing historic epistemology, or the tacitly antidemocratic strain of the eighteenth-century Enlightenment that placed the ideal of a single perfected knowledge above the autonomy of multiple ordinary human beings in everyday life. Dewey opposed this to a temporality anchored in everyday experience. His principle and interconnected concepts of "imagination" and "intelligence" constitute his idea of temporality. It is within the framework of temporality that Dewey analyzes the relationship between existence and value. "Intelligence" involves learning how to learn in the most effective manner possible. "Imagination" indicates the permanently open future and the role of the surplus of meaning beyond the strict limits of what is verifiably true and false in coping with its challenges. This includes the cultural and religious elements of meaning in human experience that form part of common sense. Growth is the productive interaction of intelligence and imagination. This is the base of conceptual pluralism. Seeing potential promise in the imaginative elements rather than an obstacle to modernity, Dewey defined the goal of reformist theory and practice in terms of "the liberation and expansion of the meanings of which experience is capable."[63] This is far from the Marquis de Condorcet's vision of Enlightenment as the "absolute perfection of the human race" through the "light of reason," freedom from "prejudice," and release "from the empire of fate," with its implication of a pure universal consciousness in a new world.[64]

The first difference in Dewey's view from the French Enlightenment-Revolutionary one is his proposing singularities in place of epistemic universals. This has far-reaching significance because it envisions reality without a fixed center. In the absence of the conventional metaphysical plateau, there is only the environment, or with globalization the multiple environments, which in the absence of a center is inherently pluralistic and operates around multiple experiences of adjustment. Dewey writes that "adjustment is no timeless state; it is a continuing process."[65] Such temporality has pluralistic implications. In a "non-recurring temporal sequence, life is no uniform uninterrupted march or flow. It is a thing of histories, each with its own plot, its own inception and movement toward its close, each having its own particular rhythmic movement; each with its own unrepeated quality pervading it throughout."[66] This is opposed to the all-unifying dialectic, which conceives the world as unfolding around a hidden inner design with a center in consciousness: "(Dialectics) argue as if self-control, self-development, went on directly as a sort of unrolling push from within. But life endures only in virtue of the support of the environment."[67] An essential plan already fixed for the future by dialectic is a form of the "antecedent" to which Dewey was opposed. He writes: "What is going on in the environment is the concern of the organism; not what is already 'there' in accomplished and finished form."[68]

Second, Dewey rejects the totalizing moment that has characterized important discourses of modernity. For Pragmatism there is no "end of history." Philosophy "has no call to create a world of 'reality' *de novo*."[69] It does not assert that

intelligence will ever dominate the course of events.... The issue is one of choice, and choice is always a question of alternatives. Because faith in a . . . final triumph is fantastic, the future remains a horizon of multiple potential openings of which the majority will necessarily remain forever undisclosed, and the others experienced relative to the intersection in existence of hazard and rule, of contingency and order . . . where life is itself a sequence of trials.[70]

There is never any such thing as a total and complete break with the past.[71] Although Dewey opposed attempts to "escape from time by recourse to traditional interests," he nevertheless insisted that "The future as well as the past can be a source of interest and consolation and give meaning to the present."[72] Dewey finds a middle way between modernity's radical promise of emancipation and the rich resources of traditional cultural and religious meanings.

The consequence of the first two differences is the rejection of the transcendental object linked to a unique truth as the basis for objectivity. Dewey spoke of "social phenomena" as "inherently historical" and "of the nature of individual temporal sequences" or singularities.[73] This entails an alternative concept of objectivity that reckons with "how it is that moral and scientific 'knowledge' can both hold of one and the same world."[74] Dewey noted that within the strict limits defining the intellectual reign of the dominant Enlightenment epistemic paradigm, "beliefs about value are . . . in the position in which beliefs about nature were before the scientific revolution" – lost in skepticism or appealing to imagined eternities.[75] He proposed a broader and pluralized concept of objectivity in an alternative to the fact-value dichotomy underlying the Enlightenment epistemic paradigm. Arguing that "scientific judgments . . . assimilated to moral (ones) is closer to common sense than . . . validity (being) denied to moral judgments because they do not square with a preconceived theory of nature," he rejected the ideal of a new universal knowledge superseding the "unfounded" world of "unscientific" belief.[76]

Putnam has explained Dewey's position in terms of the recognition that "the whole idea that the world dictates a unique 'true' way of dividing the world into objects, situations, properties, etc, is a piece of philosophical parochialism." He contests the claim "that each and every instance of objectivity must be supported by objects."[77] This is to say that objectivity need not necessarily have a fixed and finished character, nor need it correspond reductively in identity to one single thing. It is not an "Absolute Reality, fixed and complete in itself, of which our 'mental states' are bare transitory hints."[78] This traditional epistemic posture amounts to the great wall between Absolute and fleeting, or nature and experience, in producing "duplicate versions of reality, one absolute and static (and) the other phenomenal and kept continually on the jump because otherwise its own inherent nothingness would lead to its total annihilation."[79] Dewey's conceptual pluralism expands the accepted understanding of objectivity by positing the possibility of objectivity without the object. Putnam writes that "one metaphysical reason that has led many philosophers to deny the objectivity of value judgement (is that) it doesn't fit the picture of 'description of natural facts.'" Yet "certain crucial ethical statements are not descriptions." Neither valuations nor logical statements can be said to describe any object. The fact remains that ethical statements are "forms of reflection that are as fully governed by norms of truth and validity as any form of cognitive activity."[80] Beyond the limits of historic epistemology centered around the "transcendent object," objective criteria exist within the community in the Deweyan sense without the need for an imagined absolute to match the conventional paradigm of, for example, theoretical physics.

Finally, the Deweyan worldview differs in preserving a space for multiple and variable meanings. This view of the objective expanded beyond historic epistemology brings to light a second important point. As there is no single substratum for absolute truth, we may recognize how "in certain cases what exists may depend on which of various conventions we may adopt." With no absolute point of reference to establish meaning, "the *meaning* of a word is how it is used." A word "does not have a single absolutely precise use but a whole family of uses." Putnam therefore argues that "the question as to which of these ways of using 'exist' ('individual,' 'object') is *right* is one that the meanings of the words in the natural language, that is, the language that we all speak and cannot avoid speaking every day, simply leaves open." This renders any absolute distinction between fact and convention something of a dead issue: "any piece of our empirical knowledge is conventional relative to certain alternatives and factual relative to certain others." Therefore, "one thing is at once either/or in relation to other things" and this is "not in fact contradictory, if we understand each of them as belonging to a different optional language, and recognize that the two optional languages involve the choices of incompatible conventions." Moreover, "certain identity statements are left open by their meanings (ie: the uses) of the words in ordinary language, and there are equally good choices as to how openness can be closed." Thus, significantly, "that we can use both of these schemes without being required to reduce one or both of them to some single fundamental and universal ontology is the doctrine of pluralism." The doctrine of pluralism therefore expresses the remarkable flexibility and openness to multiple possibilities in everyday language and experience – which is to say, not hindered by the dogmatic and narrow essentialisms of the historic epistemological tradition. This ontological tradition must "assume that there is, somehow fixed in advance, a single 'real,' a single 'literal' sense to 'exist' (or) 'identity' – one which is cast in marble, and cannot be either contracted or expanded without defiling the statue of the god."[81]

Dewey considers this fixation on the "object" a form of negatively constraining dogma in the Western tradition in the form of the "antecedent" or "aprioristic," pure reality as a changeless and finished form. (The object of fixation can equally be when, as with Bergson or Hegel, "flux is made something to revere."[82] In either case the result is "to mythologize reality."[83]) Dewey writes that "there (need be) no assertion about *the* real object or *the* real world or *the* reality," and ultimately "an uncorrupted realism would accept such things (as error, dreams, hallucinations) as real events, and find in them no other problems than those attending the consideration of any real occurrence – namely, the problems of structure, origin, and operation." He contended that "no theory of Reality in general" is "possible or needed."[84]

This concept is significantly different from the Enlightenment notion of experience divided between the facts of scientific knowledge and the illusions of mere inherited belief. Dewey argues for a cognitive structure – grounded in surplus meaning – of considerably wider range: "experience is cognitive in a wider sense than known objects."[85] Also, "there are multiple ways of experiencing the world which do not necessarily translate into the specific conceptual apparatus that accompanies knowing about something."[86] Such expanded objectivity is made evident in that "aesthetic and moral experience reveals traits of real things as truly as does intellectual experience."[87] In short, the dominant concept of objectivity reductively conceives reality in terms of one thing, as if it were "all of the same kind."[88] Dewey argues that "knowledge that is ubiquitous, all-inclusive and monopolizing ceases to have meaning in losing all contexts."[89] We are forced to envision a single metaphysical plateau, completed as if existing in some invisible past, which transcends every community and nullifies every particularism on behalf of its absolute claim to truth. Putnam calls this cognitive posture "inflationary metaphysics" and points out the many different forms it can insidiously take, including "metaphysical explanations of the whole course of history" in Hegel's Philosophy of History, a dialectical "transcendental object."[90]

Dewey mounted his revolt against totalizing historic epistemology on the grounds that it is hostile to everyday experience: "The most serious indictment against non-empirical philosophies is that they have cast doubt over the things of ordinary experience."[91] The epistemological framework centering the known object inherently views everyday life as a "second grade conceptual system."[92] The framework is highly inflexible in that it seeks a "meaning fixed apart from use," in positing the legitimacy of the "real object" as grounded beyond the temporal and spatial flux of ordinary experience and activity.[93] Such a view, to explain ethics, must insist upon "postulating something 'non-natural,' something mysterious and sublime standing invisibly behind the goodness of persons, actions, situations, etc."[94] Moral ideas are "attributed to a world other than common reason and science."[95]

The concepts of "intelligence" and "imagination" apply directly to Dewey's ideas on the distinction between "religion" and the "religious" in *A Common Faith*. The concepts of "imagination" and "intelligence" can be fruitfully understood in opposition to *transcendent* and *foundational principles*. For Dewey, the "religious" represents the human experience, individually *as well as* collectively, which includes religious traditions and their connections to cultures and civilizations. Conversely, "religion" signifies the institutional representation of a single doctrine or dogma and its often hierarchic structure grounded in ontological claims. Accordingly, the "religious" can play an important role in a democratic public sphere (in terms of values and ideals), whereas "religion" must properly belong to the private sphere and should not encroach on the public one. In this way Dewey remains within the secular tradition without proclaiming the negation of religious values and meaning.

The condition for public participation by the religious for Dewey is a pragmatic function rather than an essentialist claim, forming part of the surplus meaning whereby "all reasoning is fundamentally imaginative."[96] The religious constitutes part of the creative element in situational inquiry where "facts are usually observed with reference to some practical end and purpose, and that end is presented only imaginatively."[97] The religious, finally, tends toward practice, opposing "beliefs as intellectual abstractions to beliefs as tendencies to act."[98] Conceptual pluralism is accordingly grounded in an existential rather than epistemic mode of analysis. Dewey's logic is a theory of inquiry, an account of how thought functions not in a purely abstract or formal mode but in the inquiries of successful science and in the problem-solving of ordinary everyday life. For Dewey, "common experience is capable of developing from within itself methods which will secure direction for itself and will create inherent standards of judgement and value."[99] Further, "real ethical questions are a species of practical question, and practical questions don't only involve valuings, they involve a complex mixture of philosophical beliefs, religious beliefs, and factual beliefs as well."[100]

It is through the concepts of "habit" and "growth" that Dewey grounds his doctrines of the religious and deliberative democracy. Rather than entangling his ideas in a complex relation to some imagined inhuman "ultimate reality" or "truth," Dewey grounds his intellectual and political ideas in an imminent conception of everyday life through a conception of "habit." For Dewey, the interplay of "imagination" and "intelligence" is provoked by a hitch in the workings of "habit." Habit includes the elements of surplus meaning that Dewey identifies with religious or cultural tradition, bodily practice, the wider expanse of the unconscious. The questions we are moved by experience to answer with a sense of urgency are necessarily situated and specific. Reflective thought is occasioned by "situations that are disturbed, troubled, ambiguous."[101]

There is therefore no simple and absolute opposition between "intelligence" and "habit" in which "reason" must vanquish unthinking "tradition," as the more extreme metaphysical tendencies in the Enlightenment quite influentially suggested. Dewey rejected any such a dichotomy and believed that the force of habit "is the stronger and deeper part of human nature than is desire for change." Further, he believed that "in most cases people respond to situations without much thought, and sometimes this may even be for the best."[102] This concept of "habit" was broadly conceived to include "not only private behavioral patterns but also heritable interpretive structures such as symbol systems, stories, beliefs, myths, metaphors, virtues, gestures, prejudices and the like."[103] Through "habits," he believed, "potential meanings are revealed and in greater proportion concealed."[104] Accordingly, meaning is collective rather than individual or "subject" centered, linked ultimately to unconscious emotions and perceptions and the natural world beyond the limits of consciousness.

The "religious" in this context is ultimately the imaginative power to envision possibilities on the collective terrain of everyday life and to act on them through social "intelligence." Dewey argued that "imagination may play upon life (as in poetry) or may enter profoundly into it (as in religious discourse)."[105] The difference between the two is in intimate relation with Dewey's conception of the "religious" as a possible mode of engaging the "imagination" to the fullest possible extent – a possibility he believes is cut short by both received supernatural and metaphysical conceptions. This "imagination" functions according to an immanent reason by calling into play "reflective thought" as "distinguished from general stream of consciousness, random chains of so-called thoughts, and prejudicial beliefs." In line with this, Dewey conceived the union of the religious and the imaginative in terms of "faith as the unification of the self through allegiance to inclusive ideal ends, which imagination presents to us and to which the human will responds as worthy of controlling our desires and choices,"[106]

As such, the religious is in itself neither inherently conservative nor revolutionary, but a way of seeing both the radical and conservative potential in all human culture. Both Ambedkar and Gandhi, in spite of their differences, employed it for radical political ends, whereas the entrenched Brahmin establishment used it coupled with religion in an attempt to hold on to power. The religious therefore means multiplicity, not historic blocks. It is rather the joining dynamism common to all cultures that Dewey calls the "religious," made especially visible in the modern period. Although nothing entirely eludes tradition, "culture lends itself as much to intelligent conservation and critical redirection as to transmission."[107] He was therefore able to oppose "socialized acts automated by rote habit on the one hand and acts of reflective morality mediated by intelligence on the other."[108] We are not in a position to either inherit or retrieve any "pure" or "absolute" form of tradition, nor are we in a position to radically reconfigure everything as it now exists into "new" form according to a blueprint of "pure reason."

Ultimately, at the core of Dewey's thought on the "imagination" is an affirmation of the principle of growth over final achievement. Growth is the counterpart to habit in Dewey's conception of deliberative democracy. The principle of growth is at the heart of Dewey's Pragmatism, in his aversion to both metaphysical and supernatural modes of thought. He deplores the "incubus of thinking of ideals as fixed, without power of growth." Just as such "fixed ideals" must exist beyond time and therefore the lived reality of our experience in some "ideal" realm, so they foster "absolutes" that demand a total and uncompromising change that can only prove destructive. Those who profess such absolute values "want something more than growth accompanied by toil and pain" and demand "final achievement." Yet for Dewey, those "who are less absolutist may be content to think that, morally speaking, growth is a higher value and ideal than is sheer attainment."[109] The capacity for growth in everyday life is Dewey's temporalized alternative to the violent moment of supreme rupture embodied in the French Revolutionary paradigm with its "end of history." It is this Deweyan alternative that we see in the extended and mass-based nonviolent struggles of Ambedkar's Dalit movement and the Chinese May 4th Movement under Dewey's direct intellectual influence, and by possible coincidence in the outlook and practice of Mahatma Gandhi, who also espoused an ideal of the "religious" over "religion" in his leadership of the Indian National Movement.

Dewey expresses the spirit of such social movements in a way that transcends the dichotomy of modernity and tradition:

Ours is the responsibility of conserving, transmitting, rectifying and expanding the heritage of values we have received that those who come after us may receive it more solid and secure, more widely accessible and more generously shared than we have received it. Here are all the elements for a religious faith that shall not be confined to sect, class, or race. Such a faith has always been implicitly the common faith of mankind. It remains to make it explicit and militant.[110]

In this relationship of transmission and accessibility, Dewey's conceptions of the religious and the democratic are united in a vision of progress not as teleologically inevitable but as the fruit of sustained awareness and continuous struggle within the limits of ordinary people's capacity. In order to achieve this ideal, it is necessary at the outset, Dewey argues, to liberate religious experience from religious dogma. We might compare this to the dogma of a national culture, equally inward looking in terms of a negatively imagined outside and inner ontological legitimacy.

This idea of the liberation of religious experience in Dewey is developed on several levels: a criticism of the "supernatural" in religion – which obstructs the "religious" – is at the same time linked to a criticism of the metaphysical or ontological basis of traditional Western thought. Like the supernatural, the ontological directs our thoughts away from the imminent realities of our lived environment and toward supposedly "hidden realities."

Dewey's criticism of both the "supernatural" in religion and the "ontological" in philosophy are components of a radical democratic project to expand the sphere of inclusion and participation in the political and social process beyond the closed confines of institutional orders that exclude sections of the population along political or economic lines. Consistent with his overall critique of historic epistemology and the supernatural, Dewey identifies the religious not with "ultimate reality" but with the fabric of everyday experience and events within the temporal flow of ordinary life as various "attitudes that may be taken toward every object and every proposed ideal or end."[111]

The religious represents for Dewey something closer to possible imaginative engagements than a doctrine of truth. He notes that people of all religious persuasions have undergone life-transforming experiences and subsequently attributed this improvement to the truth of their own religion. For him this illustrates "the use of (the religious) quality to carry a superimposed load of a particular religion." Yet, Dewey argues, "the only thing can be said to be 'proved' is the existence of some complex of conditions that have operated to effect an adjustment in life, an orientation, that brings with it a sense of security and peace." Dewey therefore concludes that the "actual religious quality in the experience described is the *effect* produced, the better adjustment in life and its conditions, not the manner and cause of its production.... It takes place in different persons in a multitude of ways."[112] This transfer for Dewey entails a radical process of opening up the human imagination within the space of our global modernity, with implications on social, cultural, and political fronts.

If this [the religious] function were rescued through emancipation from dependence on the upon specific types of beliefs and practices, from those elements that constitute a religion, many individuals would find that experiences having the force of bringing about a better, deeper and enduring adjustment in life are not so rare and infrequent as they are commonly supposed to be. They occur frequently in many significant moments of living.[113]

These insights are comparable to what Algerian philosopher Mohammed Arkoun has called "emergent reason," a world of discourse that "cannot ignore the abundant achievements of modernity (yet) neither can it disqualify *a priori* all the legacies of the living cultural traditions still linked to religious inspiration." He writes that "Emerging Reason operates, creates, and innovates in the new contexts of intercultural dialectic which opens up more possibilities for intercreativity at all levels, in all fields, all expectations, all possible politics of hope, all debates on human existence." Consequently, such pluralistic reasoning "does not necessarily emerge as an expanding evolutionary linear process of modern reasoning."[114]

Dewey writes that the core issue of *Common Faith* is the "identification of the religious with the supernatural" and the "ground for and consequences of this identification." His aim in raising this question is to "develop another conception of the nature of the religious phase of experience (which) separates it from the supernatural" for "what is genuinely religious will undergo emancipation when it is relieved from (it)."[115] Dewey therefore consciously places himself neither in the camp of those defending traditional religions nor in the so-called materialist camp of those declaring that traditional religions are entirely false, obsolete, and having nothing of value to offer in contemporary life. Dewey self-consciously opposes both camps and indeed identifies them with each other. He writes:

Aggressive atheism seems to me to have something in common with traditional supernaturalism.... What I have in mind especially is the exclusive preoccupation of both militant atheism and supernaturalism with man in isolation. (Supernaturalism) conceives of this earth as the moral center of the universe and of man as the as the apex of the whole scheme of things... (while for militant atheism the) attitude taken is often that of man living in an indifferent and hostile world and issuing blasts of defiance.[116]

The attitudes of "religion" and militant atheism that focus on man in isolation are contrasted by Dewey with what he calls a "religious attitude," which "needs the sense of connection of man, in the way of both dependence and support, with the enveloping world that the imagination feels is a universe."[117]

In *A Common Faith*, Dewey is clearly raising the problem of the existence of traditional religions within the context of modernity, where a diversity of human beings united through time and space in a dynamism, unprecedented in both its creative and destructive potential, experience a spatial and temporal relativization of their respective traditions and a confrontation with a void in meaning as well as social isolation. Dewey writes that an observer "will note that the "unseen powers" referred to (in the various religions) have been conceived in a multitude of incompatible ways" and that eliminating "the differences, nothing is left beyond the bare reference to something unseen and powerful." Dewey accordingly points out "that there is no such thing as religion in the singular," but "only a multitude of religions" which has unity only as a "miscellaneous aggregate."[118] This multicultural openness with a basis in scientific modernity nullifies the independent claim to ultimate truth of each religion on its own terms.

Yet for Dewey this crisis is only a now open confrontation with what has always been the historically evolving relativity of world religions, which previously occurred comparatively unnoticed. The problem is not, therefore, of nihilism, but of adapting the religious experience to the dynamic social and historical conditions of the present. He writes: "I gladly admit that historic religions have been relative to the conditions of social culture in which peoples lived. Indeed, what I am concerned with is to press home the logic of this method of disposal of outgrown traits of past religions." It is based on this principle of growth that Dewey conceives the distinction between the "religious" and "religion." He writes: "If so much flexibility has obtained in the past regarding an unseen power, the way it affects human destiny, and the attitudes we are to take toward it, why should it be assumed that change in conception and action has now come to an end?" This realization "compels us to ask what conception of unseen powers and our relations to them would be consonant with the best achievements and aspirations of the present."[119]

This notion of an open cognitive horizon is similar to Arkoun's insight that monotheistic "theological systems fulfill the same ideological function as the Berlin Wall (and) the walls remain solid between the communities because we have not yet developed the relevant cognitive strategies that could be used to demolish the walls and explore the real anthropological, cultural, philosophical space in a cross-cultural interpretation."[120] Arkoun's project represents an advance for the religious as a shared human experience of creativity and value formation and a departure from the limits of religion as a fixed body of dogma and closed institutional constraint.

For Dewey, the crucial point of distinction between a religion and the religious is that "a religion (and as I have just said there is no such thing as religion in general) always signifies a special body of beliefs and practices having some kind of institutional organization, loose or tight. In contrast, the adjective 'religious' denotes nothing in the way of a specifiable entity, either institutional or as a system of beliefs." Religion represents, for Dewey, a closed institutional doctrine, and the religious represents historical human imagination that connects all cultures and different forms of imagination to one another. Accordingly, Dewey calls for a transfer from the closed and insular stance of traditional religions to the open and expanding conception of the religious. In this transfer, the "idea of invisible powers would take on the meaning of all the conditions of nature and human association that support and deepen the sense of values which carry one through periods of darkness and despair to such an extent that they lose their usual depressive character."[121]

We noted before that there are two modes to the "imagination," that which supervenes and that which intervenes in life to completely interpenetrate all the elements of our being. Imagination may therefore merely "play upon life or it may enter profoundly into it." The two different possibilities accord with the relation of the imagination to the supernatural or the metaphysical. In illustrating this link, Dewey brings the received conventions of truth in Western philosophy seriously into question through a radical critique of ontology and epistemology. The changing of the physical into the metaphysical results in the limiting and weakening of the powers of the "imagination," to make the "imagination" merely supervene rather than intervene:

when conditions are adverse the to realization of our desire – and in cases of significant ideals they are extremely adverse – it is an easy way out to assume that after all they are already embedded in the ultimate structure of what is, and that appearances to the contrary are *merely* appearances. Imagination then merely supervenes and is freed from the responsibility for intervening.[122]

The truth status of religion is conceived in terms of an intellectual object that exists beyond the limits of ordinary perception in an idealized and transcendent higher reality, or the "supernatural." The grounding of the truth of faith as an invisible intellectual object, or the "supernatural," necessarily results in the development of systemic theological propositions to which belief is attached and assent given. There is, then, a very direct link between the supernatural and religious dogma, just as the concept of Platonic forms produces the legacy of metaphysics in Western thought. Finally, these worldviews all share the core idea of the "transcendent object" as a basis for truth.

This view of the truth of faith necessarily implies one total and all-inclusive basis for truth as such, and here Dewey takes issue and proposes what is rather a varied and pluralized conception of objectivity without a totalizing center. The issue of ethics, for Dewey, is not to be comprehended in terms of an intellectual object as the religious and philosophical traditions would have it. Dewey recognizes the existential value of religious experience in lived life as a constraining cultural framework providing ethical guidance, imaginative resources for interpretation, and inner peace. Yet he argues that "the authority of an ideal over choice and conduct is the authority of an ideal, not a fact, of a truth guaranteed in intellect." It follows that "there is a difference between belief that is a conviction that some end should be supreme over conduct, and belief that some object or being exists as a truth for the intellect."[123] According to Deweyan conceptual pluralism, both are different aspects of objectivity, and neither need be collapsed into the other. It follows that "if men had associated their ideas about values with practical activities instead of with cognition of antecedent Being, they would *not* have been troubled by the findings of science."[124]

Dewey envisioned the "religious" as something inherently expanding and open, without fixed or irreducible content. He argued that "faith in the continued disclosing of truth through directed cooperative human endeavour is more religious in quality than is any faith in a completed revelation." The closed doctrinal character of organized religion would therefore necessarily produce a barrier to the realization of this ideal. Dewey wrote that: "Some fixed doctrinal apparatus is necessary for *a* religion. But faith in the possibilities of continued and rigorous inquiry does not limit access to truth to any channel or scheme of things. It does not first say that truth is universal and then add that there is but one road to it."[125]

It follows that the "doctrinal method is... limited and private" while the "method of intelligence is open and public," linking religion to the religious within a broad secular context.[126] It is based in the "imagination," of which Dewey says that "the only meaning which can be assigned... is that things unrealized in fact have the power to stir us."[127] The imagination is the "converting (of) physical and brute relationships into connections of meanings characteristic of the possibilities of nature." It is when "appetite is perceived in its meanings, in the consequences it induces, and these consequences are experimented with in reflective imagination, some being seen to be consistent with one another, and hence capable of co-existence and of serially ordered achievement... when this estate is attained, we live on the human plane, responding to things in their meanings."[128] Dewey's hope lay in such an imagination beyond the exclusionary restraints of both the metaphysical and the supernatural, and yet within the existing horizon of human cultures in their historic diversity as expressed through the ongoing experience of lived life directed to democratic social ends.

Dewey's view of modern society therefore was concerned with its pluralistic and communicative potential, which is to say its degree of inclusiveness and the possibilities of intelligent direction in its immanent dynamism. In the context of globalization, there are severe challenges to be reckoned with. Dewey conceived democracy as inextricably political and social, because "only in a democracy does everyone have a chance to make his or her contribution to the discussion" while "huge inequalities in wealth and power... effectively block the interests and complaints of the most oppressed from serious consideration."[129]

Dewey produced a framework of philosophical immanence rather than transcendence. Putnam writes that the difference between Dewey and "not just the Enlightenment, but the whole conception of ethics or moral philosophy that dominated and still dominates the thinking of the great majority of philosophers down to the present day" involves his refusal to attribute a frozen or transcendental "objectivity" to the "familiar ethical concepts *right, wrong, just, unjust, good, bad, right, duty, obligation,* and the rest."[130] For Dewey, the world has no hidden or intrinsic essence to be represented of an ethical, epistemological, or other nature. This view is opposed to the dichotomies and extremes that metaphysical and supernatural visions of reality tend to produce, with complete transmutations and regenerations expected to come about by way of conformity with a transcendental ideal. In championing everyday life over "higher values" Dewey mainly criticized "*identification* of the ideal with a particular Being, especially when that identification makes necessary the conclusion that that this Being is outside of nature." He wrote that the "ideal itself has roots in natural conditions; it emerges when the imagination idealizes existence by laying hold of the possibilities offered to thought and action." The process does not require any "external criteria and guarantee of their goodness. They are had, they exist as good, and out of them we frame our ideal ends."[131]

For Putnam, ethics has a specific sense. He writes:

the glorification of warfare and *machismo* may, indeed, be older in the history of human cultures than the emphasis on alleviating suffering regardless of the class or gender of the sufferer, but it is this latter outlook, which has deep roots in the great religious traditions of the world – not only in the religious traditions of the West, but in Islam, Confucianism, Hinduism, and Buddhism as well – to which I shall refer by the name ethics.

He notes that this "ethics is precisely the morality that Nietzsche deplored, and regarded as a weakness or even a sickness." One of the focuses of Putnam's analysis is the philosopher Levinas, who wrote *Otherwise than Being; or Beyond Essence*. The central theme of Levinas's philosophy is that "all attempts to reduce ethics to a theory of being, or to base ethics on a theory of being, upon ontology, *either* in the traditional or in the Heideggerian sense, are disastrous failures."[132] The implications of Dewey's work for democracy and modernity certainly bear this claim out and point us in positive new directions. There are multiple and transient ends that are guided by democracy as a flexible ethic rather than any set universal principle. We cannot identify democracy with the presence or absence of a particular culture. Democracy is fundamentally a matter of growth and self-realization that requires the cultivation of intelligent habits in individuals and the maintenance of social structures that encourage continuous inquiry.

6

Enlightenment and Moral Politics

> The model that definitely had the best results was democracy. Therefore,
> it was natural to go for what we thought had better results.... There were
> two main choices in our society. The first was Islam, but this is only the
> beginning of all disputes. Which Islam? What kind, and with what inclina-
> tion?... democracy has more or less proved its potential at an international
> level. It has weak points for sure, yet its merits are such that they turn this
> system into a unique model.
>
> Reza Tehrani[1]

The post–June 2009 election uprising in Iran, now referred to as the Green
Movement, offers a new vision of social change that can be articulated
and theorized as an alternative to discourses of secular authoritarianism
and religious "fundamentalism." The Green Movement situates itself as a
post-Islamist and postsecular movement that has developed out of thirty
years of having a religious state in power and reflects a unique pattern of
thinking on Iran's substitution of a totalizing notion of religion for what
was once imagined as secular tyranny. The Green movement presents a
moral politics very similar to John Dewey's universal ideal in *A Common
Faith*, where a worldly democratic politics may also include the participation of multiple religious and nonreligious meanings and experiences.[2]
The postelection movement in Iran showed a democratic openness to
those who practice religion combined with a rejection of the sectarian
and exclusivist claims of narrow religious institutions based in rigid dogmas that monopolize power. This seems to be what Reza Tehrani, a
religious intellectual, expressed in the preceding quotation. We see a pragmatic and open view of religion and different way of living in the world.

For Reza Tehrani, as a believer, Islam is the beginning and not the end of questions, and provides no foreordained outcome on either the political or historical level. There is no question of rejecting Islam, as if historical religion were merely a psychological spell to be broken by the forcing of a "new" and "objective" consciousness. Islam nevertheless exists as a choice open to integration with other component political-intellectual elements to be selected on a pragmatic and ethical basis. We see a secular openness to everyday life, empowered by a historically grounded commitment to moral politics in which democracy and Islam aspire jointly to the ideals of justice and freedom.

Positive and practical achievements of secularism and Enlightenment (rule of law, respect for election process, and human rights) are embraced by the Green Movement without defining itself explicitly and exclusively as "philosophically secular." This only confirms that neither the secular nor the religious are essentially fixed categories: in practice they interact contingently through multiple connections. Only at the ideological level can religion and the secular be conceived as conceptually or practically pure objects, and even as inevitable rivals for public power. This way of approaching religion and secularism leaves the door open to using the resources and historical experiences of both without uncritically accepting every aspect of what these two systems of thinking and doing imply. The Green Movement may be viewed as Islamic while being connected to a specific historical time and precise secular ideas on the norms of political power – thereby combining elements of both Islam and secularism. The definition of Islam remains open ended and influenced by a moral vision corresponding to Foucault's concept of a "moral politics:" the nonteleological invention (not discovery) of a "manner of being" or "way of life;" the embodiment of a philosophical way of life supported by neither dogmatic tradition nor reason. At the intersection of subjectivity and forms of governmentality, this is a politics at its core on the side of the governed. Symbolically charged and mass based, it is nevertheless silent and peaceful, and determined in its moral commitment to give democratic voice to the Iranian public. Mir Hussein Mousavi, a leader of the Green Movement, courageously rejects use of Islam as a justification for political dictatorship while his supporters participated in a massive public show of respect at the death of Shi'i cleric Ayatollah Montazeri. We see in this show of respect for a political adversary an ethical gesture of nonviolence that forms part of a broader planetary awakening to an emerging post–Velvet Revolution and postcolonial ethic of democratic reconciliation.[3]

This ethic of democratic reconciliation has multiple historical roots from around the world. In the modern context, it may be traced most significantly to the profound philosophical spirit of nonviolent mass politics to emerge with the Indian national independence movement under Mahatma Gandhi and Jawaharlal Nehru. On the basis of India's multireligious and multilingual condition, Gandhi insisted strongly on a boundary between religious institutions and the affairs of the state. Yet Gandhi derived his public morality of tolerance from a diverse template of religious and philosophical sources: from Jainism, Christianity, and Islam as well as Hinduism, and not least from the European Enlightenment itself. This stance presented Gandhi as an anomaly between dogmatically secular modernizers such as Mao, Stalin, or Ataturk who fit clearly into a then-prevalent universal political science category.

Today, movements such as the Green Movement in Iran and recent nonviolent religious movements in Myanmar and Thailand reflect the consolidating ethic of democratic reconciliation that is one of the most significant developments of recent times. We can therefore make sense of the recent Iranian experience by comparing it to the Indian experience in a way that subverts the dominant teleological dichotomies of modernity in terms of religion/secularism, tradition/modernity and opens up new horizons for democratic politics. It is a politics where the local and cosmopolitan meet, close to Dewey's notion of democracy in which a broader historical spirit of human traditions assists with the unfolding of a popular grassroots and democratic politics.

We can no longer plausibly retain the view that democracy stands alone, on the bow of an advancing ship, in icy winds, and that the advancing ship is knowledge based on pure and unmixed scientific understanding. Somewhere behind the ship, smaller and smaller, is an island of self-induced illusions, separated from the ship's onward passage by an ocean that we call modern progress.

In view of these new and rooted democratic forms that combine the local and the cosmopolitan, we are forced to rethink modernity as a multicentered phenomenon in which there is no aberrant or deviant modernity with respect to an "original" Eurocentric baseline. The problem of modernity seeds a rich harvest of questions for historical inquiry, in its refusal to yield to any single cultural or even scientific definition, and this is at least equally so regarding its origins. Modernity never stemmed from a single source, later to proliferate into many forms, but initially grew into existence through a myriad of specific but interrelated historical becomings: from the English Revolutionary Puritans guided by the new

Baconian scientific spirit to Mulla Sadra in Iran declaring that existence precedes essence in a causally self-contained nature and so paving the way intellectually for secularized movements for social change. Looking at these roughly coterminous seventeenth-century events, which combined profound religious belief with unsettling new temporal and secular understandings, we can say that the cultural pluralism of modernity confronts us acutely now because it was embodied from the outset by a multiplicity too often reductively conceived as a single ideal or impulse. For both the ideas and institutions developed from the seventeenth-century English Revolution and the Iranian cultural Renaissance, as merely two examples and however remotely, offer multithreaded intellectual links to events taking shape in the world now – including the Green Movement in Iran.

The paradigm of the French Revolution, meanwhile, long accepted as the prime mover, was presented in the form of a single governing principle grounded in Reason as a universal norm of human progress. Robespierre himself adopted such a totalizing line, insisting that "nothing has been accomplished so long as anything remains to be accomplished."[4] Classical theories of modernity similarly interpreted the convergence of industrial societies on the assumption that a single expansion of European modernity would prevail throughout the world, as if the pattern were indelibly set by the West's Great Revolutions. Yet freedom is a never-ending work, all the more likely to crumble the moment we take its security for granted, and defined in ongoing manner by the contingencies of geographic space and historical time. There were accordingly numerous traditions of Enlightenment from the very outset, beyond the geographic and cultural limits of the West, which blossomed into many, with varied and important practical implications grounded in differing ethical stances. As we increasingly face the hard reality today that neither human freedom nor human nature are in any way "self-evident" truths, it is time to look at these varying traditions critically and selectively in order to affirm some over others based on the sometimes brutal lessons of historical experience from the past several hundred years.

Following the dominant French Revolutionary paradigm, modernity was for a long time routinely presented in a caricatured and simplified manner as the unified march of progress and reason, a view given considerable imaginative impetus by the vivid Hegelian narrative of "Ultimate Reality" and "progress" fused into a single forward march including, in some mysterious and not always favorable fashion, "everyone and everything." Guided by this certainly exhilarating if largely fanciful ideology cum unthought, the hegemonic modernist intellectual impulse found expression in ideologies as diverse as Marxism, anarchism, and even fascism, while surfacing in more subdued form as liberal developmentalist and modernization theories, all united in centering a teleological totality of historical progress. These discourses operated within the complex structural setting of broad macro-institutional transformations: capitalism and industrialization, the modern state-law complex, the private sphere of the family and "childhood," and Europe as a world power engaging the non-European world on far from symmetric terms of exploration, plunder, and exploitation, or the knowledge/power conjunction. A radically one-sided machinery of representation in which "the Orient was first appropriated 'textually' by Europeans in the post-Enlightenment period" played a central role in these developments).

A tacit conception of "epistemic revolution" lurked at the heart of the shaping French Revolutionary paradigm, in the ideal of total emancipation from the randomness and confusion of bygone ages. Fontenelle reflected that much of the heritage of the European past in Greco-Roman traditions was "but dreams and fantastic imaginings."[5] The unifying ideal of modernity presented Enlightenment as a revolt against the "unreason of earlier ages – reason was to replace religious authorities, sacred texts and traditions as the criterion by which all things were to be judged." At the center of this is a particular philosophical vision of historical time in which events no longer could happen by accident: science became the guiding power of historical change grounded in the "certainty" of consciousness or positive knowledge. Cartesian thought eliminated accidents from nature, positing a purely mathematical and deductive core to reality, while openly promoting science as the panacea for increasing French state power and commercial development. The violence implied in the closed historicist and state-centered principle of agency was allegedly justified by the ends to be achieved, as all irrational forms of knowledge were to be flushed away into the oblivion of memories of once-ruling public illusion.

Yet precisely here was the snag, for there was no exogenous means for reaching a universal consensus on what beliefs constituted illusion, and the concept of "science" in this hegemonic modernist worldview was often more theological than scientific. We see an Archimedean intellectual substructure: Archimedes declared that he could move the universe if he were only given some position outside of it.[6] In Comtean positivism as an ideal for radical political change, a narrowly monolithic ideal of science came to prevail with "the firmest possible foundation" based on "the invariability of the laws of nature...against all danger from subjective chimeras."[7] It was only a matter of time before the epistemic posture of modernist certainty began to turn on itself with a corrosive relativism, to the great satisfaction of an entire generation of post–World War 2 French intellectuals who were disillusioned with the Rights of Man and the legacy of the Republic in the face of a deluge of social and political scandal, hypocrisy, and near national collapse. The all-consuming post-structuralist obsession with debunking the "universal" metanarrative of Enlightenment became, from a useful undoing of reification, an intellectual impasse and "totality" complex in itself. In localizing a tradition that had claimed universality based on then-existing power dynamics, it does not follow that the tradition has nothing further to offer within the broader family of myriad other traditions. Specifically Western ideas of individual liberty, democracy, and progress remain equally important despite their having gained global hegemony in conjunction with the process of European colonial expansion. Those concepts should be analyzed critically but not rejected. We find that there are modern traditions of Enlightenment evolved from globally diverse experience that do not squeeze "hope" into the role of a meaningless subjective illusion in comparison to "universal reality." The struggle for democracy should be linked to solidarity through hope and not claims to ultimate truth.

The sheer physical power and transfixing spectacle of the French Revolution as a centripetal historical moment at once illuminated its epistemic heritage in the absolute knowledge-virtue construct of French Enlightenment and threw into obscurity the roots of that well-known Enlightenment in the earlier and relatively unexplored British Enlightenment. This featured initially Locke on the eve of the 1688 Glorious Revolution and then the third Earl of Shaftesbury and his followers in the early eighteenth century as a new postreconstruction generation groped its way intellectually and practically to a new secular social dynamic. This period may not have the spectacular quality of the late eighteenth-century French Revolution, but we find in it the proposal of an alternative ethical and epistemic engagement to the social and political turmoil of modernity. It is one that is more open to possibilities from the past and the future. This new intellectual framework was set in train in horrified response to the seventeenth-century religious wars over ultimate truth and the accompanying reactive doctrines of skepticism and atomism. It found political expression in the Glorious Revolution of 1688 as at once a secular-representative settlement favoring Parliament over the Crown and an attempt to divert the potential dangers arising from efforts at mass democratic gain over the proceeding decades. In Gertrude Himmelfarb's *The Roads to Modernity*, we find the histories of several Enlightenments that show the fuller span of European Enlightenment discourses in this time of collapsing agriculture, trade, industry, and political authority, and the creative struggle to create adaptive new institutional forms.[8]

Britain experienced the upheaval of civil war and revolution in the seventeenth century, the centrifugal undermining of a weak central state between Crown, Parliament, emerging globally linked class interests, and regional powers, and in the eighteenth experienced the perhaps even greater terrors of the emerging Industrial Revolution and the final radical displacement it inflicted on the rural population already unsettled by enclosures. Through these unprecedented and socially traumatic experiences, British Enlightenment intellectuals tried to navigate and negotiate between the old and the new in a way that drew on the community's existing resources and kept the future open. France, entangled with Britain in growing colonial rivalry, experienced first the centralizing absolutist arrogance of Louis XIV in his efforts to crush the untamed French outlands and ultimately the catastrophic bankruptcy at the close of the eighteenth century that created conditions for the French Revolution. Each following unique historical patterns, yet locked into a spreading global dynamic, these nations in the making both experienced state collapse, war, authoritarian and democratic moments of power, and the unprecedented destructive quality of modernity in its power to violently displace and render dependent entire populations. Iran, too, has experienced variations on all of these things through a related global system of power linkages and responded in various democratic and authoritarian ways that draw from multiple local-global resources of experience from Japan to India to Germany. India's fate, as Britain's first and most valuable colony, involved Iran from possibly as early as the seventeenth century in the game of colonial power politics/unconscious economic substructures of domination involving Britain, Russia, and other players. Yet the relation between India and Iran is far deeper than this, going back to ancient history in cultural, social, and economic overlap. In the sixteenth century, notably, an influx of educated Persian refugees entered the court of Indian Emperor Akbar and introduced philosophical ideas that helped nurture the Mughal Empire's most far reaching experiment in religious tolerance.

In the proliferating intersections of subjectivity and forms of governability that constituted multiple Enlightenment discourses (concerned with degrees of democratic modernity), the British Enlightenment represented the most open ended regarding the contributions of religion and tradition to a modern democratic future. This is why it is of special relevance in explaining the new radical democratic discourses within the global Enlightenment tradition in Iran today. Because in the British Enlightenment we do not find a war waged against the past, doubt is cast on the prevailing notion of Enlightenment as "epistemic revolution" inflicting irreversible rupture. There is a fragile restraining wall of inherited ideology that preserves this simplification concerning "rupture" – the same one by which a generation of Western (and other) scholars were able to interpret the Iranian Revolution as simply "backward looking," rather than seeing a simultaneity of tradition, creatively re-rendered, and modern currents, radically reframed, which partly deserved its Foucauldian label of "postmodern." A glimpse into the British Enlightenment provides an alternative and more nuanced reflection of later historical events such as the Iranian Revolution, beyond the simple binaries of modernity/ tradition, reason/unreason, and so forth, which have often passed for certainties legitimized by the postfact epistemic reconstruction of the French Revolution as the "defining moment" of modernity. This defining moment was also an eclipsing force with its own outer regions of the unthought, the greatest occlusion being the tendency for professed metaphysical certainty to exclude the combination of pragmatic scientific generalization and ordinary human hope. This chapter seeks to demonstrate the overshadowed alternative history of Enlightenment as a "narrative of hope" rather than a claim to epistemic certainty.

Himmelfarb identifies three Enlightenments behind the ushering in of modernity – a "sociology of virtue" in Britain, a "politics of liberty" in America, and an "ideology of reason" in France – which persist in shaping the intellectual air that we breathe even to the present day, and with importantly differing outcomes. These three also, in some measure, overlap, feed off of, and directly challenge one another, in different variations. The indication is that there has never been, from the very beginning, any successive flow of essential historic forms pitting, for example, religion against liberty or reason, but rather specific contexts in which these multiple elements interact in differing and changing ways at a variety of levels. Thus, in Nehruvian Indian democracy we find a combination of a politics of liberty and sociology of virtue. There is the legally enframed constitution guaranteeing liberty combined with special provisions for permitting the unique legal conjunctures that accord with specific religious concerns. As a policy framework, this has lent itself to good and ill in different contexts, but it represents the highly creative interface between a modern secular legal system and the concern with negotiating traditional religious values and practices.[9]

For those who view modernity as a single project that can only be defined in terms of secular rationalism, or the ideology of secularism, this may unsettle certain presuppositions. But a look at the Enlightenment in its fuller complexity should caution us against any overly ideological or philosophical conception of modernity and its possibilities. A closer look at the various Enlightenments also opens up the possibility of envisioning modernity in terms of certain religious values, such as caring, tolerance, and cooperation; these cognitive attitudes may function to activate a more democratic collective imaginary in a society struggling with the challenges of modernity. These reflections point to the desirability of specificity and pragmatics characterized by a humble approach in reckoning with political modernity, rather than any vision of absolute human regeneration or final overcoming of the gap between transcendental and mundane orders.

While valuing the democratic heritage of the French Revolution, we can recognize that the French experience of Enlightenment has been privileged over the other eighteenth-century Enlightenments in Britain and America. In view of these diverse manifestations, it is necessary to therefore be critical of the French Enlightenment and Revolutionary traditions as one among several. Only thereby can we be fully cognizant of the differences that exist between these Enlightenments, and their corresponding legacies. The British Enlightenment may be viewed in fuller terms, recast beyond the more narrowly conceived and often cited Scottish Enlightenment, and expanded in its the cast of characters. Himmelfarb identifies the third Earl of Shaftesbury as the father of the British Enlightenment.[10] With his *An Inquiry Concerning Virtue, or Merit* (1699), intended to refute Locke's "tabula rasa" concept, Shaftesbury generated the initial terms of what became the core belief of the British Enlightenment: a "belief in a "moral sense" that was presumed to be if not innate in the human mind (as Shaftesbury and Francis Hutcheson thought), then so entrenched in human sensibility, in the form of sympathy or fellow feeling (as Adam Smith and David Hume had it), as to have the same compelling force as innate ideas." For Shaftesbury, "virtue derived not from religion, self-interest, sensation or reason" but from the immediate and primary source of the "moral sense," the "sense of right and wrong," which is a "social affection."[11] When Bishop Berkeley, Francis Hutcheson, Edward Gibbon, and Adam Smith condemned Mandeville's *Fable of the Bees* (1705), an attack on Shaftesbury's idea of the "moral sense," it expressed this shared social ethic "that was the distinctive feature of the British Enlightenment."[12] Hutcheson's contribution to this debate was *An Inquiry Concerning the Original of Our Ideas of Beauty and Virtue*, with the subtitle *In which the Principles of the Late Earl of Shaftesbury Are Explained and Defended.*[13] In this work "moral sense is antecedant to interest because it is universal to all men."[14] This view is coupled with a mistrust of the frailty of reason: "Notwithstanding the mighty reason we boast of above other animals, its processes are far too slow, too full of doubt and hesitation, to serve us in every exigency, either for our own preservation, without the external senses, or to direct our actions for the good of the whole, without the moral sense."[15] Similarly, Bishop Butler argued that reason alone is not "a sufficient motive of virtue in such a creature as man."[16] Thomas Reid argued that "common sense, and not reason, was the unique quality of the "plain man." For Hume, there existed a "moral taste" common to all men while "a fallacy of philosophy, ancient as well as modern, (was) to regard reason as the main motive or principle of human behavior, for reason alone could never prevail over the will and passions or provide incentive for virtue."[17] Adam Smith declared it "altogether absurd and unintelligible to suppose that the first perceptions of right and wrong can be derived from reason," while "it is . . . to feel much for others and little for ourselves . . . that constitutes the perfection of human nature."[18] All of these views express the ongoing crisis in traditional modes of being and thought, the uncertainty around accepted patterns in the face of unprecedented change, and negotiate between such traditional patterns and new criteria of scientific rationality with its promise of restored security. In this negotiation, the centrality of ethical virtue is retained: the ancient ethical notion of virtue begins with following given rules or models within a specific social context, but then requires the development of a disposition to decide and act via an understanding pertaining to each unique case. In distinction from the successive and value-free moments of modern instrumental reason, for virtue the power of reason participates within an overall unity of meaning in moral education, development of affect, and personal-public becoming. Such a flexible principle, put into early modern idiom by the British Enlightenment to negotiate between the changing present and the traditional past, is more suited to societies in transition such as Iran.

In establishing the "unique character and historic importance" of the British Enlightenment – and indeed its historical primacy in the entire

event of "Enlightenment" – Himmelfarb aims to "redefine the very idea
of Enlightenment" according to such a principle of virtue:

In the usual litany of traits associated with the Enlightenment – reason, rights,
nature, liberty, equality, tolerance, science, progress – reason invariably heads the
list. What is conspicuously absent is virtue. Yet it was virtue, rather than reason,
that took precedence for the British, not personal[19] virtue but the "social virtues"
– compassion, benevolence, sympathy – which, the British philosophers believed,
naturally, instinctively, habitually bound people to each other.[20]

The primary category of virtue, as opposed to reason, presents the initial
point of departure for comparing the British and the French experiences of
Enlightenment. From this point of elementary divergence, a considerable
array of meaningful differences unfold. These three Enlightenments arose
"at a critical moment in history (and) represented alternative approaches
to modernity, alternative habits of mind and heart, of consciousness and
sensibility."[21] According to Himmelfarb, to recognize the British experience is to "restore (the Enlightenment) to its progenitor."[22] The British
Enlightenment, originating in the early eighteenth century, "took a form
very different from that of its counterpart on the Continent (or from
that of its offspring overseas)."[23] In this approach reason had "a secondary, instrumental role rather than the primary, determinant one that
the (French) *philosophes* gave to it."[24]

On account of the highly belated and narrow use of the term "Enlightenment" in English – it did not come into proper use until the early
twentieth century – the British Enlightenment has been habitually overlooked by accident of lacking a name, in addition to its more subdued
social manifestation in a myriad of social reform movements rather than
a single violent revolution such as in 1789. The approach of the British
Enlightenment constituted sociology at least as much as a philosophy,
being "concerned with man in relation to society, (and looking) to the
social virtues for the basis of a healthy and humane society."[25] This stands
in contrast with the French philosophes, who had "the more exalted mission (of making) reason the governing principle of society as well as mind,
to 'rationalize,' as it were, the world."[26] In this way Himmelfarb contrasts
the British "sociology of virtue" with the French "ideology of reason."
The first produced a nonrevolutionary and reformist temper while the
second produced the Revolution of 1789. In the case of the American
Enlightenment, the "politics of liberty" produced the founding political traditions of the Republic based on the *Federalist* and the American

Constitution. At stake in this sketch of "distinctive Enlightenments" with "shared common traits" but "profoundly different social and political implications and consequences" is the contention that ideas, ideologies, and cultural imageries in a sense produce social realities. Himmelfarb identifies where the three Enlightenments, based on their various members, at times overlap and could have taken different roads. For example, "the Americans could have injected into their Revolution a larger utopian mission, rather than the pragmatic, cautious temper conspicuous in the *Federalist* and the Constitution." Thus, although to "appreciate the distinctiveness of these Enlightenments is to appreciate as well the uniqueness of each historical situation," Himmelfarb explains that the reason why "the countries did not take these paths had a good deal to do with the ideas and attitudes that prevailed among the influential thinkers, polemicists, and political leaders in each of these countries, who helped frame the terms of the discourse and thus affect the temper of the time."[27]

In taking this angle, Himmelfarb directs attention to the "social ethic explicit or implicit in each of these Enlightenments."[28] At the core of her argument we find an ethical analysis of roads to modernity and an articulation of the possibilities these social ethics presuppose. It is, moreover, by way of redefining the British Enlightenment through a social ethic of virtue that the author includes within it such unconventional figures as Edmund Burke, who is normally considered a Counter-Enlightenment thinker, and, even more controversially, John Wesley, the evangelical theologian and founder of Methodism. The basis for including Burke is his view of the primacy of sympathy: "It is by the first of these passions (sympathy) that we enter into the concerns of others; that we are moved as they are moved, and are never suffered to be indifferent spectators of almost anything which men can do or suffer."[29] He can also be identified with the broader British Enlightenment by his views on reason: "What would become of the world if the practice of all moral duties, and the foundations of society, rested on having their reasons made clear and demonstrated to every individual."[30] Most importantly, he shares the socially inclusive outlook that Himmelfarb attributes to the British Enlightenment: "the standard of both reason and taste is the same in all human creatures."[31] Meanwhile, Wesley and the Methodists, in spite of differences with the moral philosophers, in "important practical matters... tended to converge (with them)." [32] From this perspective "the Enlightenment (becomes) more British" and "the British Enlightenment more inclusive" than the conventionally conceived Enlightenment centered in France.[33] This argument opens up new conceptual space beyond "the Enlightenment (being) invariably associated with the French, and the terms of discourse . . . made familiar by the *philosophes*."[34] In spite of "the existential realization or fulfillment of the French Enlightenment (being) one of the most dramatic events of modernity" and the French Revolution being "widely regarded . . . as the inauguration of the modern world," there are varied and subtler responses to the existential problematic of early modernity taking place in the surrounding historical space.[35] By contrast, the totalizing temper of the French Revolutionary paradigm is expressed in Hegel's *Philosophy of History*, where he writes that "It has been said that the French Revolution resulted from philosophy" and "Never since the sun had stood in the firmament and the planets revolved around him had it been perceived that man's existence centers in his head, i.e., in Thought, inspired by which he builds up the world of reality."[36]

This Hegelian quotation refers to a deeper issue that Himmelfarb's argument seeks to address, and that is the peculiarly modern project of total revolution by which human reality is sought to be refashioned to its very roots based on an abstract and absolute principle of metaphysical transfiguration. This tendency is the legacy of the French Revolution: "For the past two centuries, the paradigm of popular revolution, like the paradigm of Enlightenment, has been that of France."[37] This paradigm is overdetermined by a dogmatic and metaphysical conception of the primacy of Reason: "The idea of reason defined and permeated the (French) Enlightenment as no other idea did. . . . In a sense, the French Enlightenment was a belated Reformation, a Reformation fought in the cause not of a higher or purer religion but of a still higher and purer authority, reason."[38] Reason, in the *Encyclopédie*, is "not just pitted against religion, defined in opposition to religion (but) implicitly granted the same absolute, dogmatic status as religion."[39] The philosophes themselves were a "cohesive group" with a "coherent character and purpose," a self-conscious "vanguard . . . of the French Enlightenment."[40] These views corresponded to, the author quotes Edward Gibbon as recalling, an "intolerant zeal" and a preaching of "the tenets of atheism with the bigotry of dogmatists."[41] We see an external or totalizing conception of Reason that can only be imposed as a scientific certainty, in contrast with an internal or emergent reason that develops on the basis of overlapping consensus drawn from the existing value resources structuring already existing public communities. The first tends to a violent marginalization of tradition under the guidance of experts, and the second to a democratization of it through broad public participation.

This external Reason is contrasted with the American Revolution, the Founders of which were "practical men of affairs."[42] Himmelfarb paraphrases Edmund Burke's claim that "Unlike the American Revolution, which was a political revolution, the French Revolution . . . was nothing less than a moral revolution, a total revolution, a revolution of sentiment and sensibility penetrating into every aspect of life."[43] The primary document of the American Revolution, *The Federalist*, was "designed for a specific purpose and a specific country" and its speculations "grew out of immediate, practical concerns and were advanced modestly and even tentatively."[44] The *Encyclopédie*, by contrast, preoccupied with the most abstract principles, aimed to "collect all the knowledge that now lies scattered over the face of the earth, to make known its general structure to the men among whom we live, and to transmit it to those who will come after us."[45] Such loftily abstract and universal ambitions are a far cry from Alexander Hamilton's warning to avoid "the comerical pursuit of a perfect plan."[46] The American Enlightenment, which owed its heritage to the British tradition, understood the practical and theoretical as closely related. In France, however, where the philosophes could not aspire to influence public policy, there was rather an aspiration to "bold and imaginative thinking, unconstrained by such practical considerations as how their ideas might be translated into reality."[47] The discipline of sociology, anchored within the limits of specificity and pragmatics, is thus contrasted with a philosophical vision, which is virtually unlimited in its creative designs on humanity as such. Thus, Rousseau wrote of the philosophical legislator's role "of changing human nature, of transforming each individual."[48] Robespierre later echoed these words when he spoke of "the necessity of bringing about a complete regeneration, and, if I may express myself so, of creating a new people."[49] Among the philosophes only Montesquieu, whose *Spirit of the Laws* derived from the British model, did not "appeal to reason as the fundamental principle of politics and society" and approached his subject sociologically in terms of "physical and historical circumstances."[50]

This matter of an abstract sovereignty of reason versus a politics of pragmatism raises the important issue of the complex religious dimension to the Enlightenments. The Enlightenments that appeared in "Britain or America, where reason did not have that preeminent role, and where religion, whether as dogma or as institution, was not the paramount enemy," were "latitudinarian, compatible with a large spectrum of belief and disbelief."[51] Himmelfarb writes that "For the British moral philosophers, and for the American Founders, reason was an instrument for the attainment of the larger social end, not the end itself. And for both, religion was an ally, not an enemy."[52] Significantly, in light of this, "There was no *Kulturkampf* in those countries to distract and divide the populace, pitting the past against the present, confronting enlightened sentiment with retrograde institutions, and creating an unbridgeable divide between reason and religion."[53] In Himmelfarb's account, the French Enlightenment prioritized a strongly metaphysical conception of reason; it is this intellectual legacy, hostile to religion, that has been enshrined as the *only* paradigm for a society's historic transition to modernity. Yet the experience of the other two Enlightenments, often overlooked by modernizers and historians, proves that this dogma is not necessarily so. It seems indeed likely that such a dogma could prove harmful by creating an inevitable yet unnecessary clash between religion and the forces of modernization.

We thus have a clear vision of historical multiplicity, that is, of three distinct Enlightenments each defined by its own inner tendencies and outer circumstances. Himmelfarb explains these differences in terms of distinct national contexts:

the very different political characters of the countries and the relationship of classes within those political systems; the nature and authority of the churches and their role in the state; economics at various levels of industrialism and subject to different kinds and degrees of government regulation; and all the other historical and social circumstances that were unique to each country and helped shape its temper and character.[54]

This thesis opens up the vista to a highly pluralistic understanding of modernity, or rather modernities, and undoes much of what has passed for the "inevitabilities" of any nation's movement to modernity. The entire sense of a single passage of development characterized by certain inevitable tendencies is brought into question – that is to say, the dominant philosophy of history that has for a long time now retained the "modern imagination" in something of a viselike grip. For if it is true that the French Enlightenment has superimposed itself as a model for modernity, pitting the "modern" present of "reason" against the "retrograde" past of "tradition," whereas the overlooked British Enlightenment presents an opposing tale and possibility of religion's moral and social utility actually paving the way to a successful realization of modernity, then certainly we are less at pains to explain why national modernities of every description follow unique courses in which the play of historical forces interpenetrate in every conceivable fashion in utter defiance of the dogma about how modernity must evolve and what it must look like.

Just as the French Revolutionary paradigm of universal Rationality must assume a single and fixed road to modernity, so it is also implied that the truth and the fulfillment of the human future is "already there." All of our human struggles are the attempt to conform to this truth in a final moment of fulfillment, and ethics as the experimental outcome of will and choice can have no very great role. Conversely, if the human struggle for a road to a democratic modernity is without such "final ends," as the British Enlightenment argued, then the most important resource for human solidarity is in hope.

This also points to the very real power of ideas in achieving social change. The social implications of these different roads to modernity are important with regard to the democratic character of the politics they foment. According to the dogma of reason expressed in the *Encyclopédie*, the common people were the "ignorant and stupefied" multitude, whose voice was that of "wickedness, stupidity, inhumanity, unreason, and prejudice."[55] Himmelfarb writes: "The people were uneducable because they were unenlightened. They were unenlightened because they were incapable of the kind of reason that the *philosophes* took to be the essence of enlightenment. And they were incapable of reason because they were mired in the prejudices and superstitions, the miracles and barbarities, of religion."[56] Thus Diderot wrote: "The general mass of men are not so made that they can either promote or understand this forward march of the human spirit."[57] Himmelfarb quotes Tocqueville as saying that the philosophes believed that "religious zeal . . . will be extinguished as freedom and enlightenment increase." Yet, in his observations, America disproved that theory and he wrote: "Among us (the French) I had seen the spirit of religion and the spirit of freedom almost always move in contrary directions. Here I found them united intimately with one another: they reigned together on the same soil."[58] All of this would suggest that the antipathy to religion is not inherent in modernity as such but very likely ideological and context-specific, as with the authoritarian and repressive character of the Catholic Church in prerevolutionary France. Yet the antireligious ideology of the French Enlightenment proved to be, as the foregoing quotations show, elitist in character and hostile to the common people and the everyday world. Classes were seen as divided by a chasm of superstition and ignorance. At the root of this problem in the "ideology of reason" is not reason itself. Rather, it would hold true for any idea anchored in a totalizing metaphysics that disdains the ordinary realities of everyday life for the sake of a projected "higher goal." Any such a political ideology is more than likely to create a similarly elitist chasm.

Conversely, Himmelfarb argues, "For the British philosophers, that social chasm was bridged by the moral sense and common sense that were presumed to be innate in all people, in the lower classes as well as the upper."[59] The thought and religious feeling of the broad public in Britain did not receive the same hostility as in France because the British Enlightenment throve, according to Roy Porter, "*within* piety."[60] He wrote: "There was no need to overthrow religion itself, because there was no pope, no inquisition, no Jesuits, no monopolistic priesthood."[61] Thus, while in France "Reason was inherently subversive, looking to an ideal future and contemptuous of the deficiencies of the present, to say nothing of the past (and) disdainful also of the beliefs and practices of the uneducated and the lowborn," the British moral philosophy was "reformist rather than subversive, respectful of the past and present while looking forward to a more enlightened future (and) egalitarian (in) the moral sense and common sense being shared by all men."[62] That is to say, it was grounded in a hope that might be broadly shared, and not narrowly conceived metaphysical claims about the nature of ultimate reality that would inevitably alienate many. The public moral sense, without offering any guarantee of epistemic certainty, nevertheless represents the scope for the production of internal reasons within a given community undergoing modern transformation and negotiating between tradition and change. For such a civil social process to meet the challenge of change effectively, a democratic rather than an authoritarian state is a prerequisite.

These researches highlight that there are different approaches to modernity and that, historically, modernities in the Western world have been achieved in a variety of ways. Modernity, then, is not a single project, and there is no defensible ground for arguing that it must be defined exclusively in terms of secular rationalism – or any other ideology likely to exclude and alienate a large section of the modernizing society in question. Modernity is not an "idea" or "ideology" to be imposed from above, and such dogmas leave little room for its social and institutional representation. Modernity is a hope without final guarantees, where the good society is the ongoing fruit of struggle and wakefulness and cannot be taken for granted. From this perspective, the appropriate theoretical approach to the politics of modernity is a sociological analysis based on a specific and pragmatic orientation, and not an abstract philosophical vision that seeks to produce a rebirth either of society or of humanity as a whole. Moreover, the researches of *The Roads to Modernity* indicate that if we understand modernity in terms of its democratic vision, perhaps certain religious values can help in achieving that democratic modernity.

From the contrast between the comparatively open tradition of British Enlightenment, grounded in a modern politics of hope, and the closed totality of the French "ideology of Reason," we may shift the discussion to a twentieth-century struggle for national emancipation that also grounded itself in an open-ended politics of hope: the Indian National Independence Movement under Mahatma Gandhi and the postindependence Indian Republic under Jawaharlal Nehru. The Indian experience of nation-making is relevant to Iran from several standpoints: both experienced coterminous foreign imperial domination, India as a formal colony and Iran as part of an informal empire (impeded from full colonization by interimperialist rivalry among other issues); and both consequently struggled to build a modern nation out of the ruins of a traditional "universal" empire based on a wide ideological template ranging from authoritarian modernism to moderate Enlightenment efforts to reconcile traditional beliefs/practices with modern scientific-technological and politico-economic change. And out of these struggles emerged mass independence movements that formed powerful democratic traditions in both countries, which experienced a variety of ideological and practical leadership from which today we may draw important lessons.

Today, Iran faces a new crossroad in its political history. The second section of this chapter therefore offers a study of two geographically remote social movements, India and the United States, sharing considerable affinity on the level of thought, which have both succeeded in deeply transforming their respective social contexts in the name of a pluralistically conceived democratic modernity that challenges both a totalizing Western hegemony and nativist ideologies of "authenticity" and "radical" countermodernity. Iran may draw important lessons from these examples, particularly as the country has its own indigenous heritage of nonviolent mass resistance (as we see during the Constitutional Revolution and later in the democratic interim of 1941–53).

The Indian national movement with its deep intellectual foundations in Indian political thought – represented in the ideas of Nehru and Gandhi but realized in Indian democracy today – and the civil rights movement in the United States to transform race relations under Martin Luther King are both practical and real experiences of pluralistic and nonviolent but radical and democratic movements for change grounded in "narratives of hope." Each of them at once drew from existing local traditions while rethinking them critically, and at the same time remained open to all kinds of ideas from diverse traditions and sources from around the world. Each, in sum, was deeply conscious of the many and complex implications of "globalization" and sought to make use of this condition in order to effect a radical democratic transfiguration of their society (and ultimately, they hoped, the world), one that in effect challenged certain precepts and practices of the dominant paradigm of Western modernity as embodied in the French Revolutionary nationalist legacy.

In addition, both movements became the target of narrowly conceived nationalist groups claiming more narrowly to stand for the "authentic" essence of the local culture and preaching a politics of violence in its name. Finally, these movements and discourses significantly did not reject religious experience as something "other" to modernity, but employed it as a peaceful means in the struggle for a democratic modernity. In this way they broke with certain "scientific" or "materialist" dogmas enshrined in dominant discourses of modernity and development, while drawing on a lesser known Enlightenment heritage in which religion within certain limits may contribute meaningfully as a positive force for social change. In fact, the Indian National Movement drew on a wide diversity of sources, both Indian and Western, as well as from other cultures. These movements thereby showed an alternative face of modernity and Enlightenment heritage in which the perpetually transforming energies and imagination of the present are not destined by inner necessity to do violence to the "traditional" past in the name of a future logocentrically imagined to be grounded in a bifurcation of "reason" and "culture," "West" and "East," or any other such tacitly violent binary. Indeed, Gandhi's entire life struggle was conceived in opposition not to "enemies" but to such violence in both deed and thought.

A conception of violence as the road to social change is far from alien to the tradition of Western political thought. Indeed, as King noted, the frequent "method that has been used in history is that of rising up against the oppressor with corroding hatred and physical violence. Now of course we know all about this method in Western civilization because in a sense it has been the hallmark of its grandeur, and the inseparable twin of western materialism."[63] The violence of the French Revolution, within the larger context of what Jacques Godechot has called the "the western revolutions," both embodied the birth of modernity and established the prototype of the modern political experience of total social transformation between freedom and terror. King was deeply aware of the ever present and problematic character of this heritage in Western experience. He devoted considerable thought to it and called frequent attention to its meaning in public addresses: "One of the most persistent philosophical debates of the centuries has been over the question of ends and means.... In a real sense, the means represent the ideal in the making and the end in process."[64] For King, it was critical that the means used to achieve radical change must conform in tendency to the end to be achieved because the ends and means are ultimately one. This essentially spiritual conviction inherited from Gandhi put King at radical philosophical odds with much that is mainstream in Western political thought and practice, at once making him deeply rethink the "Western" metaphysical and ethical tradition as well as reach outside of it to "Asian" intellectual heritages of thought through his fascination with the modern Indian experience of political struggle. And, as with the Indian National Movement, King's courageous and prolonged struggle brought profound and positive results that point to an alternative mode of political action for modern conflict resolution.

In analyzing the implications of the relationships between the thought of King, Nehru, and Gandhi, we can glimpse the error in conceiving key twentieth-century "Western" and "Asian" thought and practice as being insular, separate, or complete in themselves and see how both have in fact been deeply and irreversibly intermingled in the often occluding and conflicting experience of the passage though modernity. The historically evolving epistemes of "modern thought" as actually lived by so many people through the perpetual disintegration and struggle of modern experience are far more broad and diverse than we often imagine and are becoming ever more so over time, with diverging roads of a sometimes hidden nature – what Arkoun calls the "unthought" – where very often an enormous amount is at stake on a practical and ethical level.

At the core of King's dilemma over the heritage of modernity we find the central discourse of ends and means that is given expression in Hegel's meta-narrative of historical development. Gandhi, who was the principal influence behind King's philosophy and practice of nonviolence, endeavored equally to help India fight British colonialism in such a way that Indians did not become the victims of the means they used to achieve liberation. This is in unfortunate and marked contrast to many other twentieth-century revolutions, and wars purportedly waged in the name of liberation, in which the extreme violence of the means, considered to be justified by the ends, ultimately subjected entire populations to inconceivable forms of brutality and terror in which those imagined ideal ends were entirely betrayed on every level. These experiences point to the broad importance of the questions raised theoretically and applied in practice according to strict principle by men such as King and Gandhi. Gandhi's thought, on the philosophical level, similarly and importantly involved a radical reconstruction of the political problem of ends and means as it relates to the passage to modernity. The flexibility afforded by this reconstruction permitted Gandhi, like King in the United States, to reconcile a moral vision that included history and traditions with a modern vision of a democratic future for India. Such a flexible assemblage of pragmatically integrated thought and belief, invented and reinvented, would be unthinkable within the forward-moving razor-sharp coils of a Hegelian dialectic of development toward Absolute Knowledge, in which everything finds its place strictly preordained and much is cast by the wayside on "metaphysical grounds."

It can be argued that Gandhi and King rethought the question of modernity along the lines of Dewey's concept of "deliberative democracy," in which reason has a real but limited and creative function, rather than the Reason of an overarching and universalizing historical system and "End" as conceived so influentially by Hegel. The study of Indian independence and the American civil rights movement provides, following Arkoun's thought, insight into the "limits and arbitrary aspects of hegemonic reason and is involved in the most useful debates on the passage from the *Phenomenology of the Mind*, trapped in the "mytho-historico-transcendental thematic," to "the social institution of the mind."[65] This chapter analyzes the social discourses and movements of Indian independence and American civil rights in terms of the implications for democratic modernities beyond the imprisoning dogma of a single dominant tradition of conceptualizing modernity grounded in a fixed historical trajectory favoring the West.

The thought of Hegel is especially useful for this task in a number of ways. Hegel was at once one of the Enlightenment's deepest thinkers but also one of its deepest critics. He conceived key issues of modernity in terms of multiple aspects and perspectives. Crucially, he combined a discourse of transcendent Reason with a powerful preoccupation with "finding a way home," thereby expressing at once the principal ideas of both Enlightenment and counter-Enlightenment romanticism in a single philosophical system. As the key philosopher of *historical* modernity, he assembled the totalizing elements implicit in Enlightenment within a massive frame of historic development in which all civilizations were consigned to subordinate and transient status within the West's advancing orbit. His powerful worldview therefore provides the ideal counterpoint for the ideas to be discussed here.

In spite of the massive scope of Hegel's thought, in the context of this essay the focus inevitably is on Hegel's views and attitudes toward non-Western cultures within the epistemic framework of modernity as he conceived it. These views were articulated implicitly in *Phenomenology of Spirit*, and very explicitly in *Lectures on the Philosophy of History*.[66] These views of non-Western civilizations are far from peripheral in Hegel's thought on modernity. Indeed, at their most extreme they can be construed as a form of the "epistemic violence," or "inner violence," that thinkers such as Gandhi and King were at pains to point out and exorcise from social thought and political practice. Being grounded in a historical framework, it is useful to consider the implications of Hegel's historical discourses against the also powerfully conceived narrative of history expressed in Jawaharlal Nehru's masterpiece on modernity and history, *The Discovery of India*. This book may be said to contain, as a historical vision, much in the way of the principle of openness that we find in the approaches of Gandhi and King, as well as in the philosophical articulations of Dewey.

Phenomenology of Spirit does not follow the conventional pattern of logical argumentation in which statements have a predicative relation to one another. Rather, the arguments it contains are dialectical: a continuous changing of forms based on inner tensions in which phases of transition yield to higher forms. These levels of gradation are made obsolete as they are consumed in the mounting ascent toward the summit of Absolute Knowledge. Thus, unconventionally, none of the many parts of the argument are claimed to be true, whereas each is indispensable to the final outcome that is the absolute self-realization of the totality of reality itself. To challenge the truth claim of dialectical arguments of transition is neither to necessarily disagree with their original author nor to challenge the final conclusions of the argument as a whole. Yet insofar as the overall argument is a steady ascent to higher levels, we can perceive where elements of human experience are metaphysically relegated to an inherently subordinate or inferior status in an epistemic hierarchy. So it is with "images" in Hegel, or "picture thought," which is excluded from "true thought" and the movement of "pure reason." An indispensable part of the human mind and potential for problem solving, the imagination, is thereby downgraded and exiled from legitimate participation. It is ultimately in this way that the binary of a pure and autonomous Reason set against an inferior and unreasoning tradition is reproduced within the setting of a universal historical advance. This hierarchical ordering of modes of thought and experience is the "closed" element in Hegel's metaphysics that played itself out more graphically as a justification of colonialism as the "work of the Spirit" in the *Philosophy of History*, echoing the more abstract formulation of the principle in *Phenomenology*.

Such metaphysical ranking of human experience and ways of thought was a primary object of criticism in the pragmatist philosophy of Dewey. Dewey's pragmatic reason, with its equal consideration for imagination and abstract thought in coping with social problems, turns out in its flexibility to be far closer to the genuine experience of the social activists who brought such broad and positive changes to the United States and India, respectively, through the movements for civil rights and national independence. These movements were essentially creative and open as well as critical in their attitudes to tradition, modernity, and social democracy. Meanwhile, the fixing of a rigid metaphysical primacy to one aspect of human cognition to the degradation of all others proves rather a hindrance to the human creative potential in struggling with the perpetual challenges to democratic reconstruction faced by societies everywhere through the "crisis of modernity." For, once put into practice, the claim to a legitimacy grounded in a pure or higher "Reason" invariably hides a lesser interest and functions with a lesser or greater degree of totalitarian character. Implicitly, then, this chapter compares the idea complexes of these two giants of modern thought, Hegel and Dewey, through the lifeworks of men who were both social activists and thinkers, Gandhi, Nehru, and King.

Gandhi, King, and the Problem of "Inner Violence"

The problem of "inner violence" is something unfamiliar in Western philosophical, political, and even religious traditions. In India, this idea has deep historical and cultural roots even though Gandhi adapted it to conditions of modern political struggle. The conventional Western notion would be that our inner thoughts and imaginings are a private matter, beyond the legitimate concern of the broader society of which we are a part, and in any case unable to have substantial effect regardless of their inner content. It is our conduct that is the point of concern insofar as following the law marks the boundaries of our identities as criminal or decent citizen. It is in this sense that an individual carrying apocalyptic thoughts or fantasies in his head is immaterial so long as it is never manifested outwardly. He might be a model citizen in spite of his thoughts. The controversies that have arisen from certain individuals writing down and publishing their "scandalous" thoughts show the limits of this conventional boundary at the threshold of the "invisible." In the Western religious context, the problem of heretical thoughts could once have been counted as a public transgression, but this notion runs decidedly contrary to the modern secular worldview. The dystopia of Orwell's *1984* showed a police state preoccupied with controlling people's inner thoughts at the deepest possible level to the point of controlling their experience of basic reality. Yet Orwell's vision draws attention rather to the problem of a modern information war than to the significance of violence in one's inner thoughts and its harm to the "soul" and hence "reality." Broadly defined, it is perhaps the New Age movement of the twentieth century that most influentially tried to propagate a popular discourse on the problem of the "soul" in Western material society. Yet none of these examples gets near to the intensity and seriousness with which Gandhi engaged and articulated the problem, indeed placing it at the center of a public political struggle for national independence and the creation of the Indian Republic.

Reflecting on these examples helps to illuminate the importance for Gandhi of the problem of "inner violence" as an urgent and primary issue of political practice in what has been called "the most colossal experiment in world history." For him, our unseen thoughts can and do hurt ourselves and others, and this must be addressed on both the personal and political planes. Interestingly, Gandhi's conception of inner violence was developed in significant part through his contacts with people in the Western New Age movement. The views circulated in this milieu were themselves idealized "Orientalist" notions of a "spiritual" India. Yet Gandhi's idea of "inner violence" is not necessarily so mystical and may be compared, for example, to the idea of "episteme." For Gandhi, "forms of structural and conceptual (epistemic) violence" are "embedded in words, images, and social structures of domination and exclusion."[67] Unreflected structures of thought are therefore inherited collectively and institutionally and shape not only points of view but also practice. We are responsible for what we think and imagine, perhaps particularly concerning something we do not see directly. Gandhi's concern with "inner violence" was a concern with the effects of such unreflected legacies and the possibility of undoing them. In this sense, his thought functions as a simultaneous point and counterpoint to the radical shift in intellectual thought triggered by Edward Said's *Orientalism*. Gandhi at once

borrowed heavily and uncritically from the received "Orientalist" episteme, radically reversing its official values while retaining its basic ideas
and imagery, and advanced a critique of Western metaphysical thought
that attacked its very foundations in "Reason" and "civilization" as being
inherently violent, because exclusive, at the most basic conceptual level.
At the same time, Gandhi was a strong believer in reason with a low-
ercase "r" and argued that it should be applied to all aspects of social
life, including religion. He consistently argued in favor of social dialogue
and was committed to both civil liberties and democratic functioning
throughout his active political life.

Steger has described the "first systematic construction of Gandhi's
idealized vision of India" as "a fantastic image comprised of liberal, orientalist, and folkloric fragments."[68] He shows that Gandhi drew "his
main inspiration from writings of various European thinkers as well as
daily readings of the *Bhagavad Gita*" and that his "mature views on
morality derive in large part from his contacts with British 'New Age'
circles."[69] He evolved a "myth of the regenerated nation, rooted in the
spiritual and moral virtues of 'ancient Indian civilization'" and a "vision
of India as a glorious civilization devoted to vegetarianism and spiritual
perfection."[70] Ultimately, in constructing "ancient Indian civilization as
the morally pure Other to 'modern civilization,'" a "golden age" sunken
into a "dark age," and promoting a "return to...the simple virtues of
Indian villagers," Gandhi reversed "colonial meanings of ancient and
modern." Steger argues that this "affirmative orientalist imagery contributed greatly to the popular appeal of Gandhi's myth." In these aspects
of Gandhi's thought, we see a romanticism with regard to an imagined
past and a reproduction of a permanent ontological difference separating
an essential "East" and "West," a view itself reflecting colonial ideologies, highlighting an imaginative reconstruction of cultural identity not
uncommon to much nationalist discourse throughout the period of decolonization. Indeed, the paradigm continues its various mutations into our
day. Thus Gandhi's rediscovery and reimagining of his "own" tradition
"cannot be separated from the dominant nineteenth-century British discourse on India."[71] An Orientalist image of purity was similarly affirmed
as Gandhi at times described the "world in terms of an epic struggle
between Ram and Ravana, good and evil," with India as having a special
role in redeeming the world.

Yet on a deeper level we find in Gandhi's discourse, more remarkably,
a radical reevaluation of the concept of means-ends. This consisted, in
sum, of Gandhi's refusal of a basic dualism of means and ends and an

insistence on a politics derived from moral experience as lived. At this point we are not very far from the "moral sense" of the British Enlightenment. Gandhi's rejection of a dualism on the fundamental level of means-ends functioned to ethically counterbalance the more superficial dualistic aspects that may be considered the practical drawbacks and ethical risks of his philosophy. For it was the dualistic essentialism of French Revolutionary rationalist ideology that saw legitimate political struggle as waged on behalf of total truth against a world of conspirators and enemies incarnating a dying and irrational past. For Gandhi, very much like the Deweyan philosophy of deliberative democracy, a conception of pragmatic values prevails in which the means should justify the ends in the steady advance of democratic social freedoms. It is thus that Gandhi was able not only to shake the very foundations of the British Empire and to "make (the Indian) people into a nation," but to do so through radical forms of nonviolence in which emancipation was not won at the appalling and damaging cost of enormous loss of human life.

There was inevitably a "tension between ethical inclusivism and nationalist exclusivism" in Gandhi's philosophy, which may explain the tensions between a sometimes Manichean language and a claim to being "as broad as the universe." Yet the underlying identity of means-ends in the name of nonviolence amounts also to a radically inclusive ethical principle that constitutes the democratic core of the philosophy. This underlying framework accounts for a flexibility in which "political ideas arose 'in conversation' with established traditions as a mixture of agency and structure, the old and the new, the dying and the not-yet-born."[72] This power to modify and integrate traditions and institutions conveys the principle of refusing "inner violence," as ideas of whatever variety are tested by their practical effectiveness in lived situations rather than judged out of hand based on sweeping metaphysical categories. Gandhi was thus able to reconcile his moral vision (including history and traditions) with a modern vision of the future of India.

Gandhi's doctrine of "nonviolence" was equal parts a philosophy of cosmological dimensions, a way of life, and a practical political discourse of nationalism intended to achieve the specific end of driving the British Empire out of India without inflicting suffering and death on either Indians or other nationalities in the process. He wrote that the "task before nationalists is clear. They have to win over by their genuine love all of the minorities, including Englishmen. Indian nationalism, if it is to remain non-violent, cannot be exclusive."[73] In the pacifist tradition of Tolstoy and Thoreau, yet in a creative reimagining of his Indian national heritage,

Gandhi went against the current of received paradigms of insurrection in seeking at all costs freedom without terror for *anyone*. This is why for him the fundamental principle of nonviolence is inclusiveness, and such a principle cannot permit a dualism of means and ends. In this context a "Reason" that is pure or independent of the practical realities of living could only subvert the ethical integrity and intellectual pluralism of the democratic movement. We see the threads, though they may be invisible, linking the problem of "inner violence" to a refusal of dualism of means-ends: that is, of claims to "higher reality" to which everyday life must be sacrificed in any form.

Gandhi's concept of "Ahimsa," which "took him into a realm (of nonviolence) much higher than simply non-killing" to the precept of harboring no "uncharitable thought even in connection with one who may consider himself to be your enemy," became a guiding influence in the thought and struggle of King. Like Gandhi, King's thought and practice was preoccupied with the "internal spirit of violence" and countered it to the "principle of love."[74] King extended this principle to the realm of politics in a bid for radical transformation of his society, calling for a "strongly active spirituality" or "dynamically aggressive spirituality." In so doing, he held fast to the conviction that "violence solves no social problems. It merely creates new and more complicated ones."[75] It is hence "impractical and immoral."[76] King inherited Gandhi's concept of democratic inclusion as articulated through a religious vision. Insisting that there was a "basic tension not between races" but between "justice and injustice," he called for the use of "Christian methods" and "Christian weapons."[77] What is remarkable about both religious visions is that, far from being grounded in any dogmatic theological certainty, they are inherently and consciously open to difference and grounded in a spirit of shared public hope. In this sense they are at once linked to the "moral sense" of the British Enlightenment while also stepping beyond its reformist politics to a more radical mass mobilization that nevertheless remains strictly nonviolent and, remarkably, more secular in character than many so-called secular political manifestations that make some claim to absolute knowledge of truth.

These movements were not essentialist, insisting on one truth to the exclusion of all others, but hermeneutical and flexible. The vision of Christianity for King was an interpretation derived from both local American Southern Baptist tradition and the spiritual influence of Gandhi's reconstruction of Hinduism. He writes: "I had come to see early that the Christian doctrine of love operating through the Gandhian method of non-violence was one of the most potent weapons available to the Negro in his struggle for freedom." Hence, "Christ furnished the spirit and motivation, while Gandhi furnished the method."[78] King attested to a "fascination with the Orient as a child" and conceived his struggle in broadly international terms as the "common cause of minority and colonial peoples in America, Africa, and Asia struggling to throw off racialism and imperialism."[79] The fundamental aim of his politics was to "enlarge democracy for all people."[80]

King's religious teaching was a creative interpretation of the Christian tradition. He opposed a "narrow uncritical Biblicism."[81] Yet he affirmed the essential importance of the tradition to his work, stating that "(racial discrimination) is a cancerous disease that prevents us from realizing the sublime principles of our Judeo-Christian tradition."[82] A religious conviction formed the core of his existential and political understanding: "Human worth lies in relatedness to God. An individual has value because he has value to God."[83] This relation was, however, for King, a creative one, founded on what he called "*Agape*" or love as "the most powerful creative force in the universe." He wrote that "*Agape* does not recognize value, it creates it."[84]

Agape was conceived by King as "an overflowing love which is purely spontaneous, unmotivated, groundless, and creative. It is not set in motion by any function of its object."[85] It is therefore neither a higher reality separated from ordinary experience by a barrier nor a force that favors any particular people over others. King understood it at the most general level as "some creative force which works for universal wholeness" and argued that whether "we call it an unconscious process, an impersonal Brahman, or a Personal Being of matchless power and infinite love, there is a creative force in this universe that works to bring the disconnected aspects of reality into a harmonious whole."[86] He accordingly believed that the "universe is on the side of justice." He captured this conviction in an interpretive view of history based on the image of Christ's suffering and redemption: "This belief that God is on the side of truth and justice comes down to us from the long tradition of our Christian faith. . . . Evil may so shape events that Caesar will occupy a palace and Christ a cross, but one day that same Christ will rise up and split history into A.D. and B.C., so that even the life of Caesar may be dated by his name."[87]

Finally, King's social religion is grounded in a practical politics of democratic modernity aiming at inclusion. His writings emphasized the crisis of modernity at the root of human struggles for freedom: "Continents (have) erupted under the pressures of a billion people pressing in from the past to enter modern society. In nations of both the East and the West, long-established political and social structures were fissured and changed."[88]

In this democratic struggle for inclusion, religion would play, for him, a crucial role. He argued that "Any religion that professes to be concerned about the souls of men and is not concerned about the slums that damn them, the economic conditions that strangle them and the social conditions that cripple them is a spiritually moribund religion awaiting burial."[89] Religion for King was indispensable to the value of life, yet religion disengaged from life's struggles could have no value. He believed the "universe to be under the control of loving purpose."[90] Yet King was aware of certain dangers in combining religious belief with political action. He warned against "identifying the kingdom of God with a particular social and economic system."[91] This point of view, again, points to a politics of hope.

Moreover, he insisted that social progress was not inevitable and required the diligent efforts of those seeking change: "individuals in the struggle must come to realize that it is necessary to aid time, that without this kind of aid, time itself will become and ally of the insurgent and primitive forces of social stagnation." The future was to be decided by human action, and King placed primacy on pragmatic experience over doctrine. It was a creative process, he repeatedly emphasized, in which events compelled man "to change his image of himself."[92] The appropriate responses to these changes were to be found through direct experience. Regarding the experience of the Montgomery bus boycott, King stated that "Living through the actual experience of the protest, non-violence became more than a method to which I gave intellectual assent; it became a commitment to a way of life. Many issues I had not cleared up intellectually concerning non-violence were now solved in the sphere of political action."[93]

Action is not undertaken for its own sake, as with Sorelian vitalism, but nevertheless driven by the basic resource of hope rather than conformity to doctrine.

This pragmatic approach was shared by both King and Gandhi and brought them both close to the world of everyday life. Both of them believed the struggle for liberation to "be rooted in a moral 'soul-force' or 'truth-force,'" a power that encompassed the universe itself.[94] Yet neither of them insisted on one interpretation of the meaning of that force to the exclusion of other possible views. If anything, it was the opposite: they insisted in principle on the all-inclusive nature of that force, an understanding not unlike Dewey's conception in *A Common Faith*. King insisted on the necessity to "risk our lives to become witness to the truth as we see it."[95] Gandhi, grounded in the same epistemic basis of truth as an ongoing and permanently undecided process, accordingly pledged his life "to the nonviolent search for truth."[96] For him, as well as King, the path of nonviolence was truth, and hence the unbreakable link between our inner experience and the social world. No one can know absolute truth, a view in harmony with the British Enlightenment beginning with Lockean secularism following the theologically driven horrors of the English Civil War. Such a view of truth presupposes a humble relation to events in which they are engaged critically in the cause of justice but not reduced dogmatically to any single ontological or epistemic interpretation any more than they are bent by physical force. Gandhi warned us to be alert to a deeper layer of conceptual violence: "Our violence in word and deed is but a feeble echo of the surging violence of thought in us."[97]

King wrote of modernity as a "world of geographical togetherness," and reality as "spiritually one" or a "single process" in which the "end is reconciliation."[98] For Gandhi, "Belief in non-violence is based on the assumption that human nature in its essence is one and therefore unfailingly responds to the advance of love."[99]

Gandhi and King are really saying that the universe is a single process riven with conflict but moving toward an absolute oneness, and that this process can only begin and end in our soul and not through the violent changing of others. Yet it is altogether a social process. Hegel is saying something with a superficial resemblance but inwardly very different. For him there is also a cosmic force that moves toward oneness, or reconciliation, and he too was decidedly concerned with the meaning of the self in modernity. Yet Gandhi and King use a principle of inclusion, and Hegel uses the dialectic. The dialectic must transcend and hence stratify, whereas the principle of inclusion must "be" in peace with what "is." Yet both are activist philosophies of a kind. It is a very thorny but important difference, because the first is metaphysical and the second immanent. Hence, Hegel may justify dialectically European colonialism as a necessary stage on the path to the "Spirit."[100] For Gandhi and King, such a violent means is inconceivable with any end of reconciliation and will invariably produce further violence. Here, then, we glimpse the real significance of the means-ends issue that Gandhi and King raise so forcefully, that Dewey explored at length in his writings on ethics and experience, and that Hegel as well as Nehru presented from what are opposed points of view on the subjects of modernity and history. This means-ends problem is also the issue of a "narrative of hope" versus a narrative of essential truth, for any "truth" so convinced of its supremacy as to exclude the possibility of debate with other points of view necessarily considers any means acceptable in its ascendance to ultimate power.

Nehru, Hegel, and the Concept of Modern History

Regarding modern Indian history, Khilnani has written that "Imperial and post-imperial accounts," which have "suffused the sensibilities of popular and specialist writings about India," tell of "a revival of the passions of community, religion and caste, stalking the scene in old and pristine form, the ageless subjects of India's history, ancient and modern." This story, he writes, "sustains a historicist nostalgia" and a "sense that without the carapace of imperial authority, things fall apart."[101]

These narratives of "ageless subjects," such as we find popularized in works of V. S. Naipaul, leave no doubt as to "origins." Underlying such narratives is the idea that as events have happened, they must have a principle or essential cause. By extension, an essence is sought underlying different cultures or civilizations. Samuel Huntington did this, echoing Bernard Lewis, in his popular and influential essay on the "Clash of Civilizations." Increasingly historians have become suspicious of this notion, which supposes an idea of "necessity" in history. Nehru expressed doubt about this manner of interpreting history when he wrote that "It seems absurd... to talk of an impulse, or an idea of life, underlying the growth of Indian civilization. Even the life of an individual draws sustenance from a hundred sources."[102] Nehru's thinking is strongly antiessentialist, particularly his later thought, and he led the new Indian Republic in a democratic experiment decidedly wedded to the politics of hope. This is why Nehru's thought and policy was consistently context specific and flexible within the changing context at the same time as it was principled, and he welcomed a wide diversity of religious and political viewpoints in the process of nation-making so long as they operated within the democratic process and eschewed violence.

Nehru, as a socialist, was very conscious of the coterminous Soviet and Chinese experiments and was deeply disturbed by the metaphysical dogmatism that drove them to commit acts of brutal violence against their own populations. He addressed this problem regularly in his "Letters to the Chief Ministers." He observed that these regimes functioned according to dogmas that denied the element of contingency and experiment in the uncertain passage of human practice in time, which were precisely his own grounds for renouncing violence in the footsteps of Gandhi and the National Movement.

The strange and dangerous metaphysical dogmatism that seems to successfully embrace the dynamism modernity is striking in Hegel and survived in tacit form into the doctrines of Marx, despite Althusser's insistence on the late Marx as a pure figure of scientific certainty beyond the "ideological taint" of humanism. In the writings of Hegel, we find a coupling of the "sheerly contingent" with "universal notional shapes that are evinced in fact and history" that "align themselves and lead on to one another" and "can in fact ultimately be regarded as distinguishable facets of a single all-inclusive universal or concept." By way of this chain, "all dialectic thought-paths lead to the Absolute Idea." We thereby have an idea of the "logically necessary" determining the "path . . . taken in the past and terminating in the present." Outside of this advance, the "contingently historical" dissolves with the unreality of a dream.[103] Hegel perhaps captured this central idea of "necessity" in history more vividly and influentially than any other writer, with a "literary genius" and "swayed in his choice of words by a burgeoning unconscious."[104]

Khilnani observes that "over the past generation the presumption that a single shared sense of India – a unifying concept and idea – can at once define the facts that need recounting and provide the collective subject for the Indian story has lost all credibility." The historical observer confronts an impasse in which there is "on the one hand, the old opposition between the monochromy of the post-imperial imagination and that of the nationalist histories of a unified people" and "on the other hand, set against both, the pointillism of the new Indian historians, ever more ingeniously trawling and re-reading the archives for examples of 'resistance' to the ideas of nation and state."[105] Khilnani may well be speaking of some of the communalist tendencies in describing nationalism in this way; but the nationalist discourse articulated by Nehru was certainly pluralistically conceived from the very outset.

The "post-imperial imagination" is a "nostalgic vision of India" that is "reflected casually and unthinkingly in journalistic evocations of 'eternal India,' of 'political dynasties' and 'feudal corruption'." This in turn is contrasted to a "percussive nationalism" for which "1947 marked a keypoint on a still building crescendo, a thrilling movement to a brighter future, where a settled and defined modern Indian nation, mature in its 'emotional integration,' would come to preside over its own destiny."[106] In fact, both Gandhi and Nehru insisted that the nation could not and

should not be defined; that "definition" must remain as open and mutating as time its moving self. Such a fixed character to national identity is
certainly more in a Hegelian sense of "what must be conceived as what is
realizing itself in what is individual and empirical, and as responsible both
for the being and intelligibility of the later."[107] Hegel thought in terms
of an underlying "universal" existing "*beneath* the surface of natural
objects, as the essences or forces which explain them." In this way, history itself as a larger subjectivity is endowed with consciousness, purpose,
and origin, and accordingly each "meaningful" historical event must have
its particular origin, to be explained in these terms. The development of
the individual necessarily involves the achieving of inner identity with
the movement of the historical universal, an identity that in itself merely
affirms that the two – or many – really are one. The end is ultimately
the origin in the great "Idea." This "Idea" does not depend on hope to
achieve its ends – it is already "ultimate reality," as it were, functioning
in disguise. It is the rational universalism of the French Revolutionary
legacy.

Roger Chartier has questioned such a historical logic. He asks that
we shift the focus of our reflections: supposing we pursue the origins
not of events themselves, as if we could find a pure and unifying ground
of origin behind them, but rather of the manner in which events were
received and thought about by the people involved. This point of view
presupposes no essence or innate purpose to ideas in themselves, but
emphasizes the importance of how they are received and by which people
in a given time and place; in sum, how ideas are created and recreated
with practical use in the context of social and economic forces that are
themselves important without necessarily being fundamental. This is far
closer to Nehru's understanding of events, ideas, and history. It is a world
where hope, and not "ultimate reality," is paramount.

Nehru in many respects played a central role in defining the new Indian
society of postindependence. He strived to create and sustain a balanced
view of local/global, state/society, and tradition/modernity. In writing
The Discovery of India, he offered a unified narrative on Indian history
that elaborates the diversity of India's history with the aim of articulating
a democratic vision for the future of India. Like Gandhi, Nehru had a
deep sense of Indian history and appreciation for its cultural traditions
and articulated these in terms that were inclusively open to all cultures
and religious traditions. In addition, even as the leader of the struggle
against colonialism, he was not afraid of borrowing ideas from European
intellectuals and in fact had a deep understanding of Western cultural

and intellectual traditions. For Nehru as for Gandhi, England was not the enemy. Above all, he articulated these discourses with an emphasis on the importance of a democratic Indian state and thereby contributed enormously to the intellectual foundations of postcolonial Indian democracy.

Khilnani writes: "In the first instance, the history of independent India can be seen, most narrowly but also most sharply, as the history of a state: one of the first, largest and poorest of the many created by the ebb of European empire after the Second World War."[108] Nehru set the goal of creating a unifying yet open and plural narrative around Indian traditions and history that would be inclusive of all Indian cultures, and thus he endeavored to lay the ground for an Indian enlightenment. In this endeavor, he created "a remarkably stable democracy, the largest in the world, despite the country's linguistic, cultural, ethnic, and administrative heterogeneity."[109]

Nehru's discourse began from the conventional premise of articulating a national identity from out of the experience of colonialism and the many chaotic becomings of modernity. He asked, "What is India, apart from her physical and geographical aspects? . . . How does she fit into the modern world?" Coming from a European education in England at Harrow School and Cambridge, Nehru was aware of the ambiguity of his identity as an Indian nationalist calling for Independence. He wrote:

India was in my blood and there was much in her that instinctively thrilled me. And yet I approached her almost as an alien critic, full of dislike for the present as well as for many of the relics of the past that I saw. To some extent I came to her via the West, and looked at her as a friendly Westerner might have done. I was eager and anxious to change her outlook and appearance and give her the garb of modernity.[110]

Nehru is hence candid about the inevitable contradiction of his role in the movement for Indian independence, looking these sensitive issues directly in the face rather than yielding to the social and inner pressure of striking an "authentic" pose. This candidness itself testifies to an openness with regard to the real forces in play, including Western and colonial ones, rather than the option of an "epistemic violence" that amounts to a kind of frigid denial as to the depths of what has changed and the resulting roads of nostalgia.

Thereby avoiding at the outset the trap of discourses of authenticity, Nehru conceived the future of independent India in terms of "a desire for synthesis between the old and the new."[111] Although seeking to reform many Indian customs, for Nehru the project of Indian modernity did not entail any necessary destruction or "transcendence" of India's traditions. On the other hand, nor were traditions something frozen, but an important part of an ongoing evolution. He wrote that: "Traditions have to be accepted to a large extent and adapted and transformed to meet new conditions and ways of thought."[112] This is an example of reflexive modernity, neither warring with the traditional past nor venerating it as a frozen imagining of lost certainty. In contrast to a dialectical view in which tradition is something modernity must "negate or go beyond," Nehru adopted a far more Deweyan view in which modernity is to be dealt with in terms of "proximate questions, not ultimate." Questions of this type are not "concerned with framing a general theory of reality, knowledge and values once and for all, but with finding how authentic beliefs about existence as they currently exist can operate fruitfully and efficaciously in connection with the practical problems that are urgent in actual life."[113] This epistemic framework is integral to "narratives of hope."

Nehru's inclination to "absorb new ideas while retaining the old" is linked to a view of history in which peoples are continually "mixing with each other and slowly changing." In Nehru's vision of history, there are no pure forms, and therefore the future must also be open. As for a "higher" national identity, it is something "partly true" yet with the substance of a dream, which is to say imaginary: "Whether there was something like an Indian dream through the ages, vivid and full of life or sometimes reduced to the murmurings of troubled sleep, I do not know. Every people and every nation has some such belief or myth of national destiny and perhaps it is partly true in each case."[114] This is a very different point of view from the Hegelian, in which history is the "logical growth of notions out of notions" leading to the "notional integration" in "Absolute Knowledge or the Absolute Idea, the test of whose absoluteness consists simply in the fact that nothing further remains to be taken care of," or the end of history.[115]

For Hegel, the mind is a place of forms, or pure ideas that move history toward the final term in which it will "discover itself in its object and its object in itself."[116] This condition is one of a "pure thought" aligned to necessity and beyond the contingency and accident that is expressed in so-called "picture-thinking, whose nature it is to run through the Accidents and Predicates."[117] This is a central theme that runs through the *Phenomenology*. Hegel writes that: "The habit of picture-thinking, when it is interrupted by the Notion, finds it just as irksome as does formalistic thinking that argues back and forth in thoughts that have no actuality. That habit should be called material thinking, a contingent consciousness that is absorbed only in material stuff, and therefore finds it hard to lift the (thinking) self clear of such matter, and to be with itself alone."[118] There is a binary therefore set up from the outset in Hegel's system between imagination and a more pure form of reason in the Notion in which imagination is inherently of lesser value. We also notice here that "habit" is contrasted to "forward movement," and the "pure" (with itself alone) with the "impure." Summing up these negative qualities, the imagination is relegated to the arbitrary level of nature, along with those non-Western cultures that are always still mired in nature and belong to an earlier moment in the development of the Spirit, lost in the "visionary dreaming" of the "anti-human, the merely animal, (which) consists of staying within the spheres of feeling." Meanwhile, "true thoughts...are only to be won through the labour of the Notion. Only the Notion can produce the universality of knowledge which is neither common vagueness nor the inadequacy of ordinary common sense, but a fully developed, perfected cognition."[119] Conversely, hope is very much a product of the imagination and anyone without the certainty of absolute truth – anyone immersed in ordinary rather than supernatural experience – cannot very well manage without it.

This Hegelian epistemic view of knowledge as the subject of a universal historical progression is at best totalizing. As well as degrading ordinary experience in favor of an esoteric level of knowledge, it implies a view of the past in which considerable parts are to be damned to the oblivion of meaninglessness *tout court*. History is in some sense here a great machine driven by an inner "causal" process of elimination to attain an eventual and final purity of identity. Nehru adopted a quite different perspective on history. Regarding the relation of the past to the future, he writes of being able to

trace the threads which bound (the lives of Indian people) to the past, even while their eyes were turned toward the future. Everywhere I found a cultural background which had exerted a powerful influence on their lives. This background was a mixture of popular philosophy, tradition, history, myth, and legend, and it was not possible to draw a line between any of these.

Nehru identifies a socially shared imaginary background with variations in content depending on social positioning: "If my mind was full of pictures from recorded history and more or less ascertained fact, I realized that even the illiterate peasant had a picture gallery in his mind, though largely drawn from myth and tradition."[120] On observing this phenomenon, Nehru neither subjects it to the absolute dismissal that the Hegelian system would demand nor affirms it with the blindly romantic and manipulative enthusiasm of the cultural nationalist of authenticity. Rather, he esteems it pragmatically in saying: "This imagined history and mixture of fact and legend became widely known and gave to the people a strong and abiding cultural background . . . (and also) a wooliness of mind where fact was concerned." Yet it "becomes symbolically true and tells us of the minds and hearts and purposes of the people of that particular epoch."[121] It is a matter for neither abolition nor frozen veneration, but rather a part of the ongoing process and experience of education that is modern culture and society, or what Dewey has called "education as growth."[122] Such a point of view does not consider the thinking of everyday life to be of inferior standing to some higher knowledge of reality, but rather to be the fertile soil out of which positive ideas and change can grow. According to Nehru, social change cannot effectively grow without it, and it is the ground of such change.

Nehru sums up such an approach in his description of an early Indian philosophy whose influence can still be traced:

The approach was one of experiment based on personal experience. . . . What that experience was, and whether it was a vision or a realization of some aspects of truth and reality, or was merely a phantasm of the imagination, I do not know. . . . What interests me more is the approach, which was not authoritarian or dogmatic but was an attempt to discover for oneself what lay behind the external aspect of life.[123]

This is principally a pragmatic approach with many possible applications.

Underlying Nehru's view of India's future, then, is this flexible view of the past in which "India was not isolated, and throughout this long period of history she had continuous and living contacts with Iranians and Greeks, Chinese and Central Asians and others."[124] Nehru argues that "The coming of new races with a different background brought a new driving force to India's tired mind and spirit, and out of that impact arose new problems and new attempts at a solution."[125]

Yet Nehru does not simply promote openness and diversity in modernity for its own sake, and makes the defining principle for its dynamism that of "growth." He argues that "The extreme tolerance of every kind of belief and practice, every superstition and folly, had its injurious side also, for this perpetuated many an evil custom and prevented people from getting rid of the traditional burdens which prevented growth."[126]

This is growth, however, not in the Hegelian sense of a total revolution in pursuit of a higher purity or perfected cognition, but rather in the Deweyan sense: "We are never interested in changing the *whole* environment; there is much that we take for granted and accept as it already is. On this background our activities focus at certain points in an endeavor to introduce needed changes."[127] Such a permission of the random element could never be abided in a Hegelian idea of "growth" in which all "meaningful" movement is necessarily toward an absolute: growth is "not a passive Subject inertly supporting the accidents; it is, on the contrary, the self-moving Notion."[128]

For Hegel, the ordinary experience of everyday life is to be left behind on the road to the highest possible purified understanding, an absolute: "It is in self-consciousness, in the Notion of Spirit, that consciousness first finds its turning-point, where it leaves behind the colourful show of the sensuous here-and-now."[129] In doing so it moves toward "the *essence* or as the *in-itself.*"[130] This is a view quite apart from that of Nehru, who expresses an underlying attitude to metaphysics in his thought in a discussion of Buddhism: "everything continually changes and life in all its forms is a stream of becoming. Reality is not something that is permanent and unchanging . . . but a thing of forces and movements, a succession of sequences."[131] Such a view attributes meaning to each event because of its particularity and uniqueness in the flow of time. For Hegel, however, for whom "The True is the whole (but) the whole is nothing other than the essence consummating itself through its development," meaning can be conceived on nothing less than the colossal scale of an "absolute reality" itself or the "totality of reality," something inevitably imaginary in spite of claims to have transcended the imagination.[132] We see, then, two very different views of what makes the nation.

At the base of these differing views are opposing ideas of identity. For Nehru, identity is hybrid and plural. He writes that: "It would seem that every outside element that has come to India and been absorbed by India has given something to India and taken much from her; it has contributed to its own and India's strength." In the case of India and Iran, "the relationship precedes even the beginnings of Indo-Aryan civilization."[133] Throughout *The Discovery of India*, Nehru traces many forms of inter-relations between India and Iran, Greece, China, and Arabia, pointing to a diversity of origins in both Indian culture and throughout the broad region included in the narrative. The origins of historical developments are to be traced to multiple points, forces, or movements and can thereby never be conceived of as "pure." Conversely, for Hegel, the historical process is ultimately "the interaction of pure knowing with itself," a single and pure origin and end.[134] For Nehru, "otherness" is a source of continuous stimulus and growth. For Hegel, for whom "the *single* individual consciousness is *in itself* Absolute Essence," "otherness" is something to be systematically overcome by way of the universal dialectic.[135] Hegel writes that: "self-consciousness is all reality, not merely *for itself* but *in itself,* only through *becoming* this reality.... It demonstrates itself to be this *along the path* in which first, in the dialectical movement of 'meaning,' perceiving and understanding, otherness as an *intrinsic being* vanishes."[136] In this view in which "truth is only the whole movement of thought, *knowing* itself," we have wandered quite far from the inclusive "truth as we see it" according to the thought of Gandhi and King, as well as the British moral philosophers with their notion of a universal moral sense.[137] For all of these points of view require a substratum in hope.

These opposed views also center on the differences between immanence and transcendence. Immanence focuses on the meaning of each event, with expanding and shrinking levels of scope depending on the point of view, but with no absolute meaning possible. Yet transcendence interprets meaning only on the level of the absolute, and every "little" thing inside must be understood in terms of that absolute as a final aim. Never mind if it needs to be crushed to make the pattern work. At the same time, this difference concerns conceptions of multiple origins versus a single origin, or a mixed-up origin versus a pure origin. A pure origin is a single cause, an overriding principle.

In spite of these differences, Hegel and Nehru share basic concerns in the two works cited here. Both are concerned with the relation between individual and society in the context of modernity and the ethical implications of this problem. This is also to say the problem of modernity and tradition. Equally, both are concerned with writing a kind of "living history" as opposed to a "meticulous chronicle of facts."[138]

Concerning the first point, perhaps the central theme of *Phenomenology* is the relation of the particular to the universal; or the individual to society. With the end of ancient Greek civilization, an inner harmony between individual and society was lost. and the entire historical dialectic is the process of regaining this lost experience of social harmony, yet on a higher and less naïve level, as it were the final level. Hegel speaks of ancient Greece as one "in whose name alone the cultivated man of Europe (and in particular we Germans) feels at home."[139]

In less flamboyant terms, Nehru is preoccupied with the same problem, writing of one who "had no duty to, or conception of, society as a whole, and no attempt was made to make him feel his solidarity with it. This idea is perhaps largely a modern development and cannot be found in any ancient society."[140] Yet Nehru does not propose any final solution to this problem and leaves it open.

Hegel, on the other hand, seeks to resolve it by way of the dialectic. He believes that "something fundamental was lost as well as gained in the transition from the outlook of the ancient to the outlook of the modern world" and is determined to confront "why we left 'beauty' behind and what form the final realization of Spirit is required to take."[141] The *Phenomenology* takes us through all of these phases, from the beautiful and harmonious innocence of Greece and its final inner dissolution through to the fatal divisions of Rome and Stoicism, through the "plant" and "animal" religions of Asia representing an earlier stage of religious development, into the chaotic free-for-all of the French Revolution, to the sublime and purified expression of a Christianity beyond images toward the end. All of it is basically a preoccupation with the modern meaning of being "at home" in the world, the story of the Spirit looking for a home.

Yet in claiming allegiance to the "absolute," Hegel finally must equate himself with the existing powers that be, and thus writes that "It is in fact in the life of a people or nation . . . that the Notion has its complete reality."[142] Democracy is concerned with time and change, and this final frozen moment will surely destroy it. Although Nehru too proposed the state as a solution to this dilemma, it was not conceived in the exclusive terms of a pure Notion or absolute identity that by design excludes so much "dross" from the progressive passage of history. For Nehru, the nation-state retained its legitimacy only so long as it involved the participation of every level of society, and mistakes were the inevitable price to be paid for self-reliance among the public. This, again, returns us to the elementary philosophical difference over means-ends and the problem of "inner violence." To impose a "perfect solution" on the population is, from Nehru's point of view, merely a form of authoritarian violence, as he repeatedly asserted with regard to the Stalinist regime in the Soviet Union. Similarly, he condemned American authoritarian intervention into national politics of developing countries for its disregard for the views of the local population.

Interestingly, in Indian history, Nehru conceives colonialism as a unique experience of rupture as it "constitutes an end to the interwovenness of Asian nations."[143] The very state that for Hegel embodied the necessary passage to Absolute Knowing was for Nehru the source of a totalitarian dissolution of intercultural fertility and national isolation.

For Nehru, modernity is principally a powerful historical impulse. He recognized both its positive and its negative values for India. Colonialism brought "an entirely different impulse from the West, which had slowly developed in Europe from the times of the Renaissance, Reformation, and political revolution in England, and was taking shape in the beginnings of the industrial revolution. The American and French Revolutions were to carry this further."[144] Yet the "British who came to India were not political or social revolutionaries; they were conservatives representing the most reactionary social class in England."[145] Nehru thus identifies the two inextricable faces of modernity: the democratic face in the home country and the dictatorial face in the colonies leading to a "simultaneous engendering of conservativism and revolution."[146] In conceiving the colonial experience in terms of an obstacle to greater possibility through democratic modernity and remembering Indian history as a pluralistic field of intercultural relations, Nehru was able to look positively beyond the dark experiences of colonialism to a different, pluralistic, and democratic future.

It is demonstrated in his fixation on ancient Greece as the single great origin of all things good and meaningful in the world, the singular point of departure for a historical odyssey in which universal meaning is sought and ultimately obtained within the frontiers of the "West." Meanwhile outside it is only the howling fury and blind libido of nature waiting to be conquered.

This tendency toward such a narrow and fanciful construction of history is one of the principal points that Nehru takes issue with: in *The Discovery of India*, he calls for a wider internationalism. In criticizing the limits of the "classical mind," Nehru writes that: "Ancient Greece is supposed to be the fountain-head of European civilization and much has been written about the fundamental difference between the Orient and the Occident. I do not understand this; a great deal of it seems to be vague and unscientific.... Many European thinkers imagined that all that was worthwhile had its origin in Greece and Rome."[147] Such thinking cuts off the real and complex interconnection between the world's cultures in history and shrinks the actuality of events down to a frequently reproduced caricature. It is the tacit yet absolute Orientalism of the *Phenomenology* as a treatise not only of "universal history" but "total reality," absorbed deeply and perhaps unconsciously through the dominant imaginary episteme of the time, that truly undermines any claim of the work to a democratic pluralism in its analysis of modernity. Its success as what is by now an unconscious historical paradigm rests on a set of ignorant and Orientalist assumptions that are by the sheer abundance of their reproduction taken to be plausible.

Nehru's conception of history opens an alternative passage in thinking to the historians of the nineteenth-century Raj and their notions about India, which continue to be recycled by such influential writers as V. S. Naipaul, concerning "essential" antagonisms between a "pure" Indian Hinduism and the brutal pillaging of an "alien" Islam. The same can be said for the communalists with their fascist programs. Looking through the lens of Nehru's thought, we may comprehend more readily, for example, how the elite Hindu culture of Vijayanagara was already "deeply transformed through nearly two centuries of intense and creative interaction with the Islamic world."[148] It would be nonsense to ignore the reality of conflict and hostility between cultures and peoples. Yet the continuing legacy of Orientalist-inspired colonial narratives occludes the broader background reality of hybridity and interaction between cultures, tending to freeze cultural identities into mutually excluding and hostile entities. Nehru's thought invites us to look beyond such imaginary boundaries to a broader and more inclusive understanding of modernity, expressing the practical embodiment of a narrative of hope with profound roots in the Enlightenment in both its Western and non-Western articulations that go much further back than the typical eighteenth-century treatises on Enlightenment would suggest. If the Enlightenment is in its core timeless and variable values, it is also a struggle without end that we have inherited and that can occur only within the limits of time – with no final answers except for our inextinguishable hope, and whoever cares to remember in times to come. There is no certainty of being or Reason doing so on our behalf.

7

Conclusion

This study addresses the curious genealogy of a dominant body of intellectual thought in the Middle East today and the significant political quandary to which it has contributed: a regime based on a politics of authenticity. Iranian intellectuals and, more spectacularly, political upheaval and transformation since the 1979 revolution have provided much of the momentum for this discursive centering of an object of knowledge conceived to have fixed ontological attributes: the "West." This basically metaphysical word can be used freely without requiring further elaboration, and everyone already knows to what it refers. Yet *this* "West" – as the product of this particular Middle Eastern historical and political experience and the discourse to which it has given birth – is not unlike the concept of the "Orient" as "other" produced through colonialism in the sense of being a homogeneous and principally imaginative construct. It is therefore similarly problematic in being dangerously reductive and constitutes an obstacle to genuine communication that would take into account sociological realities, the passage of historical time, and everyday life. With the recent upsurge in democratic movements in Iran, the centrality of the concept "West" in defining Iranian political stakes is challenged by other long-term intellectual currents in the Iranian tradition centering democratic change and openness – a development that reignites hopes for Iran's future as a pluralistic society.

The narrow concept of "West" as alien "other," however, persists at the center of the convoluted Iranian intellectual climate and attempts to constrain political action to a set of very narrow options. As a result of this, too many intellectuals in the Muslim world still confuse the violent

colonial legacy of Western modernity with its democratic narrative, possibilities, and the actually existing civil institutions. In the current junc-
ture where the Iranian population is reaching out at the practical level and
seeking more democratic alternatives to the current regime, it is essential
to demystify the existing intellectual paradigm and political regime in its
claims to "authenticity." In this way it is possible to critically discon-
nect the cognitive attitudes of Iranian Muslim and secular intellectuals
from the damaging heritage of counter-Enlightenment as expressed in
Heidegger and other thinkers – to produce new channels for production
of political thought and meaning.

The reigning confusion around the nature of modernity and the
West has led Iranian politics into a series of theoretically confusing
and politically self-destructive problems. Intellectuals, in having adopted
the intellectual habits of the paranoid ontological paradigm of counter-
Enlightenment, confuse the specific foreign policy problems of America
and Europe with the supposed values of modernity and enlightenment as
such. Where the U.S. policy in the Middle East inflicts political oppression, many Iranian intellectuals make an automatic link to human rights –
for example – as then being also an oppressive discourse. A causal relationship is imagined between any political practice of Western countries
and modern democratic ideas, ideals, or institutions – in a way that would
never be imagined for the practices of states in the Islamic world or the
practices and ideas of Islam. Such a mode of thinking has the severe draw-
back of conceiving any alternative politics, including fascism, as being
morally and practically the equivalent of liberal democratic institutions.

This perplexing condition is the result of intellectuals having spent
too much time and energy demonizing Western modernity and thereby
creating a highly confusing situation where *any* alternative to Western
modernity (or liberalism) becomes intellectually attractive and at times
very popular. We may understand many malicious and abusive discourses
grounded in hatred as sustained by the more sophisticated if gravely
flawed intellectual substratum analyzed in this study. This highly distorted and dangerously simple notion of political options, coupled with
the popular imagination to which it is linked, fails to make any distinction between democratic modernity and a West-centric modernity. As a
driving force for political action, such an intellectual framework is fatally
self-defeating and destructive.

Yet strong democratic alternatives in Iranian politics and intellectual
thought have existed and may receive a surge of new life through the
deconstruction of the paradigm of counter-Enlightenment authenticity.

This study has aimed to highlight the distinction between democratic modernity as a broad human potential and the historically dominant West-centric variant, and the dire peril in remaining blind to this distinction through the denial or ignorance invariably linked to ideologies of authenticity.

What we have done in the various chapters is to present three different discourses about the modern world:

1. *West-centric modernity*: This has been the historically dominant discourse pulled into critical explicitness from the unconscious obscurity of the "unthought" through the wave of poststructuralist critiques initiated by Edward Said's *Orientalism*. As a highly influential discourse, it boasts the names and important contributions of such illustrious figures as the French Enlightenment thinker and jurist Montesquieu, the key philosopher of modernity Hegel, and more recent high-profile scholars such as Bernard Lewis. It influenced the domestic policies of important national leaders from Kemal Ataturk to the Shah of Iran. It would be a mistake to confuse the discourse with Western thought as such. As we show in the study of three Enlightenments, the Western Enlightenment itself contained seminal threads that, although inadequately acknowledged in comparison with more politically constructed and venerated discourses, are themselves open in ways that the West-centric episteme of modernity is not. There are ample discourses within the Western tradition that tacitly or otherwise attempt to refute the West-centric paradigm of modernity and map out alternatives. Moreover, this term obviously indicates a powerful and often unconscious historical tendency rather than any conscious organizational affiliation, and it would be mistaken to assert that those thinkers who have partaken in it are necessarily therefore unworthy of serious attention in their own right as thinkers, or that their work does not potentially contain multiple aspects. All the same, this very strong current in Western thought must be interrogated wherever possible and undone because of the epistemic violence it inflicts on an imagined past and the actual political violence it inspires against non-Western cultures and societies deemed by a twisted logic to be of that "premodern" past deserving of being scrapped on the road to a "great tomorrow." In this study we have paid particular attention to the "means-end" ethical aspect of this debate and tried to show via the thought of Dewey,

Gandhi, and M. L. King that Hegelian "quantum leaps" beyond heritage into some "pure beginning" are invariably a violent disaster, comparing unfavorably to sociologically guided pragmatic approaches that take heritage into account as productive terrain for communication, action, and democratic transformation.

2. *Negation of modernity:* As I have endeavored to show, this tendency is hardly indigenous to the Middle East or even to the non-Western world. Authoritarian discourses in the Islamic world are strongly influenced by the radical anti-Enlightenment discourses of the West. The "negation of modernity" episteme has its origins in a powerful Western discourse dating back to the beginnings of Enlightenment itself. This has found an especial political resonance in those societies experiencing violent modernization from above that, guided by a West-centric ideology of modernity, seeks to abolish or stifle local tradition in the name of a "transcendental" idea of "universalist" modernity. The tragedy of movements inspired by the negation of universal modernity, or "nativist" ideology, is that often they create political tyrannies just as bad as, or worse than, the ones they are intended to replace. In sum, they reproduce the totalizing logic of the West-centric paradigm of modernity in a dialectical fashion that harbors ingrained forms of violent exclusion and can thereby lead only to dangerous and politically oppressive "local" forms. These highly creative and often very colorful political discourses representing an "authentic tradition," invariably dreamed up by intellectuals, come in an enormously wide variety, from ethnic nationalist to religious. Thus I have aimed to demonstrate how unstable all discourses of authenticity necessarily are. They form part of what is a hermeneutic endeavor, yet seek to enshrine themselves with an ontological seal with grave political ramifications. Articulated in the setting of the modern nation-state and intended to "resolve" the tensions of modernity, they invariably produce intolerance, narrow-mindedness, and violence in a smashing of the liberal freedoms that are among the chief gains of the legacy of Enlightenment. One of the functions of this study has been to highlight the elementary precepts of this discourse, expressed at its most philosophically sophisticated in Heidegger's *Being and Time.* By so identifying its defining structure as well as its practical and ethical consequences I hope to alert those of good conscience who might otherwise be swayed under its influence. In

sum, I have sought to highlight the lethal dark side of "radical" alternatives to democracy and liberalism.

3. *A more open, pluralistic and democratic modernity:* This study rejects the idea that a democratic change requires the metaphysical or even epistemological transformation of societies. This intellectual preoccupation presents an elitist obstacle to democratic change and fails to recognize the value of existing cultural resources of meaning and value. To illustrate this, we emphasize the philosophical ideas of Dewey and the practical thought of Gandhi and King, as well as the social and historical thought of Nehru, to show that alternative interpretations of the Enlightenment heritage can help to build a democratic society if the approach is sociologically grounded in everyday life rather than ontological or epistemological.

The chapter on Dewey's "conceptual pluralism" and religion, a relatively neglected if important discourse, opens up a vista to the "unthought" of both Islamist radical discourses and secular modernist-West-centric discourses in terms of traditions, including religion, and democratic political possibility in today's modern societies. Dewey's ideas offer in philosophical form a "middle path" between opposed polemical perspectives that are a ghostly afterlife of a colonial dialectic of "universal" and "local," toward an alternative frame for conceptualization and dialogue. In today's climate of growing international violence, where verbal dialogue has too often already been cast by the wayside as either futile or impossible in the context of a "clash of civilizations," this space is of urgent importance. Dewey as a thinker challenged a deeply entrenched aspect of not only Western but also – as the two are more historically interwoven than is commonly supposed – Islamic thought in a metaphysical dualism. The critique of both received metaphysics and religion called for by Dewey offers a framework that, while building on the democratic achievements of the seventeenth- and eighteenth-century Enlightenment, also opens the democratic promise of the Enlightenment up beyond its narrowly Eurocentric metaphysical anchor to non-Western cultures and forms of reason. As a philosopher of modernity, Dewey opens alternative roads to both the hegemonic paradigm inherited from an era of unchallenged Western dominance and the narrow and poisonous dream of a "return to roots" philosophically enshrined in Heidegger's *Being and Time*.

Dewey is in many ways the twentieth-century philosopher of a radical democratic pluralism. His thought envisions a reading of historical experience in terms of multiple trajectories. In a chapter on the historian Gertrude Himmelfarb's study of the Enlightenment, we can see how a historical movement or epistemic shift occurs through multiple tendencies, but how by way of a kind of selective memory one tendency surfaces as the dominant or official version in a play of writing/text/reading. The work of historical memory is to bring into focus "forgotten" elements in the shadowy margins of historical narrative and thereby to change the meaning for contemporary practice of a historical process or set of events.

In the case of the Enlightenment, we can see how a totalized tendency involving a transcendent Reason gained discursive ascendancy, and that this was largely because of the awesome and ground-shaking dimensions of the French Revolution. Revolutionary historical events in a sense create the intellectuals they claim as their inspiration. Yet the persistence of a shaping unconscious ideological influence engendered by these constructions shows how an equally energetic and conscious work of historical reflection is called for to release alternative possibilities of interpretation, action, and communication. In the case of the Enlightenment, the far less metaphysically dogmatic streams of British and American Enlightenment thought, in their sociological concreteness, offer a far wider possible range of application for traditional and religious culture in the creation of democratic modernity than the absolutist idea of a total Reason and hence total beginning at the core of French Enlightenment thought. This study alerts us, again, to the importance of a history of systems of thought, as much in the Islamic as in the Western context, the two of which in any case overlap considerably more frequently than the often falsely opposed labels would lead us to suspect. By inquiring into systems of thought, we may undo the reliance not only on such labels, but also on the unconscious intellectual habits that sustain their hold over both imagination and intellect in academic and popular thought.

A rereading of the ideas and work of key twentieth-century figures Gandhi and M. L. King shows not only their shared vision, but the broader system of thought to which they both gave a living articulation. This system of thought, of which they made such a practical success as a means of achieving a democratic modernity in their societies, is also articulated theoretically as a philosophical position by Dewey in relation to Western intellectual thought and by Arkoun in relation to received Islamic tradition. Although there is no identical core uniting these diverse thinkers and activists, there are nevertheless basic precepts and dispositions in relation to the problems of modernity and tradition that distinguish them as being members of what may loosely be called a movement of thought committed to a radical democratic politics based on the permission of all possible sources of meaning. Equally, they all focus on a concrete pragmatics of social reconstruction and avoid the totalizing metaphysical and epistemological constructs that have often wrought tragedy. This system of thought, as a historical framework, is given powerful articulation by Nehru, whose work provides interesting contrast to the Hegelian expression of the Eurocentric paradigm of history tied to the Western hegemony of an earlier era. The basic precepts of such a West-centric paradigm reanimate themselves in the "clash of civilizations" thesis set in the midst of the highly destructive and misguided U.S. war efforts in the Middle East intended to control oil resources and impose some abstractly conceived model of "democracy" by force of sheer violence. Nehru's thought, on the other hand, paved the way for the Indian democracy that today is an "effervescent bridgehead of liberty on the Asian continent."

By articulating the already available theoretical and practical dimensions of a more open and nonviolent paradigmatic road to democratic modernity, I hope to encourage moral and spiritual alternatives to the violent and worn-out "philosophy of history" that attempts to freeze all growth in social experience to a notion of some fixed underlying substance of an ontological or epistemic variety.

Where this is concerned, Iran and other Islamic societies face a peculiar intellectual impasse. That many key concepts behind this may be found in an analysis of Heidegger's principle work *Being and Time* reveals the error in conceiving either "East" or "West" as independently evolving historical entities and any framework that excludes either the one or the other in a study of the formation of modernity. It is necessary to be at once context specific and sensitive to global networks on numerous levels that render impossible any notion of a society as being outside of modernity or in isolation from globalized history. This historical aspect of the "thought"/"unthought" is at perhaps the defining level in constructing modernity as an obstacle to communication: the notion of an unchanging historicity, excluding all outside reality and consigning it to a limbo or nothingness, that begins in the world of classical Greece and Rome, and that is called "Western civilization" as a historical entity almost endowed with its own "subjectivity."

Heidegger's *Being and Time* left strictly intact the historical horizons of this episteme while radically remarking the frontier between the

"thought" and the "unthought" at the crucial level of truth by constructing an alternative to universal modernity in a discourse of "authenticity,"
objective knowledge to ontological understanding, and so forth. Inher-
iting the Heideggerian paradigm, Fardid and other Iranian intellectuals
expanded the boundaries of the historical frontier beyond the "West"
to include the "East" in the context of a struggle in Islamic societies
over the very definition of Islam. Presenting this to the outside world as
a "resurgence of Islam," Fardid in fact preserved intact and exploited
the Heideggerian move of endowing an ontological sanction to claim an
ultimate legitimacy in the ceaseless contest over meaning that defines the
pace and texture of modern social experience at every level.

This militant vision of Islam based on a peculiarly Heideggerian "spiritual superiority" is of course a historically constructed discourse, subject
to the limits of "thought" and "unthought" as are all discourses, and
with a genealogical ancestry linking back through successive interpretations and uses that arise within the transfiguring particularity of historical
events. Only by grasping this does it become possible to appreciate Islam
as a living and pluralistic reality in which there are equally, though more
"quietly," calls from "Islamic" thinkers for new Qu'ranic hermeneutics
and the democratization of contemporary Middle Eastern societies. In
sum, the Islamist discourse of authenticity can only be properly understood in the context of a larger political, cultural, and hermeneutical
process of the construction of identity involving individuals and institutions in contemporary Islamic societies. The popular struggle for a
more democratic social order in Iran today contributes to the practical undoing of such a totalizing identity politics, and intellectuals must
meet this momentum on the theoretical level through creatively engaging systems and channels of meaning production in fast-evolving Islamic
societies.

By tracing modern Islamic discourses through the reformist thought
of Jamal al-Din Afghani, Muhammad Abduh, and Abd al-Hamid ibn
Badis, written in the European colonial context with the aim of inspiring an "awakening" to reconcile Islam with modern science, we find a
seismic epistemic rupture with regard to the "new" universe of Islamic
thinkers (Arkoun, Fazlur Rahman, Nasr Hamid Abu Zayd), who rather
engage the problem of Islamic culture's historical construction and hence
deal in a radical hermeneutics rather than traditional apologetics. If the
early thinkers wanted to embrace "Western" science while preserving
a "traditional" Islamic identity, the newer thinkers question and reconstruct that very Islamic identity in itself. This shows a radically different

approach to the continuing problematic of modernity that has also characterized newly arising self-reflective discourses in Western settings that are more well known (Deleuze, Foucault, etc.). Yet these developments in different societies are interlinked and are prone to similar weaknesses and strengths, which have nevertheless different consequences in their respective social contexts.

Arkoun's intellectual project is inspired by two basic questions that haunted him during his student years in Algeria: How is the Arab-Muslim identity that claimed to define the Algerian nationalist movement to be understood? How are we to determine in what measure modern civilization, represented in Algeria by colonial power, can be understood as a universal civilization? Later, as a student in Paris working with March Bloch and Lucien Febvre, he applied a structuralist critique to the dominant nationalist ideology of the Algerian revolution on the grounds of its denial of difference within Algerian society and Islam. From these beginnings Arkoun went on to evolve a powerful and influential hermeneutical critique of prevailing Islamic and nationalist discourses in Islamic societies that participates in a larger epistemic transfiguration that is currently underway.

This epistemic transfiguration in Islamic societies is hardly surprising, as the "new" thinkers have inhabited a different world in which Islamic countries, now having gained independence, nevertheless exist under states that stifle even the faintest hope of democratic reform. These states, the result of nationalist revolutions, at times socialist, Marxist, or even Islamist, have been welded into place through the political games of local elites and Western nations that often enough perceived secular or democratic political expressions as contrary to their interests in the region. In this context, the "new" thinkers confront local tyrants who either claim to speak on behalf of a "true" Islam or aggressively seek to "undo" religion in the name of a monstrous "secularism," as well as corrupted defenders of Islamic orthodoxy and Islamist militants who argue for the theological legitimacy of a totalitarian "Islamic state." In sum, a widespread crisis of legitimacy in Islamic cultures has effected the transition from a reformist apologetics in the colonial context to a project of radical hermeneutics expressing a vast spectrum of often-opposed political tendencies, from the democratically and spiritually inspired autocritique of Arkoun to the anarcho-fascist ideology of cosmic destruction articulated, alas more famously, by Osama bin Laden. The centrifugal historical moment that burst forth on the world scene and revolutionized the very terms of not only Islamic political discourse but the framework of received Western sociology itself was of course the Iranian Revolution of 1979 – something still far from having been adequately interpreted in the full significance of the impasse to which it has led us.

The problematic of democracy in the transition from a colonial or neo-colonial dialectic of center-periphery to a set of competing hermeneutical horizons within a common experience of modernity mapped out in this study concern the tensions and alternative futures of modernity's evolution in both non-Western societies and the West itself. This study has offered an outline of some aspects of a transforming historical epistemology, tracing certain limits between the "thought" and the "unthought," with initial specific reference to contemporary Iranian intellectual discourses but also referring more broadly to the dangerous discursive interzone of Western and Middle Eastern (and non-Western generally) peoples and states in an era overshadowed by the ongoing tragedy of the U.S. war in Iraq. In terms of geopolitics, this discursive interzone holds a great deal at stake for the future of both Middle Eastern and Western societies in terms of democratic promise and authoritarian terror on the highly uncertain, but certainly shared, horizon of tomorrow's world.

Notes

Introduction: Political Islam's Romance with the "West"

1. Corbin visited Iran for the next 25 years and had regular meetings with Tabataba'i and other Iranian intellectuals.
2. Ayatollah Morteza Motahari (1920–79) was a leading clerical and political figure during the 1978 Revolution and a close disciple of Ayatollah Khomeini. He was assassinated after the Revolution by a radical Islamic group. Ayatollah Seyed Mohammad Hussein Beheshti (1928–81) was a leading architect of the Islamic Republic in Iran. He was head of Iranian judicial system after the Revolution. He too was assassinated together with more than seventy members of the Islamic Republic party on June 28, 1981.
3. Seyyed Hussein Nasr (1933–) is a prominent scholar of Islamic philosophy. He was a university president and held other senior positions in the government in the 1960s and 70s. He is currently a professor of Islamic Studies at George Washington University. Dariush Shayegan (1935–) is one of Iran's prominent scholars of comparative religion. Shayegan studied with Henry Corbin in Paris and wrote a book about him and his works.
4. Shari'ati was largely influenced by Louis Massignon (1883–1962) and his unique interpretation of Islam. However, Henry Corbin was a student of Massignon, and he held the position of Islamic Studies Chair at the Sorbonne after Massignon's death.
5. See J. G. A. Pocock, "Post-Puritan England and the Problem of Enlightenment," in *Culture and Politics from Puritanism to the Enlightenment*, edited by Perez Zagorin. University of California Press, 1980.

1. Intellectuals and the Politics of Despair

1. Homa Katouzian, *Mossadeq and the Struggle for Power in Iran* (London: I. B. Tauris, 2009), p. 11.
2. Ahmad Fardid, "Shadegg-e Hedayat dar Chaleh-ye-harz-e Farense [Sadeq Hedayat's descent into the cesspool of French literature]," *Ettela't* (February 19, 1974).

3. Ahmad Fardid, "Chand porsesh dar bab-e farhange-e Sharq [A few questions on the culture of the East]," transcribed by Reza Davari, *Farhang-e va
Zendegi* 7 (1971), 32–9, p. 33.

4. Al-e Ahmad, in fact, did not understand the Fardidist notion of Westoxication. For Fardid, Gharbzadegi represented the influence of Greek ideas in the
Islamic world, and its genealogy dated back to a much earlier time.

5. Al-e Ahmad. "Masalan Sharh-e Ahvalat," in Hamid Tabrizi, *Jalal Al-e
Ahmad: Mardi dar Kesha kesh-e Tarikh-e Moaser* [Jalal Al-e Ahmad: A Man
in Troubled Contemporary History] (Tabriz: Nashr-e Kave, 1978), p. 63.

6. Mehrzad Boroujerdi, *Iranian Intellectuals and the West: The Tormented
Triumph of Nativism* (Syracuse, NY: Syracuse University Press, 1996), p. 9.

7. Quoted in Boroujerdi, pp. 148–9.

8. Boroujerdi, p. 149.

9. Boroujerdi, p. 150.

10. Dariush Shayegan, *Asiya Bar Barabar-e Gharb* [Asia Facing the West]
(Tehran: Amir Kabir, 1977), p. 168.

11. Shayegan, "Din va falsefeh va elm dar Sharq va Gharg" [Religion, philosophy
and science in East and West]. *Alefba* (Tehran) 1st ser., no. 6 (2536/1977),
101–9, p. 108. Quoted in Boroujerdi, p. 149.

12. Shayegan, *Asia Facing the West*, p. 150.

13. Ibid., p. 149.

14. Ibid., p. 150.

15. Ibid., p. 151.

16. Ibid.

17. Ibid., p. 152.

18. Ibid.

19. Ibid.

20. Ibid.

21. Aramesh Dustdar (under the pseudonym Babak Bamdadan), "Emtena' e
tafakkor e dini" [The Impossibility of Religious Thinking], *Alephba* (Paris),
1, 1982.

22. Aramesh Dustdar, *Derakhshesh hay-e tire* [Dark Sparkles] (Cologne,
Germany: Andishe Azad Publication, 1993), p. XII.

23. Javad Tabatabai, *Ibn-Khaldun va olum-e ejtemai* [Essay on Ibn-Khaldun:
The Impossibility of the Social Sciences in Islam] (Tehran: Tarh-e No, 1995),
pp. 47–8.

24. Max Weber also reverts to this sort of reductionism when discussing Islam.
For a critique of this approach see Marshall Hodgson, *The Venture of Islam*
(Chicago: University of Chicago Press, 1974).

2. The Crisis of the Nativist Imagination

1. Rimbaud. Poesies. *Une saison en enfer. Illuminations* (Gallimard, 1999),
pp. 177–8.

2. Ibid., p. 179.

3. Ibid., p. 192.

4. Ibid., p. 200.

5. Ibid.
6. Tayeb Salih, *Season of Migration to the North* (New Hampshire: Heinemann, 1970)., p. 1.
7. Edward W. Said, *Orientalism. Western Conceptions of the Orient* (New Delhi, Penguin, 2001), p. 1.
8. Ibid., p. 135.
9. Lois Parkinson and Wendy B. Faris, editors, *Magical Realism: Theory, History, Community* (Durham, NC: Duke University Press, 1995), p. 497.
10. Said, *Orientalism*, p. 5.
11. Parkinson and Faris, *Magical Realism*, p. 497.
12. Salih, *Season of Migration*, pp. 17, 14–15, 46.
13. Frederic Jameson, *Late Marxism* (London: Verso, 1990), p. 30.
14. Ervand Abrahamian, *Iran between Two Revolutions* (Princeton, NJ: Princeton University Press, 1982), p. 105.
15. Abrahamian. *Iran between Two Revolutions*, pp. 123–4.
16. Ibid., p. 1.
17. Mohammed Arkoun, *The Unthought in Contemporary Islamic Thought* (London: Saqi Books, 2002), p. 18.
18. Said, *Orientalism*, p. 332.
19. Ibid.
20. Paul Ricoeur, *Memory, History, Forgetting* (Chicago: University of Chicago Press., 2004), p. 149.
21. Salih, *Season of Migration*, p. 5.
22. Ibid., p. 125.
23. **AU: Please provide note text.**
24. Said, *Orientalism*, p. 1.
25. Salih, *Season of Migration*, p. 92.
26. Ibid., p. 33.
27. Patricia Geesey, "Cultural hybridity and contamination in Tayeb Salih's *Mawsim al-hijra ila al-Shamal* (*Season of Migration to the North*)," *Research in African Literatures* 28 (1997), 135.
28. Salih, *Season of Migration*, p. 49.
29. Geesey, "Cultural hybridity," 132.
30. Ibid.
31. Ibid., 4.
32. Ibid., 2.
33. Ibid.
34. Ibid., 48, 102.
35. Ibid., 11
36. Ibid., 4.
37. John Dewey, *The Philosophy of John Dewey*, edited by John J. McDermott (Chicago: University of Chicago Press, 1979), p. 89.
38. David L. Pike, *Passage through Hell: Modernist Descents, Medieval Underworlds* (Ithaca, NY: Cornell University Press, 1997), p. 38.
39. Salih, *Season of Migration*, p. 30.
40. Ibid., p. 29.
41. Ibid., p. 33.

42. Ibid., p. 134.
43. Geesey, "Cultural hybridity," 137.
44. Arkoun, *The Unthought*, p. 20.
45. Zamora, Lois Parkinson, and Wendy B. Faris, *Magical Realism: Theory, History, Community* (Durham, NC: Duke University Press, 1995), p. 498.
46. Salih, *Season of Migration*, p. 33.
47. Ibid., p. 50.
48. Ibid., p. 108.
49. Ibid., p. 130.
50. Ricoeur, *Memory, History, Forgetting*, p. 41.
51. Salih, *Season of Migration*, p. 165.
52. Ibid., p. 150.
53. Ibid., p. 168.

3. Modernity beyond Nativism and Universalism

1. John Dewey, *The Philosophy of John Dewey*, edited by John J. McDermott (Chicago: University of Chicago Press, 1973), p. 295.
2. Hillary Putnam, *Ethics Without Ontology* (Cambridge, MA: Harvard University Press, 2004), p. 84.
3. Georg Wilhelm Hegel, *Phenomenology of Spirit* (Motilal Banarsidass, 1998), p. 212.
4. Rachid Benzine, *Les Nouveaux Penseurs de l'Islam* [New Thinkers of Islam], (Albin Michel, 2004), p. 114.
5. Ibid., p. 59.
6. Ibid., p. 118.

4. Heidegger and Iran: The Dark Side of Being and Belonging

1. Ali Shari'ati, *Collected Work*, Vol. 4 [in Persian] (Elham, 1994), p. 254.
2. Richard Wolin, *The Seduction of Unreason. The Intellectual Romance with Fascism from Nietzsche to Postmodernism* (Princeton, NJ: Princeton University Press, 2004), p. 2.
3. Ibid., p. 5.
4. Ibid., p. 286.
5. Ibid., p. 285.
6. Ibid., p. 284.
7. Richard Wolin, *The Politics of Being: The Political Thought of Martin Heidegger* (New York: Columbia University Press, 1990), p. 17.
8. Wolin, *The Seduction of Unreason*, p. 30.
9. Friedrich Nietzsche, *The Will to Power*, trans. Walter Kaufmann (New York: Vintage, 1967), p. 612. Quoted in Wolin, *The Seduction of Unreason*, p. 31.
10. Ibid., p. 3.
11. Wolin, *The Politics of Being*, p. 16.
12. Martin Heidegger, "The Self Assertion of the German University," translated by Keith Harris, *Review of Metaphysics*, 38 (1985), 467–502, p. 480. Quoted

in *The Cambridge Companion to Heidegger*, edited by Charles Guignon (Cambridge, UK: Cambridge University Press, 1993), p. 277.

13. Martin Heidegger, *Beitrage zur Philosophie. Gesamtausgabe*, p. 38. Quoted in Wolin, *The Politics of Being*, p. 25.
14. Wolin, *The Politics of Being*, p. 23.
15. Ibid., p. 24.
16. Ibid., p. 25.
17. Ibid., p. 22.
18. Ibid., p. 27.
19. Ibid., p. 23.
20. Ibid., p. 27.
21. Martin Heidegger, *Being and Time*, translated by Joan Stambaugh (Albany: State University of New York Press, 1996), p. 18.
22. Ibid., p. 281.
23. Ibid., p. 17.
24. Ibid., p. 358.
25. Ibid., p. 357.
26. Ibid., p. 356.
27. Ibid., p. 358.
28. Wolin, *The Politics of Being*, p. 17.
29. Heidegger, *Being and Time*, pp. 169–70.
30. **AU: Please provide note text.**
31. Ibid., p. 351.
32. Michael Inwood, *A Heidegger Dictionary* (Oxford: Blackwell, 1999), pp. 6–7.
33. Martin Heidegger, *Schellings Abhandlung über das Wesen der menschlichen Freiheit* (1809) (Tübingen: Niemeyer, 1971)/*Schelling's Treatise on the Essence of Human Freedom*, translated by J. Stambaugh (Athens, OH: Ohio University Press, 1985), pp. 31/25. Quoted in Inwood, *A Heidegger Dictionary*, pp. 6–7.
34. Martin Heidegger, *An Introduction to Metaphysics*, translated by Ralph Manheim (New Haven, CT: Yale University Press, 1959), p. 203.
35. Martin Heidegger, *Nietzsche*, vol. II: *The Eternal Recurrence of the Same*, translated by D. F. Krell (San Francisco: Harper & Row, 1984). Quoted in Inwood, *A Heidegger Dictionary*, p. 185.
36. Martin Heidegger, *Beitrage zur Philosophie (Vom Ereignis)*, edited by F.-W. von Herrmann (1989), manuscripts of 1936–8. Quoted in Inwood, *A Heidegger Dictionary*, p. 211.
37. Heidegger, *Being and Time*, p. 19.
38. Ibid., p. 161.
39. Ibid., p. 163.
40. Ibid., p. 166.
41. Wolin, *The Politics of Being*, pp. 21–2.
42. Ibid., p. 20.
43. " 'Only a god can save us': *Der Spiegel*'s interview with Martin Heidegger (1976)," in *Heidegger: The Man and the Thinker* (Chicago: Precedent, 1981), p. 24.

44. Heidegger, *Being and Time*, pp. 67–8.
45. Ibid., p. 71.
46. Ibid., p. 65.
47. Michael Polanyi. *Personal Knowledge. Towards a Post-Critical Philosophy* (Chicago: University of Chicago Press, 1974 [1958]), p. 39.
48. Ibid., p. 202.
49. Ibid., p. 41.
50. Ibid., p. 119.
51. Ibid., p. 235.
52. Wolin, *The Politics of Being*, pp. 28–9.
53. Heidegger, *Being and Time*, p. 240.
54. Wolin, *The Politics of Being*, p. 28.
55. Heidegger, *Being and Time*, p. 351.
56. Ibid., p. 357.
57. Ibid., p. 284.
58. Ibid., p. 275.
59. Wolin, *The Politics of Being*, p. 39.
60. Winfried Franzen, *Von der Existenzialontologie zur Seinsgeschichte*, p. 10. Quoted in Wolin, *The Politics of Being*, p. 21.
61. Heidegger, *Being and Time*, p. 202.
62. Ibid., p. 353.
63. Ibid., p. 299.
64. Ibid., p. 15.
65. Ibid., p. 283.
66. Ibid., p. 20.
67. Ibid., p. 41.
68. Ibid., p. 31.
69. Ibid.
70. Ibid., p. 255.
71. "Something to steer by" (review of *John Dewey and the High Tide of American Liberalism* by Alan Ryan), *London Review of Books* (June 20, 1996), 7.
72. Heidegger, *Being and Time*, p. 292.
73. Ibid., p. 31.
74. Ibid., p. 287.
75. Ibid., p. 5.
76. Ibid., p. 3.
77. Ibid., p. 24.
78. Ibid., p. 3.
79. Ibid., p. 264.
80. Ibid., p. 235.
81. Wolin, *The Politics of Being*, p. 40.
82. Heidegger, *Being and Time*, p. 175.
83. Ibid., p. 266.
84. Ibid., pp. 351–2.
85. Ibid., p. 351.
86. "Only a god can save us," p. 24.

87. Heidegger, *Being and Time*, p. 214.

88. Ibid., p. 358.

89. Ibid., p. 259.

90. Ibid., p. 286.

91. Ibid., p. 301.

92. Ibid., p. 351.

93. Friedrich Nietzsche, *Beyond Good and Evil. Prelude to a Philosophy of the Future,* translated by Walter Kaufmann (New York: Vintage Books, 1989), pp. 2–3.

94. Heidegger, *Being and Time*, p. 272.

95. Martin Heidegger, "On the essence of truth," in *Basic Writings*, p. 116.

96. Ibid., p. 120.

97. Ibid., p. 127.

98. Heidegger, *Beitrage zur Philosophie,* quoted in Inwood.

99. Heidegger, "On the essence of truth," p. 127.

100. Ibid., p. 129.

101. Ibid., p. 124.

102. Ibid., p. 130.

103. Ibid., p. 132.

104. Ibid., p. 109.

105. Ibid., p. 132.

106. Ibid., p. 124.

107. Ibid., p. 138.

108. Heidegger, *Being and Time*, p. 276.

109. Ibid., p. 273.

110. Ibid., p. 358.

111. Ibid., p. 352.

112. Ibid., p. 299.

113. Martin Heidegger, "The origin of the work of art," in *Basic Writings*, p. 143.

114. Thomas Sheehan, "Reading a life: Heidegger and hard times," in *The Cambridge Companion to Heidegger* (Cambridge University Press, 1993), p. 83.

115. Ibid., p. 76

116. Heidegger, "Only a god can save us," p. 57.

117. Heidegger, "The origin of the work of art," p. 167.

118. Heidegger, *An Introduction to Metaphysics*, p. 203.

119. Heidegger, "The origin of the work of art," p. 180.

120. Ibid., p. 186.

121. Quoted in Inwood, p. 120.

122. John D. Caputo, "Heidegger and theology," in *The Cambridge Companion to Heidegger* (Cambridge University Press, 1993), p. 272.

123. Sheehan, "Reading a life," p. 78.

124. Hans-Georg Gadamer, *Philosophical Hermeneutics*, translated by David E. Linge (Berkeley: University of California Press, 1976), p. 214.

125. Caputo, "Heidegger and theology," p. 277.

126. Wolin, *The Politics of Being*, p. 75.

127. Quoted in Wolin, *The Politics of Being*, p. 75.

128. Sheehan, "Reading a life," p. 278.

129. Heidegger, "The origin of the work of art," p. 166.
130. Heidegger, *Poetry, Language, and Thought*, p. 91.
131. Soroush is influenced by analytical philosophy and is critical of the German tradition. However, he too imagines the West in terms of its spiritual decline and rejects secularism as inauthentic. The fact that Soroush embraces a democratic project for Iran represent his critical philosophical stand against Heideggerian critique of modernity.
132. Ahmad Fardid, *Soqut-e-Hedayat dar Chaleh-ye harz-e adabiyyat-e Faranse* [Sadeq Hedayat's descent into the cesspool of French literature]. *Ettela'at* (February 24, 1974), 19.
133. Quoted in Mehrzad Boroujerdi, *Iranian Intellectuals and the West. The Tormented triumph of Nativism* (New York: Syracuse University Press, 1996), p. 64.
134. Ibid.
135. Reza Baraheni, *Qessehnevisi*, 2nd ed. (Tehran: Ashrafi, 1969), p. 465.
136. Quoted in Boroujerdi, *Iranian Intellectuals and the West*, p. 68.
137. Jalal Al-e Ahmad, *Gharbzadegi (Occidentosis)* (Ravagh Publishers, 1972), p. 15.
138. Heidegger, *Introduction to Metaphysics*, p. 28; Al-e Ahmad, *Occidentosis*, p. 28.
139. Al-e Ahmad, *Gharbzadegi*, p. 31.
140. Ibid., p. 34.
141. Ibid., p. 31.
142. Ibid., p. 59.
143. Ibid., p. 31.
144. Al-e Ahmad, *Dar Khedmat va Khyanat-ye Rowshanfekran*, vol. 2, p. 149.
145. Al-e Ahmad, *Gharbzadegi*, p. 78.
146. Ibid., p. 79.
147. Al-e Ahmad, *Lost in the Crowd*, p. 64.
148. Ali Shari'ati, *Marxism and Other Western Fallacies: An Islamic Critique*, p. 32.
149. Ali Shari'ati, *On the Sociology of Islam*, p. 119.
150. Shari'ati, *Marxism and Other Western Fallacies*, p. 95.
151. Ibid., p. 67.
152. Shari'ati, *On the Sociology of Islam*, p. 79.

5. Democracy and Religion in the Thought of John Dewey

1. AU: Please provide note text.
2. John Dewey, *The Philosophy of John Dewey*, edited by John J. McDermott (Chicago: University of Chicago Press, 1973), p. 289.
3. Ibid., p. 50.
4. Ibid., p. 209.
5. John Dewey, *A Common Faith* (New Haven, CT: Yale University Press, 1934), p. 25.
6. Steven Fesmire, *John Dewey and Moral Imagination. Pragmatism in Ethics* (Bloomington: Indiana University Press, 2003), p. 28.

7. Dewey, *A Common Faith*, p. 86.
8. Dewey, *The Philosophy of John Dewey*, p. 336.
9. Fesmire, *John Dewey and Moral Imagination*, p. 49.
10. John Dewey, "What I Believe." Quoted in Fesmire, *John Dewey and Moral Imagination*, p. 9.
11. Dewey, *A Common Faith*, p. 48.
12. Ibid., p. 75.
13. Dewey, *The Philosophy of John Dewey*, p. 382.
14. Dewey, *A Common Faith*, p. 79.
15. Dewey, *The Philosophy of John Dewey*, p. 311.
16. Fesmire, *John Dewey and Moral Imagination*, p. 3.
17. Ibid., p. 4.
18. Dewey, *The Philosophy of John Dewey*, p. 209.
19. Dewey, *A Common Faith*, p. 18.
20. Dewey, *The Philosophy of John Dewey*, p. 74.
21. Ibid., p. 91.
22. Ibid., p. 337.
23. Ibid., p. 19.
24. Ibid., p. 185.
25. Ibid., p. 342.
26. Ibid., pp. 34–6.
27. Ibid., p. 38.
28. Martin Heidegger, "Letter on Humanism." In *Basic Writings*, p. 260.
29. Martin Heidegger, "On the Essence of Truth." In *Basic Writings*, p. 116.
30. Dewey, *The Philosophy of John Dewey*, p. 281.
31. Ibid., p. 328.
32. Ibid., p. 311.
33. Ibid., p. 577.
34. Ibid., p. 339.
35. Ibid., pp. 77, 78.
36. Ibid., p. 339.
37. Ibid., p. 339.
38. Ibid., p. 347.
39. Ibid., p. 339.
40. Ibid., p. 337.
41. Dewey, *A Common Faith*, p. 15.
42. Fesmire, *John Dewey and Moral Imagination*, p. 3.
43. Dewey, *The Philosophy of John Dewey*, p. 280.
44. Ibid., pp. 213–14.
45. Ibid., p. 224.
46. Fesmire, *John Dewey and Moral Imagination*, p. 12.
47. Ibid., p. 11.
48. Hillary Putnam, *Ethics without Ontology* (Cambridge, MA: Harvard University Press, 2004), pp. 97–8.
49. Fesmire, *John Dewey and Moral Imagination*, p. 28.
50. Dewey, *The Philosophy of John Dewey*, p. 50.
51. Ibid., pp. 56–7.

52. Fesmire, *John Dewey and Moral Imagination*, p. 50.
53. Dewey, *The Philosophy of John Dewey*, p. 66.
54. Ibid., p. 50.
55. Ibid., p. 411.
56. Ibid., p. 415.
57. Mohammed Arkoun, *The Unthought in Contemporary Islamic Thought* (London: Saqi Books, 2002), p. 18.
58. Dewey, *The Philosophy of John Dewey*, p. 13.
59. See Partha Chatterjee, *Nationalist Thought and the Colonial World. A Derivative Discourse* (University of Minnesota, 1986) and Ashis Nandy, "The Intimate Enemy," in *Exiled at Home* (Delhi: Oxford University Press, 2005).
60. Dewey, *The Philosophy of John Dewey*, p. 29.
61. Meera Nanda, *Prophets Facing Backward. Postmodern Critiques of Science and Hindu Nationalism in India* (New Brunswick, NJ: Rutgers University, 2003), p. 190.
62. Ibid., pp. 183–96.
63. Dewey, *The Philosophy of John Dewey*, p. 337.
64. Marquis de Condorcet, *The Future Progress of the Human Mind*. In *The Portable Enlightenment Reader*, edited by Isaac Kramnick (New York: Penguin, 1995), pp. 26–38.
65. Dewey, *The Philosophy of John Dewey*, p. 64.
66. Ibid., p. 555.
67. Ibid., p. 62.
68. Ibid., p. 64.
69. Ibid., p. 335.
70. Ibid., p. 353.
71. Ibid., p. 589.
72. Ibid., p. 56.
73. Ibid., pp. 410–411.
74. Ibid., p. 214.
75. Ibid., p. 577.
76. Ibid., p. 214.
77. Putnam, *Ethics without Ontology*, p. 51.
78. Dewey, *The Philosophy of John Dewey*, p. 190.
79. Ibid., p. 218.
80. Putnam, *Ethics without Ontology*, pp. 72–7.
81. Ibid., pp. 37–49.
82. Dewey, *The Philosophy of John Dewey*, p. 284.
83. Ibid., p. 193.
84. Ibid., pp. 86, 89.
85. Ibid., p. 241.
86. Ibid., p. xxvii.
87. Ibid., p. 264.
88. Ibid., p. 265.
89. Ibid., pp. 265–6.
90. Putnam, *Ethics without Ontology*, p. 19.
91. Dewey, *The Philosophy of John Dewey*, p. 276.

92. Putnam, *Ethics without Ontology*, p. 85.
93. Ibid., p. 47.
94. Ibid., p. 18.
95. Dewey, *The Philosophy of John Dewey*, p. 214.
96. Fesmire, *John Dewey and Moral Imagination*, p. 5.
97. Dewey, *A Common Faith*, p. 18.
98. Fesmire, *John Dewey and Moral Imagination*, p. 28.
99. Dewey, *The Philosophy of John Dewey*, p. 276.
100. Putnam, *Ethics without Ontology*, p. 75.
101. Fesmire, *John Dewey and Moral Imagination*, p. 35.
102. Ibid., p. 18.
103. Ibid., p. 10.
104. Ibid., pp. 10–11.
105. Dewey, *A Common Faith*, p. 17.
106. Ibid., p. 33.
107. Fesmire, *John Dewey and Moral Imagination*, p. 23.
108. Ibid., p. 5.
109. Dewey, *A Common Faith*, p. 56.
110. Ibid., p. 87.
111. Ibid., p. 10.
112. Ibid, pp. 12–14.
113. Ibid. p. 11.
114. Arkoun, *The Unthought in Contemporary Islamic Thought*, p. 28.
115. Dewey, *A Common Faith*, p. 2.
116. Ibid., pp. 52–3.
117. Ibid., p. 53.
118. Ibid., pp. 4–7.
119. Ibid., p. 6.
120. Arkoun, *The Unthought in Contemporary Islamic Thought*, p. 76.
121. Dewey, *A Common Faith*, pp. 9, 15.
122. Ibid., p. 22.
123. Ibid., p. 21.
124. Dewey, *The Philosophy of John Dewey*, p. 383.
125. Dewey, *A Common Faith*, p. 26.
126. Ibid., p. 39.
127. Ibid., p. 43.
128. Dewey, *The Philosophy of John Dewey*, p. 311.
129. Putnam, *Ethics without Ontology*, p. 105.
130. Ibid., p. 106.
131. Dewey, *A Common Faith*, p. 48.
132. Putnam, *Ethics without Ontology*, pp. 51, 23–4.

6. Enlightenment and Moral Politics

1. Interview with Reza Tehrani, Tehran, summer 1998.
2. John Dewey, *A Common Faith* (New Haven, CT: Yale University Press, 1934).

3. For an in-depth study of this new political tendency, see Ari Sitas, *The Ethic of Reconciliation* (Durban: Madiba, 2008).

4. *Speeches of Maximilien Robespierre* (New York: International Publishers, 1927), p. 61.

5. Paul Hazard, *The European Mind. 1680–1715* (New York: Fordham University Press, 1990), p. 70.

6. See Akeel Bilgrami on this concept.

7. Auguste Comte, "A General View of Positivism," in *The Great Political Theories*, edited by Michael Curtis (New York: Harper Perennial, 1962), p. 147.

8. Gertrude Himmelfarb, *The Roads to Modernity: The British, French, and American Enlightenments* (New York: Knopf, 2004).

9. For detailed discussions of such institutions in India, see *Secularism and its Critics*, edited by Rajeev Bhargana (New Delhi: Oxford, 1999).

10. Himmelfarb, *The Roads to Modernity*, p. 3.

11. Ibid., p. 5.

12. Ibid., p. 6.

13. Ibid., p. 7.

14. Ibid., p. 8.

15. Ibid., p. 9.

16. Ibid., p. 10.

17. Ibid., p. 11.

18. Ibid., p. 12.

19. **AU: Please provide note text.**

20. Ibid., p. 13.

21. Ibid., p. 14.

22. Ibid., p. 15.

23. Ibid., p. 16.

24. Ibid., p. 17.

25. Ibid., p. 18.

26. Ibid., p. 19.

27. Ibid., p. 20.

28. Ibid., p. 21.

29. Ibid., p. 22.

30. Ibid., p. 23.

31. Ibid., p. 24.

32. Ibid., p. 25.

33. Ibid., p. 26.

34. Ibid., p. 27.

35. Ibid., p. 28.

36. Ibid., p. 29.

37. Ibid., p. 30.

38. Ibid., p. 31.

39. Ibid., p. 32.

40. Ibid., p. 33.

41. Ibid., p. 34.

42. Ibid., p. 35.

43. Ibid., p. 36.
44. Ibid., p. 37.
45. Ibid., p. 38.
46. Ibid., p. 39.
47. Ibid., p. 40.
48. Ibid., p. 41.
49. Ibid., p. 42.
50. Ibid., p. 43.
51. Ibid., p. 44.
52. Ibid., p. 45.
53. Ibid., p. 46.
54. Ibid., p. 47.
55. Ibid., p. 48.
56. Ibid., p. 49.
57. Ibid., p. 50.
58. Ibid., p. 51.
59. Ibid., p. 52.
60. Ibid., p. 53.
61. Ibid., p. 54.
62. Ibid., p. 55.
63. Martin Luther King, Jr., *A Testament of Hope: The Essential Writings and Speeches of Martin Luther King, Jr.* (New York: HarperOne, 1990), p. 44.
64. Ibid., p. 102.
65. Mohammad Arkoun, *The Unthought in Contemporary Islamic Thought* (London: Saqi Books, 2002), p. 20.
66. For an analysis of Hegel's Philosophy of History along these lines, see Mirsepassi, *Intellectual Discourse and the Politics of Modernization: Negotiating Modernity in Iran* (Cambridge, UK: Cambridge University Press, 2008).
67. Manfred Steger, *Gandhi's Dilemma: Nonviolent Principles and Nationalist Power* (New York: Palgrave Macmillan, 2000), p. 6.
68. Ibid., p. 36.
69. Ibid., pp. 8, 35.
70. Ibid., pp. 8, 11.
71. Ibid., p. 29.
72. Ibid., p. 16.
73. Ibid., p. 5.
74. King, *A Testament of Hope*, p. 8.
75. Ibid., p. 7.
76. Ibid., p. 17.
77. Ibid., p. 10.
78. Ibid., pp. 16–17.
79. Ibid., pp. 23–4.
80. Ibid., p. 22.
81. Ibid., p. 36.
82. Ibid., p. 147.
83. Ibid., p. 122.
84. Ibid., p. 16.

85. Ibid., p. 19.
86. Ibid., p. 20.
87. Ibid., p. 9.
88. Ibid., p. 169.
89. Ibid., p. 38.
90. Ibid., p. 40.
91. Ibid., p. 37.
92. Ibid., p. 145.
93. Ibid., p. 38.
94. Steger, *Gandhi's Dilemma*, p. 5.
95. King, *A Testament of Hope*, p. 103.
96. Steger, *Gandhi's Dilemma*, p. x.
97. Ibid., p. 2.
98. King, *A Testament of Hope*, pp. 138–41.
99. Steger, *Gandhi's Dilemma*, p. 2.
100. G W F Hegel, *Phenomenology of Spirit*, A.V. Miller, translator (Oxford, UK: Oxford University Press, 1977), p. 522, n. 196.
101. Sunil Khilnani, *The Idea of India* (New York: Farrar, Straus and Giroux, 1999), p. 1.
102. Jawaharlal Nehru, *The Discovery of India* (New York: Penguin, 2004), p. 146.
103. Hegel, *Phenomenology of Spirit*, p. vii.
104. Ibid., p. xiii.
105. Khilnani, *The Idea of India*, pp. 2,3.
106. Ibid., p. 2.
107. Hegel, *Phenomenology of Spirit*, p. viii.
108. Khilnani, *The Idea of India*, p. 3.
109. Jan Palmowski, *Oxford Dictionary of Twentieth-Century World History*, (New York: Oxford University Press, 1997), p. 437.
110. Nehru, *The Discovery of India*, p. 41.
111. Ibid., p. 47.
112. Ibid., p. 45.
113. John Dewey, *The Philosophy of John Dewey*, edited by John J. McDermott (Chicago: University of Chicago Press, 1973), p. 385.
114. Nehru, *The Discovery of India*, p. 47.
115. Hegel, *Phenomenology of Spirit*, pp. vii, x.
116. Ibid., p. xiv.
117. Ibid., p. 37.
118. Ibid., p. 35.
119. Ibid., p. 43.
120. Nehru, *The Discovery of India*, p. 61.
121. Ibid., pp. 100, 101.
122. Dewey, *The Philosophy of John Dewey*, p. 483.
123. Ibid., p.
124. Nehru, *The Discovery of India*, p. 85.
125. Ibid., p. 93.
126. Ibid., p. 94.

127. Dewey, *The Philosophy of John Dewey*, p. 489.
128. Hegel, *Phenomenology of Spirit*, p. 37.
129. Ibid., pp. 110–111.
130. Ibid., p. 52.
131. Nehru, *The Discovery of India*, p. 130.
132. Hegel, *Phenomenology of Spirit*, p. 11.
133. Nehru, *The Discovery of India*, p. 149.
134. Hegel, *Phenomenology of Spirit*, p. 363.
135. Ibid., p. 139.
136. Hegel, *Phenomenology of Spirit*, p. 140.
137. Ibid., p. 181.
138. Nehru, *The Discovery of India*, p. 102.
139. Quoted in Paul Ricoeur, *Memory, History, Forgetting* (Chicago: University of Chicago Press, 2006), p. 370.
140. Nehru, *The Discovery of India*, p. 93.
141. Robert Stern, *Routledge Philosophy Guidebook to Hegel and the Phenomenology of Spirit* (London: Routledge, 2002).
142. Hegel, *Phenomenology of Spirit*, p. 212.
143. Ibid., p. 152.
144. Nehru, *The Discovery of India*, p. 254.
145. Ibid., pp. 314–15.
146. Ibid., p. 340.
147. Ibid.
148. Philip B. Wagoner. "A Sultan Among Hindu Kings: Dress, Titles, and the Islamicization of Hindu Culture at Vijayanagara," *Journal of Asian Studies* 55(4) (November 1996), 851–80.

Index